THEATRE EXPERIMENT

Theatre Experiment

EDITED BY MICHAEL BENEDIKT

Doubleday & Company, Inc., Garden City, New York

Library of Congress Catalog Card Number 67–19125

Printed in the United States of America

. . . the confused history of man is largely the history of conflicting senses of reality, and the scope for bewilderment becomes infinite if we include the history of literature. Our grasp of reality being as insecure as it is, we are indeed asking for trouble if we try to define imaginative literature, which is, whatever else it is, a sort of make-believe, in terms of what manifestly it is not, namely reality. Or is it? . . . When Schopenhauer completely reversed, surprisingly in terms of Plato himself, the Platonic view of the arts . . . it seemed merely the philosophical consummation of what artists and the lovers of the arts had come to feel with ever-increasing conviction: the artistic creation was closer to Reality than was the world as it appeared to the uninitiated human mind . . . and the artistic product was the more excellent, the more energetically the artist cut through the tangled trappings and frivolous futilities of the shadow-realm of appearances, the less he was distracted by personal bias and prejudice from his awful conversation with that which is truly true and really real. In other words and in two senses: the less the work of art is like "real life," the better is its chance to be like real life.

—*Erich Heller* (1965)

We're trying to bring a new spirit into the theatre
A joyfulness voluptuousness virtue—
Instead of that pessimism more than a hundred years old
And that's pretty old for such a boring thing—

. . . the full unfolding of our modern art
Often connecting in unseen ways as in life
Sounds gestures colors cries tumults
Music dancing acrobatics poetry painting
Choruses actions and multiple sets

—*Guillaume Apollinaire* (1917)
(tr. Louis Simpson)

Contents

Introduction

There is an important difference theatrically between Europe and America and one seldom recognized: it is that Realism has remained dominant in the American theatre. Just when this schism began seems plain. The reaction to Romanticism which occurred in America around the turn of the century had begun in Europe some twenty-five years earlier, producing what the French call Naturalist theatre.[1] But in Europe this shift was almost immediately eclipsed by the appearance of an Anti-Naturalist theatre, a development sometimes brought about by the theatrical Naturalists themselves. In France, for example, almost as soon as the great André Antoine opened his Théâtre Libre in 1887, Symbolism in poetry and the novel came to the fore, and Antoine—French theatrical Naturalism's patron saint himself—declared: "Just as I was the first to open my doors to the plays of Naturalism, so I shall open them to the Symbolist drama as well." In 1896, Aurélien-Marie Lugné-Poë produced Alfred Jarry's proto-Surrealist drama *Ubu Roi* at the Théâtre de l'Art; and so in France, even before the end of the nineteenth century, theatre in opposition to Naturalism was established—to become a tradition a few years later with the experiments of Apollinaire, Cocteau, and the Surrealists. In Germany, a company that translated the French theatre's very name, Die Freie Bühne, was founded in 1889 by Otto Brahm, specifically to explore the Libre's Naturalist goals. In 1906, Max Reinhardt, a former Brahm associate, opened his own playhouse, the Kammerspiele, for anti-naturalistic productions, and then gradually developed the essentials of theatrical Expressionism. In Spain,

[1] In this discussion we adopt the Gallic practice of referring to all nineteenth-century realistic drama not in its mid-nineteenth-century guise, *Réalisme,* but in its most polemical and experimental final form, *Naturalisme.*

Barcelona had its anti-naturalistic Teatro Intim by 1898; in Sweden, the Intima Theatern was opened in Stockholm in 1907; and in Russia, in the early years of the twentieth century, at the height of the Moscow Art Theatre's first fame, Vsevolod Meyerhold not only produced anti-naturalistic drama with the blessing of Stanislavski but, in fact, used Stanislavski's company.

There were virtually no American counterparts to these developments at this time. It was not until just after the start of the First World War that New York saw the establishment of three companies devoted to experiment: the Washington Square Players, the Neighborhood Playhouse, and the Provincetown Players. Efforts were also made to establish experimental theatre in Chicago, Boston, and elsewhere; but, symptomatically, perhaps the most durable of all the experimental little theatres was George Pierce Baker's 47 Workshop at Harvard. Moreover, most of the time such anti-naturalistic plays as were performed in all these theatres were European. It is by now a theatrical truism that the most theatrically effective of the indigenous new dramas of this period were the plays of the young Eugene O'Neill, then in his most realistic and possibly best phase, presented by the Provincetown group.

The American version of Naturalism was not only slow to arrive, but to some extent it ran counter to European accomplishments. In his celebrated preface to the dramatization of his novel *Thérèse Raquin* (1873), Emile Zola had prophesied in the name of Naturalism that:

> . . . the experimental and scientific spirit of the century will enter the domain of the drama, and in this lies the only possible salvation for the drama . . . we must look to the future and the future will have to do with the human problem studied in the framework of reality. The drama will either perish or become modern and realistic.[2]

The American version of the "modern and realistic" drama Zola foresaw is perfectly epitomized by the productions of David

[2] Quoted in Eric Bentley, *The Playwright as Thinker* (New York: Meridian Books, 1955), p. 6. Full text in Barrett H. Clark, *European Theories of the Drama* (New York: Appleton, 1941).

Belasco, whose accomplishment was to present plays that appeared to be taking into account the "framework of reality" of which Zola spoke, but which were decked out many of the same trappings Zola had hoped to banish forever from the theatre.[3] Zola died in 1902; Ibsen had turned to the more allusive Symbolist approach that characterizes his later dramas; Strindberg was foreshadowing both the mood and technique of Expressionism; yet at the turn of the century, with such dramas as his first great success, *The Girl I Left Behind Me* (1893), *Madame Butterfly* (1900), and *The Girl of the Golden West* (1905), Belasco was just beginning to explore his characteristic and highly influential style. The plays he produced (and sometimes wrote himself) were usually based on the most superficial, local-color aspect of environment. The three works mentioned above, for example, evoked, respectively, the French and Indian Wars, about which there was a resurgence of interest in the nineties; contemporary Japan, whose ports had recently been opened by Perry; and America's supposedly exotic "Wild West." The use of naturalistic technique in these dramas—and literally dozens of other exercises in theatrical tourism—was diametrically opposed to what Zola meant to recommend, which was a study of the intense ties between individuals and the most ordinary realities. His celebratedly veristic settings were transparently designed as the ideal arenas for the storms, earthquakes, and other natural disasters which occurred in his plays with unnatural frequency. His plots, too, were, in every sense of the word, melodramatic. Belasco's realism was basically a perpetuation of Romanticism.

Although Belasco was unrivaled in his elaborations of production mechanics, many others followed his example; by 1907, when this master of modern American commercial drama opened his theatre, the Stuyvesant (still operating today on Broadway as the Belasco Theatre), "Belascoism" was an acknowledged trend. It was a vogue that was to last a decade or more. American Naturalism did at least provide a somewhat more engaging theatrical product than did many other tendencies of the time—

[3] Belasco's Zola-ite intentions were at least initially strong: one of the first plays he directed, as early as 1879, was Zola's *L'Assommoir*.

moralizing drama, desperately "gay" and flimsy light comedy. As in Europe, Naturalism, even a debased brand, left the theatre better than it found it; and, in one playwright whose color-drenched early sea tales transcended the more simple-minded aspects of Belascoism, produced a creative figure of international stature: Eugene O'Neill. Still, the darker side of these beginnings is evident. Reading the potentially starker plays of the time one has the feeling that the spirit of popular Naturalism with its superficial and sentimentalizing aspects has affected them. And it is easy to agree with Alan S. Downer that "even the best of the serious plays written by Americans before the First World War are not more than superficially true to life as we understand it."[4]

One need not proceed as far as an assault on Naturalism to find its presence remarkable. Moreover, its presence is perhaps not as surprising as the fact that its continuation as an almost unique American theatrical phenomenon has so seldom been discussed. Indeed, a prime factor contributing to the continuation of the American naturalistic tradition has no doubt been the general lack of awareness regarding its strength. It may have come as a shock to many theatregoers who imagined themselves the witnesses of several decades of far-reaching drama when, in 1962, after more than a quarter-century of reviewing American drama, Mary McCarthy in her essay "The American Realist Playwrights," grouped as obvious realists most of the leading dramatists of the time: "Arthur Miller, Tennessee Williams, William Inge, Paddy Chayevsky—behind them, casting them in the shadow, stands the great figure of O'Neill."[5] Except for their relative outdatedness, there is no reason why such names as Maxwell Anderson, Robert Sherwood, Sidney Howard, Sidney Kingsley, Clifford Odets, Lillian Hellman, and Irwin Shaw might not have been added to this list. As McCarthy also points out, any lack of cognizance on this score is probably at least partly a function of the stances of these playwrights in regard to their own theatre strategies. "One characteristic of American realism in

[4] *Fifty Years of American Drama* (Chicago: Regnery, 1951), p. 39.
[5] *The Humanist in the Bathtub* (New York: New American Library, 1962), p. 28.

the theatre," notes McCarthy, "is that none of its practitioners currently . . . wants to call himself a realist."[6]

2

In the late twenties, however, there was at least one playwright who had begun to think logically and carefully about the situation of the American theatre. This was Thornton Wilder. In two later essays, "Some Thoughts on Playwrighting" (1941) and "A Platform and a Passion or Two" (1957) Wilder spoke out regarding his uneasiness of that time: "Toward the end of the twenties I began to lose pleasure in going to the theatre . . . I felt that something had gone wrong with it in my time and that it was fulfilling only a small part of its potentialities . . . I ceased to believe in the stories I saw presented there."[7] Wilder's disbelief was not, he indicates, based on the theatre's far-fetchedness, but quite the contrary: "I became dissatisfied with the theatre because I was unable to lend credence to such childish attempts to be 'real.'"[8]

In his own theatrical practice, Wilder works as what he calls "a rediscoverer of forgotten goods" against what he sees as the chief evil of nineteenth-century Naturalism's theatrical philosophy—the tendency to produce drama that is simply soothing—and its techniques, all of which tend to "load the stage with specific objects . . . squeeze it into [a] removed showcase."[9] "The history of the theatre," continues Wilder, "shows us that in its greatest ages the stage employed the greatest number of conventions. The stage is fundamental pretense, and it thrives on the acceptance of that fact and in the multiplication of additional pretenses. When it tries to assert that the personages in the action 'really are,' really inhabit such and such rooms, really suffer such and such emotions, it loses rather than gains credibility." Referring

[6] *Ibid.*, p. 29.
[7] *American Playwrights on Drama*, Ed. Horst Frenz (New York: Hill & Wang, 1965), p. 120.
[8] *Ibid.*, p. 124.
[9] *Ibid.*, p. 123.

to the dramatic situation not only in the late twenties, but in the mid-century as well, he notes that

> . . . the modern world is inclined to laugh condescendingly at the fact that in the plays of Racine and Corneille the gods and heroes of antiquity were dressed like courtiers under Louis XIV; that in the Elizabethan age scenery was replaced by placards notifying the audience of the location; and that a whip in the hand and a jogging motion of the body indicated that a man was on horseback in the Chinese theatre; these devices did not spring from naïveté, however, but from the vitality of the public imagination in those days and from an instinctive feeling as to where the essential and where the inessential lay in drama.[10]

In Wilder's tracing of the lost art of imaginative theatre, he blames the drama of the nineteenth century, specifically the middle-class and scientifically oriented drama of the period—a genre whose essential tenet is that reality is best explored by acts of measurement, recording and imitation:

> The trouble began in the nineteenth century and was connected with the rise of the middle classes—they wanted their theatre soothing. There's nothing wrong with the middle classes in themselves. We know that now. The United States and Scandinavia and Germany are middle-class countries . . . completely . . . When a middle-class is new . . . there is much that is wrong with it . . . Their questions about the nature of life seemed to be sufficiently answered by the demonstration of financial status and by conformity to some clearly established rules of decorum. These were precarious positions; abysses yawned on either side. The air was loud with questions that must not be asked. These audiences fashioned a theatre which could not disturb them.[11]

Wilder's solution to what he regarded as this apotheosis of middle-class drama was to compose the works included in *The Long Christmas Dinner and Other Plays* (1931), plays that in his own words, "tried to capture not verisimilitude but reality."

[10] *Ibid.*, pp. 59–60.
[11] *Ibid.*, p. 121.

3

The idea that Realism in the threatre cannot capture reality but merely "verisimilitude," and that the much vaunted arsenal of techniques employed by its stages is irrelevant, is the fundamental premise of the non-naturalistic playwright. Anti-Naturalism has its own distinct philosophy and world view. And part of its outlook is that even the most obvious reality, even the conventional reality we are most apt to acknowledge, is best captured on the stage through other means than those of either simple or—to use the well-worn critical term—"selective realism," or imitation.[12] Anti-Naturalism's initial assumption is that it is false to assume that life is best represented on a stage in which the "realer" the setting, the more "lifelike" the characters, the more "natural" the events, the better. It takes it that there is another way of approaching the theatre altogether; and one which has more to do with most of the important creative modes of the twentieth century. The significant painting of the past hundred years and the most lasting plays that followed Naturalism suggest that reality in the deepest, most essential sense is best served

[12] It is interesting that usually the last aspect of drama which those who speak of a renaissance in theatre through a "selective realism" select for change, is text. Important as settings, lighting, costumes are, obviously a fresh textual perspective must accompany such changes if they are to be coherent. An example of a work of American theatre that tends to separate stylizations of decor from textual shifts is Mordecai Gorelik's *New Theatres for Old* (New York: Samuel French, 1940). Gorelik, also a stage designer and director, regards even the most modest departures from strict Realism in script, and even the weakest of these modest departures, as evidence of the triumph of what he calls Symbolism. That, had Anti-Naturalist drama of distinction existed here in 1940, this writer might sadly enough have bridled, is suggested by Gorelik's later assault on the new French Surrealist-Absurdist drama in dialogue with Martin Esslin (New York *Times,* August 8 and 29, 1965). Actually, the main (and largely unfocused), thrust of Gorelik's curious and interesting book is to suggest that the American theatre, when it has been explorative, has been more successfully explorative in terms of decor than in its textual aspect. The internationally recognized excellence of the American musical in the years after World War II, while the American "serious" theatre floundered, confirms the continuation in recent years of this particular forte.

not by attempts at direct reproduction, but when seen through the glass of the particular medium in which the artist has chosen to work—presumably out of some enthusiasm for its special qualities in the first place.

One might term the question of a more openly theatrical theatre that is a central preoccupation of most important theatrical cultures in this century, a question of proper and appropriate design. The Naturalist playwright is an illusionist. Whatever the loftiness of his moral intention, he resembles the man who designs a building in which wood is painted to look like brick, or plastic is scored to resemble real tile; in which materials are disguised. In his eyes the proscenium set is interpreted as an actual picture frame in which a duplicate of reality is to be invoked. (Indeed, the emphasis on the proscenium arch in theatres built in the nineteenth century, on the heavy golden frame surrounding a stable and defined reality, is in some ways comparable to the heavy golden frames retained in the more realistic paintings of the period.) As the contemporary painter understands that there are many ways to fill a canvas, and that imitating reality is only one of a range of choices, the contemporary non-illusionistic playwright conceives that filling the stage with conventionally realistic characters is only one of many possible choices. Fundamentally, the difference between Naturalism and most of the important theatre that came after it is that a representative of the latter current would probably consider a basic ingredient of any honest theatrical act to be distinct acknowledgment of the theatrical medium. From the Anti-Naturalist point of view, creating in an artistically evasive, attemptedly realistic fashion may actually be the most fundamentally frivolous way to work in the theatre, as in all other arts—the insistent bleakness and much-remarked surface "seriousness of purpose" of virtually all the American Realist playwrights to the contrary.[13]

[13] This unseriousness is underlined not only by major developments in the other arts of our time, but by certain shifts in science, shifts so major that they amount to a revision of the reality-view which Naturalism claimed to reflect. The view of nature science held for most of the latter part of the nineteenth century is not the same that it holds in the twentieth century. The fixed and indubitable reality of nineteenth-century mechanistic science is

4

This anthology tries to assemble examples of pieces that show the wide variety of styles and approaches that lie outside of Naturalism. Stylistically, the plays differ from one another much more than those in most anthologies of recent American drama, and the present collection has been compiled in terms of style rather than subject or theme. The range of styles outside the canons of Naturalism is considerable, and might be grouped roughly into two categories, pre-Naturalist and post-Naturalist—categories into which they fall conveniently if not immediately very illuminatingly. The first group would include approaches theatrically operative before the mid-nineteenth century, and which contemporary playwrights have nevertheless found serviceable and meaningful. The approaches represented here include what we might loosely characterize as the Archaic (reflected in Allan Kaprow's *Gas*), the Medieval (E. E. Cummings' *Santa Claus*), the Elizabethan (reflected in the structure of Thornton Wilder's *The Long Christmas Dinner* and Robert Lowell's *Benito Cereno*); the Chinese (Wallace Stevens' *Three Travelers Watch a Sunrise*) and Japanese (Paul Goodman's *The Birthday*). Other pre-naturalistic styles, from the Greek and Roman to the Commedia dell'Arte, play over these, as well as over the other pieces here. The styles of post-Naturalism include Naturalism's *fin-de-siècle* successor, Symbolism (traces of which can be found

---

not that contemplated by Einstein and the scientists who came after him, with their relativistic and constantly changing reality. Oddly enough, even as Zola-ites were swearing their allegiance to the world-view of Victorian science, skeptics were regularly emerging not only among incipient Symbolist writers, but among the scientists themselves. The minority view, and the view held by twentieth-century science, was eloquently expressed by physicist P. G. Tait, who was perhaps speaking specifically of Naturalism when in 1876 he asserted that "nothing is more preposterously unscientific than to assert (as is constantly done by quasi-scientific writers of the present day) that with the utmost strides attempted by science we should necessarily be sensibly nearer to a conception of the ultimate nature of matter." (Quoted by James B. Conant, *Modern Science and Modern Man* [New York: Columbia University Press, 1952], p. 53.)

among the *chinoiseries* of Stevens, as well as in the linguistic hermeticism of Gertrude Stein's *What Happened*), Expressionism (an echo of which appears in the modern-morality-play personifications of Cummings; Surrealism (Ring Lardner's *The Tridget of Greva* and *Abend di Anni Nouveau*) and Absurdism (Jack Richardson's *Gallows Humor,* Rosalyn Drexler's *Hot Buttered Roll*); not to mention those recent experiments: The Theatre Piece (Ruth Krauss' *Poem-Plays; What Happened*), the Happening (*Gas;* Robert Whitman's *Flower;* Carolee Schneemann's *Meat Joy*), and their cognates. The influence of those two major theatrical streams, Artaud and the irrational-cruel, Brecht and his emphatically theatrical, Epic style are infused throughout these plays; but also, in many, hints of the timeless, non-naturalistic styles of popular theatre seem to appear. Included here are plays which evoke the naïveté of the pageant and spectacle (Kenneth Koch's *George Washington Crossing the Delaware*), and also music-hall and vaudeville (Russell Edson's *The Falling Sickness*).

The difference between non-Realism in pre-naturalistic theatre and non-Realism in post-naturalistic theatre is that in the latter we find a quality common to most essentially serious contemporary art: self-consciousness. Whereas in the earlier theatre, it is apt to be a matter of theatrical second nature, of innate Theatricalism (what Wilder doubtless referred to when speaking of "the vitality of the public imagination in those days and . . . an instinctive feeling as to where the essential and the inessential lay in drama"), in the later nineteenth and twentieth century, anti-Realism is apt to be a product of greater deliberateness. That even in part art should evolve through conscious tactics may be disillusioning from the aesthetic utopian's point of view; but the inescapable fact remains that even though twentieth-century playwrights may be working in old, pre-naturalistic modes, they will probably possess the degree of self-consciousness that justifies the characterization of their work as not merely post-Naturalist, but positively *Anti*-Naturalist.

5

In the 1830s Alexis de Tocqueville in *Democracy in America* enunciated what he thought would be an intimate connection between the American passion for democracy, the emphasis on science and commerce that he felt supported it, and the nature of the arts as a direct function of middle-class democracy. In the third book of his study, Tocqueville made some startling predictions about the sociology of American drama:

> In written productions, the literary canons of aristocracy will be gently, gradually, and, so to speak, legally modified; at the theatre they will be riotously overthrown . . . Democratic peoples . . . care but little for what occurred at Rome and Athens; they want to hear something which concerns themselves, and the delineation of the present age is what they demand . . . Most of those who frequent the amusements of the stage do not go there to seek the pleasures of the mind, but the keen emotions of the heart. They do not expect to hear a fine literary work, but to see a play; and provided the author writes the language of his country correctly enough to be understood, and that his characters excite curiosity and waken sympathy, the audience [is] satisfied. They ask no more of fiction, and immediately return to real life.[14]

When one examines the variety of sentimental Naturalism that holds sway on Broadway and is commonly known as *schmaltz,* one realizes that Tocqueville's sociologically based predictions have even come true in aesthetic terms: the plays we have sound roughly like the ones he predicted we would prefer. Still, his remarks are most startling when applied generally. In establishing the supremacy of the will of the many, Tocqueville feared that there might be a corresponding tendency to stamp out the will of the few, removing possibilities of dissent; thus, to a certain extent, democracy could conclude in contradiction. Until relatively recently, it seemed as if it were the role of the middle-

[14] *Democracy in America,* tr. Henry Reeve (New York: Schocken Books, 1961), Vol. II, pp. 95–99.

class, commercial theatre in America and most of its journalistic critics to prove that certain of De Tocqueville's dire sociopolitical predictions were justified. Few other countries succumbed as thoroughly as did the United States to a situation in which, if theatre was not bulk theatre, it was apt not to exist, much less receive sufficient or sympathetic notice in the press.

The change in the situation here was of course largely due to the development, which accelerated after the Second World War, of the off-Broadway movement. Still, the character of even this modest departure from the naturalistic norms of Broadway was soon to change in a fashion which De Tocqueville might have considered peculiarly predictable and American. The lament of one devoted off-Broadway theatregoer, Gerald Weales, provides an ample survey of the off-Broadway situation by 1962:

> There was a time when the words off-Broadway theatre called up a picture of a dedicated group, held together by esthetic or ideational concerns, determined to change the state of the theatre or the state of the world. Today, the words suggest a producing unit with a much smaller investment than Broadway demands, with a small house to play in, with special Equity contracts, with a play that is likely to be as safe as it is experimental . . . There are few off-Broadway producing groups with any continuity . . . If there has been a theatrical revolution in the last fifteen years, ironically, it has not overthrown Broadway; it has re-created off-Broadway, changed it from a state of mind to a producing apparatus so like Broadway that only the technicians who draw up contracts can find the line between them . . . Even though off-Broadway is more willing to take a chance on the unusual without the European seal of approval that Broadway demands, the bulk of off-Broadway production resembles the Broadway offerings.[15]

Weales identifies as the crucial event in this collapse the mid-1950s success of the Weill-Brecht *Threepenny Opera,* which ran to unprecedented off-Broadway crowds for no less than seven years. Though the *Threepenny Opera* never moved to Broadway

[15] *American Drama Since World War II* (New York: Harcourt, Brace & World, 1962), pp. 203–205.

physically, it is clear that there were many, both inside the theatre and out, who mentally transferred it there anyway.

From the point of view of American stage history, it is not only the existence but the stance of the European small-theatre tradition that is impressive. The fact that the image of an experimental, Anti-Naturalist off-Broadway was insufficiently defined at the very beginning, not clearly thought out, has without doubt contributed to the ease of its metamorphosis. Even today the phenomenon of off-Broadway theatre is as often as not—and even by its supporters—considered a function of geography, rather than aesthetics. Moreover, while Broadway producers with sharp-eyed consistency exclude experimental drama from their stages, off-Broadway has regularly been hospitable to playwrights whose every trait indicated that their work was a mere warm-up for Broadway—a role that television might more appropriately (and for a while in the fifties did actually) play. With the exception of a few energetic off-Broadway houses, what has prevented a reversion to a situation in which bulk theatre styles exist almost exclusively in even what has rather loosely been called "the nation's greatest theatre city" has been the newest minority theatre: the off-off-Broadway theatre, presented in tiny playhouses, or, still more bravely, in locales ranging from converted lofts to coffeehouses to churches. Of course, given a sufficiently vague view of differences between Broadway and non-commercial theatre, there is no reason why the genuineness of the off-off-Broadway renaissance, too, should not diffuse.[16]

[16] Though we have taken the present ambiguous situation of non-Broadway theatre as likely to exist throughout a nation accustomed to the hegemony of bulk theatre, it is atypical in one respect: the agony of off-Broadway is not apt to be repeated and has not been repeated in the decentralized, regional theatres that bloomed just after the close of the Second World War. Perhaps such growths are less easy and natural than in theatre-seeded New York, and therefore apt to be more alert as to the purpose of their presences; in any case, this tradition has continued to flourish, both aesthetically and otherwise. And the better university theatres, free from outside pressures at the outset, have certainly become stronger, and increasingly intent upon the experimental.

6

Throughout this introduction we have attempted to stress the importance of thinking about the character of our theatre, as well as its individual plays; and have thus evolved the definitions used in the descriptions of the Anti-Naturalist plays to follow. Actually, it would be quite as gratifying to this writer if the partisans of realistic theatre set forth its rules, goals, and limits. History suggests that this is not likely to happen, however, and we can expect that any thinking that will be done vis-à-vis either the implications of the American commercial threatre and the experimental theatre, will probably have to come from these latter realms. Continuation of the lack of viable public definition between the "Other Theatre" of Anti-Naturalism and the commercial theatre will no doubt be assured by the other recent critical tendency to regard all experimental developments, no matter how radical, as simply representing additional forms of Realism. This anthology tries in part to suggest that there are other ideas in operation, which are, at base, quite directly the *opposite* of those of Realism. It is interesting that in Europe this clear separation between the two streams has resulted in the firm establishment of a non-realistic tradition, whose playwrights appeal on their own terms to a relatively general public. The strength of the tradition is certainly such that it is inconceivable that any leading European critic would feel called upon to devote most of the preface to his collected reviews to a refutation of another leading theatre man's assertion that "I equate good plays with successful plays" (as Harold Clurman recently did with regard to remarks by Elia Kazan).[17] Equally inconceivable would be any critical willingness to relent with regard to certain crucial theatrical distinctions, as when—after making a fascinating and significant distinction between the play as written text and the play as theatricalist elaboration—this same critic allows that "a dispute today as to whether the written

[17] *Lies Like Truth* (New York: Grove Press, 1960), p. 9.

text . . . or the performance . . . would [be the most important] would probably prove more useless than to debate the question of the chicken and the egg."[18]

Hopefully, this anthology may also redress somewhat the prejudice of silence and lack of such debates, which in the American theatre has almost always acted in favor of "chicken" and against "egg." Theatre consists of course of both components, but it would seem that it is our tradition, viewing theatre with the equanimity of such convictions, to end up mostly with the chicken. That other possibilities exist, we hope to show with the following selection of experimental, Anti-Naturalist drama. And, of course, chicken or egg, this editor would be pleased should the reader enjoy the unusual and original American plays herein simply in terms of the incomparable pleasure of theatre.

Michael Benedikt
New York, 1966

[18] *Ibid.*, p. 4.

THEATRE EXPERIMENT

The Long Christmas Dinner
BY THORNTON WILDER

Thornton Wilder's statement that "the stage is fundamental pretense and . . . thrives on the acceptance of that fact and in the multiplication of additional pretenses" (*Some Thoughts on Playwrighting,* 1941) expresses the classic Anti-Naturalist point of view: that the theatre is at its best when most peculiarly itself—i.e. theatrical. For the creation of his highly theatrical brand of drama, Wilder has remarked on his great debt to pre-nineteenth century theatrical genres, especially the oriental and the Elizabethan. At the same time, his plays clearly deal in ordinary events, involving settings that are not only earthy, but endearingly local. The unique flavor of Wilder's particular anti-naturalistic style may be said to stem from these associations. Such duality pervades *The Long Christmas Dinner,* surely one of the most moving American dramas ever written. As in most of Wilder's plays, the basic premise is a problem that can best be solved with the materials specifically at the playwright's disposal. The requirement here is the representation of the life of a New England family during the Christmas season. This involves, as it often does in Wilder, telescoping time. The family is seen passing from Christmas to Christmas virtually without reference to the time elapsed and in the space of a few minutes an entire dynasty flourishes, dwindles, and dies. In such a telescoping, birth and death become necessary elements of the dramatic texture; and Wilder's symbolic representation of such events is both original and right. Wilder's frank indulgence in the pleasures of the theatrical—perhaps emblemized most unforgettably by the Stage Manager who narrates the panorama of *Our Town*—has, of course, not only won him a special place among American playwrights, but has also surely contributed greatly to making him one of the most popular of American playwrights abroad.

The Long Christmas Dinner

The dining-room of the Bayard home. Close to the footlights a long dining table is handsomely spread for Christmas dinner. The carver's place with a great turkey before it is at the spectator's right.

A door, left back, leads into the hall.

At the extreme left, by the proscenium pillar, is a strange portal trimmed with garlands of fruits and flowers. Directly opposite is another edged and hung with black velvet. The portals denote birth and death.

Ninety years are to be traversed in this play which represents in accelerated motion ninety Christmas dinners in the Bayard household. The actors are dressed in inconspicuous clothes and must indicate their gradual increase in years through their acting. Most of them carry wigs of white hair which they adjust upon their heads at the indicated moment, simply and without comment. The ladies may have shawls concealed beneath the table that they gradually draw up about their shoulders as they grow older.

Throughout the play the characters continue eating imaginary food with imaginary knives and forks.

There is no curtain. The audience arriving at the threatre sees the stage set and the table laid, though still in partial darkness. Gradually the lights in the auditorium become dim and the stage brightens until sparkling winter sunlight streams through the dining room windows.

Enter LUCIA. *She inspects the table, touching here a knife and there a fork. She talks to a servant girl who is invisible to us.*

LUCIA

I reckon we're ready now, Gertrude. We won't ring the chimes today. I'll just call them myself. (*She goes into the hall and calls*) Roderick. Mother Bayard. We're all ready. Come to dinner.

(*Enter* RODERICK *pushing* MOTHER BAYARD *in a wheel chair.*)

MOTHER BAYARD

. . . and a new horse too, Roderick. I used to think that only the wicked owned two horses. A new horse and a new house and a new wife!

RODERICK

Well, Mother, how do you like it? Our first Christmas dinner in the new house, hey?

MOTHER BAYARD

Tz-Tz-Tz! I don't know what your dear father would say!

LUCIA

Here, Mother Bayard, you sit between us.

(RODERICK *says grace.*)

MOTHER BAYARD

My dear Lucia, I can remember when there were still Indians on this very ground, and I wasn't a young girl either. I can remember when we had to cross the Mississippi on a new-made raft. I can remember when St. Louis and Kansas City were full of Indians.

LUCIA

(*tying a napkin around* MOTHER BAYARD'S *neck*)

Imagine that! There!—What a wonderful day for our first Christmas dinner: a beautiful sunny morning, snow, a splendid sermon. Dr. McCarthy preaches a splendid sermon. I cried and cried.

RODERICK

(*extending an imaginary carving-fork*)

Come now, what'll you have, Mother? A little sliver of white?

LUCIA

Every least twig is wrapped around with ice. You almost never see that. Can I cut it up for you, dear? (*over her shoulder*) Gertrude, I forgot the jelly. You know,—on the top shelf.—Mother Bayard, I found your mother's gravy-boat while we were moving. What was her name, dear? What were all your names? You were . . . a . . . Genevieve Wainright. Now your mother—

MOTHER BAYARD

Yes, you must write it down somewhere. I was Genevieve Wainright. My mother was Faith Morrison. She was the daughter of a farmer in New Hampshire who was something of a blacksmith too. And she married young John Wainright—

LUCIA

(*memorizing on her fingers*)

Genevieve Wainright. Faith Morrison.

RODERICK

It's all down in a book somewhere upstairs. We have it all. All that kind of thing is very interesting. Come, Lucia, just a little wine. Mother, a little red wine for Christmas day. Full of iron. "Take a little wine for thy stomach's sake."

LUCIA

Really, I can't get used to wine! What would my father say? But I suppose it's all right.

Enter COUSIN BRANDON *from the hall. He takes his place by* LUCIA.)

COUSIN BRANDON

(*rubbing his hands*)

Well, well, I smell turkey. My dear cousins, I can't tell you how pleasant it is to be having Christmas dinner with you all. I've lived out there in Alaska so long without relatives. Let me see, how long have you had this new house, Roderick?

RODERICK

Why, it must be . . .

MOTHER BAYARD

Five years. It's five years, children. You should keep a diary. This is your sixth Christmas dinner here.

LUCIA

Think of that, Roderick. We feel as though we had lived here twenty years.

COUSIN BRANDON

At all events it still looks as good as new.

RODERICK

(*over his carving*)

What'll you have, Brandon, light or dark?—Frieda, fill up Cousin Brandon's glass.

LUCIA

Oh, dear, I can't get used to these wines. I don't know what my father'd say, I'm sure. What'll you have, Mother Bayard?

(*During the following speeches* MOTHER BAYARD'S *chair, without any visible propulsion, starts to draw away from the table, turns toward the right, and slowly goes toward the dark portal.*)

MOTHER BAYARD

Yes, I can remember when there were Indians on this very land.

LUCIA

(*softly*)

Mother Bayard hasn't been very well lately, Roderick.

MOTHER BAYARD

My mother was a Faith Morrison. And in New Hampshire she married a young John Wainright, who was a Congregational minister. He saw her in his congregation one day . . .

LUCIA

Mother Bayard, hadn't you better lie down, dear?

MOTHER BAYARD

. . . and right in the middle of his sermon he said to himself: "I'll marry that girl." And he did, and I'm their daughter.

LUCIA

(*half rising and looking after her with anxiety*)

Just a little nap, dear?

MOTHER BAYARD

I'm all right. Just go on with your dinner. I was ten, and I said to my brother—

(*She goes out. A very slight pause.*)

COUSIN BRANDON

It's too bad it's such a cold dark day today. We almost need the lamps. I spoke to Major Lewis for a moment after church. His sciatica troubles him, but he does pretty well.

LUCIA

(*dabbing her eyes*)

I know Mother Bayard wouldn't want us to grieve for her on Christmas day, but I can't forget her sitting in her wheel chair right beside us, only a year ago. And she would be so glad to know our good news.

RODERICK

(*patting her hand*)

Now, now. It's Christmas. (*formally*) Cousin Brandon, a glass of wine with you, sir.

COUSIN BRANDON

(*half rising, lifting his glass gallantly*)

A glass of wine with you, sir.

LUCIA

Does the Major's sciatica cause him much pain?

COUSIN BRANDON

Some, perhaps. But you know his way. He says it'll be all the same in a hundred years.

LUCIA

Yes, he's a great philosopher.

RODERICK

His wife sends you a thousand thanks for her Christmas present.

LUCIA

I forget what I gave her.—Oh, yes, the workbasket!

(*Through the entrance of birth comes a nurse wheeling a perambulator trimmed with blue ribbons.* LUCIA *rushes toward it, the men following.*)

O my wonderful new baby, my darling baby! Who ever saw such a child! Quick, nurse, a boy or a girl? A boy! Roderick, what shall we call him? Really, nurse, you've never seen such a child!

RODERICK

We'll call him Charles after your father and grandfather.

LUCIA

But there are no Charleses in the Bible, Roderick.

RODERICK

Of course, there are. Surely there are.

LUCIA

Roderick!—Very well, but he will always be Samuel to me.—What miraculous hands he has! Really, they are the most beautiful hands in the world. All right, nurse. Have a good nap, my darling child.

RODERICK

Don't drop him, nurse. Brandon and I need him in our firm.

(*Exit nurse and perambulator into the hall. The others return to their chairs,* LUCIA *taking the place left vacant by* MOTHER BAYARD *and* COUSIN BRANDON *moving up beside her.* COUSIN BRANDON *puts on his white hair.*)

Lucia, a little white meat? Some stuffing? Cranberry sauce, anybody?

LUCIA

(*over her shoulder*)

Margaret, the stuffing is very good today.—Just a little, thank you.

RODERICK

Now something to wash it down. (*half rising*) Cousin Brandon, a glass of wine with you, sir. To the ladies, God bless them.

LUCIA

Thank you, kind sirs.

COUSIN BRANDON

Pity it's such an overcast day today. And no snow.

LUCIA

But the sermon was lovely. I cried and cried. Dr. Spaulding does preach such a splendid sermon.

RODERICK

I saw Major Lewis for a moment after church. He says his rheumatism comes and goes. His wife says she has something for Charles and will bring it over this afternoon.

(*Enter nurse again with perambulator. Pink ribbons. Same rush toward the left.*)

LUCIA

O my lovely new baby! Really, it never occurred to me that it might be a girl. Why, nurse, she's perfect.

RODERICK

Now call her what you choose. It's your turn.

LUCIA

Looloolooloo. Aië. Aië. Yes, this time I shall have my way. She shall be called Genevieve after your mother. Have a good nap, my treasure. (*She looks after it as the nurse wheels the perambu-*

lator into the hall.) Imagine! Sometime she'll be grown up and say "Good morning, Mother. Good morning, Father."—Really, Cousin Brandon, you don't find a baby like that every day.

COUSIN BRANDON

And the new factory.

LUCIA

A new factory? Really? Roderick, I shall be very uncomfortable if we're going to turn out to be rich. I've been afraid of that for years.—However, we mustn't talk about such things on Christmas day. I'll just take a little piece of white meat, thank you. Roderick, Charles is destined for the ministry. I'm sure of it.

RODERICK

Woman, he's only twelve. Let him have a free mind. *We* want him in the firm, I don't mind saying. Anyway, no time passes as slowly as this when you're waiting for your urchins to grow up and settle down to business.

LUCIA

I don't want time to go any faster, thank you. I love the children just as they are.—Really, Roderick, you know what the doctor said: One glass a meal. (*putting her hand over his glass*) No, Margaret, that will be all.

(RODERICK *rises, glass in hand. With a look of dismay on his face he takes a few steps toward the dark portal.*)

RODERICK

Now I wonder what's the matter with me.

LUCIA

Roderick, do be reasonable.

RODERICK

(*tottering, but with gallant irony*)

But, my dear, statistics show that we steady, moderate drinkers . . .

LUCIA

(*rises, gazing at him in anguish*)
Roderick! My dear! What . . . ?

RODERICK

(*returns to his seat with a frightened look of relief*)
Well, it's fine to be back at table with you again. How many good Christmas dinners have I had to miss upstairs? And to be back at a fine bright one, too.

LUCIA

O my dear, you gave us a very alarming time! Here's your glass of milk.—Josephine, bring Mr. Bayard his medicine from the cupboard in the library.

RODERICK

At all events, now that I'm better I'm going to start doing something about the house.

LUCIA

Roderick! You're not going to change the house?

RODERICK

Only touch it up here and there. It looks a hundred years old.
(CHARLES *enters casually from the hall. He kisses his mother's hair and sits down.*)

LUCIA

Charles, you carve the turkey, dear. Your father's not well.—You always said you hated carving, though you *are* so clever at it.
(*Father and son exchange places.*)

CHARLES

It's a great blowy morning, Mother. The wind comes over the hill like a lot of cannon.

LUCIA

And such a good sermon. I cried and cried. Mother Bayard loved a good sermon so. And she used to sing the Christmas hymns all around the year. Oh, dear, oh, dear, I've been thinking of her all morning!

RODERICK

Sh, Mother. It's Christmas day. You mustn't think of such things. —You mustn't be depressed.

LUCIA

But sad things aren't the same as depressing things. I must be getting old: I like them.

CHARLES

Uncle Brandon, you haven't anything to eat. Pass his plate, Hilda . . . and some cranberry sauce . . .

(*Enter* GENEVIEVE. *She kisses her father's temple and sits down.*)

GENEVIEVE

It's glorious. Every least twig is wrapped around with ice. You almost never see that.

LUCIA

Did you have time to deliver those presents after church, Genevieve?

GENEVIEVE

Yes, Mama. Old Mrs. Lewis sends you a thousand thanks for hers. It was just what she wanted, she said. Give me lots, Charles, lots.

RODERICK

(*rising and starting toward the dark portal*)

Statistics, ladies and gentlemen, show that we steady, moderate . . .

CHARLES

How about a little skating this afternoon, Father?

RODERICK

I'll live till I'm ninety.

LUCIA

I really don't think he ought to go skating.

RODERICK

(*at the very portal, suddenly astonished*)

Yes, but . . . but . . . not yet!

(*He goes out.*)

LUCIA

(*dabbing her eyes*)

He was so young and so clever, Cousin Brandon. (*raising her voice for* COUSIN BRANDON'S *deafness*) I say he was so young and so clever.—Never forget your father, children. He was a good man.—Well, he wouldn't want us to grieve for him today.

CHARLES

White or dark, Genevieve? Just another sliver, Mother?

LUCIA

(*putting on her white hair*)

I can remember our first Christmas dinner in this house, Genevieve. Twenty-five years ago today. Mother Bayard was sitting here in her wheel chair. She could remember when Indians lived on this very spot and when she had to cross the river on a new-made raft.

CHARLES *and* GENEVIEVE

She couldn't have, Mother. That can't be true.

LUCIA

It certainly was true—even I can remember when there was only one paved street. We were very happy to walk on boards. (*louder, to* COUSIN BRANDON) We can remember when there were no sidewalks, can't we, Cousin Brandon?

COUSIN BRANDON
(*delighted*)
Oh, yes! And those were the days.

CHARLES *and* GENEVIEVE
(*sotto voce. This is a family refrain*)
Those were the days.

LUCIA
. . . and the ball last night, Genevieve? Did you have a nice time? I hope you didn't *waltz,* dear. I think a girl in our position ought to set an example. Did Charles keep an eye on you?

GENEVIEVE
He had none left. They were all on Leonora Banning. He can't conceal it any longer, Mother. I think he's engaged to marry Leonora Banning.

CHARLES
I'm not engaged to marry anyone.

LUCIA
Well, she's very pretty.

GENEVIEVE
I shall never marry, Mother—I shall sit in this house beside you forever, as though life were one long, happy Christmas dinner.

LUCIA
O my child, you mustn't say such things!

GENEVIEVE
(*playfully*)
You don't want me? You don't want me?
(LUCIA *bursts into tears.*)
Why, Mother, how silly you are! There's nothing sad about that—what could possibly be sad about that.

LUCIA

(*drying her eyes*)

Forgive me. I'm just unpredictable, that's all.

(CHARLES *goes to the door and leads in* LEONORA BANNING.)

LEONORA

(*kissing* LUCIA'S *temple*)

Good morning, Mother Bayard. Good morning, everybody. It's really a splendid Christmas day today.

CHARLES

Little white meat? Genevieve, Mother, Leonora?

LEONORA

Every least twig is encircled with ice.—You never see that.

CHARLES

(*shouting*)

Uncle Brandon, another?—Rogers, fill my uncle's glass.

LUCIA

(*to* CHARLES)

Do what your father used to do. It would please Cousin Brandon so. You know—(*pretending to raise a glass*)—"Uncle Brandon, a glass of wine—"

CHARLES

(*rising*)

Uncle Brandon, a glass of wine with you, sir.

BRANDON

A glass of wine with you, sir. To the ladies, God bless them every one.

THE LADIES

Thank you, kind sirs.

GENEVIEVE

And if I go to Germany for my music I promise to be back for Christmas. I wouldn't miss that.

LUCIA

I hate to think of you over there all alone in those strange pensions.

GENEVIEVE

But, darling, the time will pass so fast that you'll hardly know I'm gone. I'll be back in the twinkling of an eye.

(*Enter Left, the nurse and perambulator. Green ribbons.*)

LEONORA

Oh, what an angel! The darlingest baby in the world. Do let me hold it, nurse.

(*But the nurse resolutely wheels the perambulator across the stage and out the dark door.*)

Oh, I did love it so!

(LUCIA *goes to her, puts her arm around* LEONORA'S *shoulders, and they encircle the room whispering*—LUCIA *then hands her over to* CHARLES *who conducts her on the same circuit.*)

GENEVIEVE

(*as her mother sits down,—softly*)

Isn't there anything I can do?

LUCIA

(*raises her eyebrows, ruefully*)

No, dear. Only time, only the passing of time can help in these things.

(CHARLES *and* LEONORA *return to the table.*)

Don't you think we could ask Cousin Ermengarde to come and live with us here? There's plenty for everyone and there's no reason why she should go on teaching the First Grade for ever and ever. She wouldn't be in the way, would she, Charles?

CHARLES

No, I think it would be fine.—A little more potato and gravy, anybody? A little more turkey, Mother?

(BRANDON *rises and starts slowly toward the dark portal.* LUCIA *rises and stands for a moment with her face in her hands.*)

COUSIN BRANDON

(*muttering*)

It was great to be in Alaska in those days . . .

GENEVIEVE

(*half rising, and gazing at her mother in fear*)

Mother, what is . . . ?

LUCIA

(*hurriedly*)

Hush, my dear. It will pass.—Hold fast to your music, you know. (*as* GENEVIEVE *starts toward her*) No, no. I want to be alone for a few minutes.

(*She turns and starts after* COUSIN BRANDON *toward the Right.*)

CHARLES

If the Republicans collected all their votes instead of going off into cliques among themselves, they might prevent his getting a second term.

GENEVIEVE

Charles, Mother doesn't tell us, but she hasn't been very well these days.

CHARLES

Come, Mother, we'll go to Florida for a few weeks.

(*Exit* BRANDON.)

LUCIA

(*smiling at* GENEVIEVE *and waving her hand*)

Don't be foolish. Don't grieve.

(*She clasps her hands under her chin; her lips move, whispering; she walks serenely into the portal.* GENEVIEVE *stares after her, frozen. At the same moment the nurse and perambulator enter from the Left. Pale yellow ribbons.* LEONORA *rushes to it.*)

LEONORA

O my darlings . . . twins . . . Charles, aren't they glorious! Look at them. Look at them.

GENEVIEVE

(*sinks down on the table her face buried in her arms*)

But what will I do? What's left for me to do?

CHARLES

(*bending over the basket*)

Which is which?

LEONORA

I feel as though I were the first mother who ever had twins.—Look at them now!—But why wasn't Mother Bayard allowed to stay and see them!

GENEVIEVE

(*rising suddenly distraught, loudly*)

I don't want to go on. I can't bear it.

CHARLES

(*goes to her quickly. They sit down. He whispers to her earnestly taking both her hands*)

But Genevieve, Genevieve! How frightfully Mother would feel to think that . . . Genevieve!

GENEVIEVE

(*shaking her head wildly*)

I never told her how wonderful she was. We all treated her as though she were just a friend in the house. I thought she'd be here forever.

LEONORA

(*timidly*)

Genevieve darling, do come one minute and hold my babies' hands. We shall call the girl Lucia after her grandmother,—will that please you? Do just see what adorable little hands they have.

(GENEVIEVE *collects herself and goes over to the perambulator. She smiles brokenly into the basket.*)

GENEVIEVE

They are wonderful, Leonora.

LEONORA

Give him your finger, darling. Just let him hold it.

CHARLES

And we'll call the boy Samuel.—Well, now everybody come and finish your dinners. Don't drop them, nurse; at least don't drop the boy. We need him in the firm.

LEONORA

(*stands looking after them as the nurse wheels them into the hall*)

Someday they'll be big. Imagine! They'll come in and say "Hello, Mother!" (*She makes clucking noises of rapturous consternation.*)

CHARLES

Come, a little wine, Leonora, Genevieve? Full of iron. Eduardo, fill the ladies' glasses. It certainly is a keen, cold morning. I used to go skating with Father on mornings like this and Mother would come back from church saying—

GENEVIEVE
(*dreamily*)
I know: saying "Such a splendid sermon. I cried and cried."

LEONORA
Why did she cry, dear?

GENEVIEVE
That generation all cried at sermons. It was their way.

LEONORA
Really, Genevieve?

GENEVIEVE
They had had to go since they were children and I suppose sermons reminded them of their fathers and mothers, just as Christmas dinners do us. Especially in an old house like this.

LEONORA
It really is pretty old, Charles. And so ugly, with all that ironwork filigree and that dreadful cupola.

GENEVIEVE
Charles! You aren't going to change the house!

CHARLES
No, no. I won't give up the house, but great heavens! it's fifty years old. This Spring we'll remove the cupola and build a new wing toward the tennis courts.

(*From now on* GENEVIEVE *is seen to change. She sits up more straightly. The corners of her mouth become fixed. She becomes a forthright and slightly disillusioned spinster.* CHARLES *becomes the plain business man and a little pompous.*)

LEONORA
And then couldn't we ask your dear old Cousin Ermengarde to come and live with us? She's really the self-effacing kind.

CHARLES

Ask her now. Take her out of the First Grade.

GENEVIEVE

We only seem to think of it on Christmas day with her Christmas card staring us in the face.

(*Enter Left, nurse and perambulator. Blue ribbons.*)

LEONORA

Another boy! Another boy! Here's a Roderick for you at last.

CHARLES

Roderick Brandon Bayard. A regular little fighter.

LEONORA

Goodbye, darling. Don't grow up too fast. Yes, yes. Aië, aië, aië—stay just as you are.—Thank you, nurse.

GENEVIEVE

(*who has not left the table, repeats dryly*)

Stay just as you are.

(*Exit nurse and perambulator. The others return to their places.*)

LEONORA

Now I have three children. One, two, three. Two boys and a girl. I'm collecting them. It's very exciting. (*over her shoulder*) What, Hilda? Oh, Cousin Ermengarde's come! Come in, Cousin.

(*She goes to the hall and welcomes* COUSIN ERMENGARDE *who already wears her white hair.*)

ERMENGARDE

(*shyly*)

It's such a pleasure to be with you all.

CHARLES

(*pulling out her chair for her*)

The twins have taken a great fancy to you already, Cousin.

LEONORA

The baby went to her at once.

CHARLES

Exactly how are we related, Cousin Ermengarde?—There, Genevieve, that's your specialty.—First a little more turkey and stuffing, Mother? Cranberry sauce, anybody?

GENEVIEVE

I can work it out: Grandmother Bayard was your . . .

ERMENGARDE

Your Grandmother Bayard was a second cousin of my Grandmother Haskins through the Wainrights.

CHARLES

Well, it's all in a book somewhere upstairs. All that kind of thing is awfully interesting.

GENEVIEVE

Nonsense. There are no such books. I collect my notes off gravestones, and you have to scrape a good deal of moss—let me tell you—to find one great-grandparent.

CHARLES

There's a story that my Grandmother Bayard crossed the Mississippi on a raft before there were any bridges or ferryboats. She died before Genevieve or I were born. Time certainly goes very fast in a great new country like this. Have some more cranberry sauce, Cousin Ermengarde.

ERMENGARDE

(*timidly*)

Well, time must be passing very slowly in Europe with this dreadful, dreadful war going on.

CHARLES

Perhaps an occasional war isn't so bad after all. It clears up a lot of poisons that collect in nations. It's like a boil.

ERMENGARDE

Oh, dear, oh, dear!

CHARLES

(*with relish*)

Yes, it's like a boil.—Ho! ho! Here are your twins.

(*The twins appear at the door into the hall.* SAM *is wearing the uniform of an ensign.* LUCIA *is fussing over some detail on it.*)

LUCIA

Isn't he wonderful in it, Mother?

CHARLES

Let's get a look at you.

SAM

Mother, don't let Roderick fool with my stamp album while I'm gone.

LEONORA

Now, Sam, do write a letter once in a while. Do be a good boy about that, mind.

SAM

You might send some of those cakes of yours once in a while, Cousin Ermengarde.

ERMENGARDE

(*in a flutter*)

I certainly will, my dear boy.

CHARLES

If you need any money, we have agents in Paris and London, remember.

SAM

Well, goodbye . . .

(SAM *goes briskly out through the dark portal, tossing his unneeded white hair through the door before him.* LUCIA *sits down at the table with lowered eyes.*)

ERMENGARDE

(*after a slight pause, in a low, constrained voice, making conversation*)

I spoke to Mrs. Fairchild for a moment coming out of church. Her rheumatism's a little better, she says. She sends you her warmest thanks for the Christmas present. The workbasket, wasn't it?—It was an admirable sermon. And our stained-glass window looked so beautiful, Leonora, so beautiful. Everybody spoke of it and so affectionately of Sammy. (LEONORA'S *hand goes to her mouth.*) Forgive me, Leonora, but it's better to speak of him than not to speak of him when we're all thinking of him so hard.

LEONORA

(*rising, in anguish*)

He was a mere boy. He was a mere boy, Charles.

CHARLES

My dear, my dear.

LEONORA

I want to tell him how wonderful he was. We let him go so casually. I want to tell him how we all feel about him.—Forgive me, let me walk about a minute.—Yes, of course, Ermengarde—it's best to speak of him.

LUCIA

(*in a low voice to Genevieve*)

Isn't there anything I can do?

GENEVIEVE

No, no. Only time, only the passing of time can help in these things.

(LEONORA, *straying about the room finds herself near the door to the hall at the moment that her son* RODERICK *enters. He links his arm with hers and leads her back to the table.*)

RODERICK

What's the matter, anyway? What are you all so glum about? The skating was fine today.

CHARLES

Sit down, young man. I have something to say to you.

RODERICK

Everybody was there. Lucia skated in the corners with Dan Creighton the whole time. When'll it be, Lucia, when'll it be?

LUCIA

I don't know what you mean.

RODERICK

Lucia's leaving us soon, Mother. Dan Creighton, of all people.

CHARLES

(*ominously*)

Roderick, I have something to say to you.

RODERICK

Yes, Father.

CHARLES

Is it true, Roderick, that you made yourself conspicuous last night at the Country Club—at a Christmas Eve dance, too?

LEONORA

Not now, Charles, I beg of you. This is Christmas dinner.

RODERICK
(*loudly*)

No, I didn't.

LUCIA

Really, Father, he didn't. It was that dreadful Johnny Lewis.

CHARLES

I don't want to hear about Johnny Lewis. I want to know whether a son of mine . . .

LEONORA

Charles, I beg of you . . .

CHARLES

The first family of this city!

RODERICK
(*rising*)

I hate this town and everything about it. I always did.

CHARLES

You behaved like a spoiled puppy, sir, an ill-bred spoiled puppy.

RODERICK

What did I do? What did I do that was wrong?

CHARLES

You were drunk and you were rude to the daughters of my best friends.

GENEVIEVE
(*striking the table*)

Nothing in the world deserves an ugly scene like this. Charles, I'm ashamed of you.

RODERICK

Great God, you gotta get drunk in this town to forget how dull it is. Time passes so slowly here that it stands still, that's what's the trouble.

CHARLES

Well, young man, we can employ your time. You will leave the university and you will come into the Bayard factory on January second.

RODERICK

(*at the door into the hall*)

I have better things to do than to go into your old factory. I'm going somewhere where time passes, my God! (*He goes out into the hall.*)

LEONORA

(*rising*)

Roderick, Roderick, come here just a moment.—Charles, where can he go?

LUCIA

(*rising*)

Sh, Mother. He'll come back. Now I have to go upstairs and pack my trunk.

LEONORA

I won't have any children left!

LUCIA

Sh, Mother. He'll come back. He's only gone to California or somewhere.—Cousin Ermengarde has done most of my packing —thanks a thousand times, Cousin Ermengarde. (*She kisses her mother.*) I won't be long. (*She runs out into the hall.*)

(GENEVIEVE *and* LEONORA *put on their white hair.*)

ERMENGARDE

It's a very beautiful day. On the way home from church I stopped and saw Mrs. Foster a moment. Her arthritis comes and goes.

LEONORA

Is she actually in pain, dear?

ERMENGARDE

Oh, she says it'll all be the same in a hundred years!

LEONORA

Yes, she's a brave little stoic.

CHARLES

Come now, a little white meat, Mother?—Mary, pass my cousin's plate.

LEONORA

What is it, Mary?—Oh, here's a telegram from them in Paris! "Love and Christmas greetings to all." I told them we'd be eating some of their wedding cake and thinking about them today. It seems to be all decided that they will settle down in the East, Ermengarde. I can't even have my daughter for a neighbor. They hope to build before long somewhere on the shore north of New York.

GENEVIEVE

There is no shore north of New York.

LEONORA

Well, East or West or whatever it is.

(*Pause.*)

CHARLES

My, what a dark day.

(*He puts on his white hair. Pause.*)

How slowly time passes without any young people in the house.

LEONORA

I have three children somewhere.

CHARLES

(*blunderingly offering comfort*)

Well, one of them gave his life for his country.

LEONORA

(*sadly*)

And one of them is selling aluminum in China.

GENEVIEVE

(*slowly working herself up to a hysterical crisis*)

I can stand everything but this terrible soot everywhere. We should have moved long ago. We're surrounded by factories. We have to change the window curtains every week.

LEONORA

Why, Genevieve!

GENEVIEVE

I can't stand it. I can't stand it any more. I'm going abroad. It's not only the soot that comes through the very walls of this house; it's the *thoughts,* it's the thought of what has been and what might have been here. And the feeling about this house of the years *grinding away*. My mother died yesterday—not twenty-five years ago. Oh, I'm going to live and die abroad! Yes, I'm going to be the American old maid living and dying in a pension in Munich or Florence.

ERMENGARDE

Genevieve, you're tired.

CHARLES

Come, Genevieve, take a good drink of cold water. Mary, open the window a minute.

GENEVIEVE

I'm sorry. I'm sorry. (*She hurries tearfully out into the hall.*)

ERMENGARDE

Dear Genevieve will come back to us, I think. (*She rises and starts toward the dark portal.*) You should have been out today, Leonora. It was one of those days when everything was encircled with ice. Very pretty, indeed.

(CHARLES *rises and starts after her.*)

CHARLES

Leonora, I used to go skating with Father on mornings like this. —I wish I felt a little better.

LEONORA

What! Have I got two invalids on my hands at once? Now, Cousin Ermengarde, you must get better and help me nurse Charles.

ERMENGARDE

I'll do my best. (*She turns at the very portal and comes back to the table.*)

CHARLES

Well, Leonora, I'll do what you ask. I'll write the puppy a letter of forgiveness and apology. It's Christmas day. I'll cable it. That's what I'll do. (*He goes out the dark door.*)

LEONORA

(*drying her eyes*)

Ermengarde, it's such a comfort having you here with me. Mary, I really can't eat anything. Well, perhaps, a sliver of white meat.

ERMENGARDE

(*very old*)

I spoke to Mrs. Keene for a moment coming out of church. She asked after the young people.—At church I felt very proud sitting under our windows, Leonora, and our brass tablets. The Bayard aisle,—it's a regular Bayard aisle and I love it.

LEONORA

Ermengarde, would you be very angry with me if I went and stayed with the young people a little this Spring?

ERMENGARDE

Why, no. I know how badly they want you and need you. Especially now that they're about to build a new house.

LEONORA

You wouldn't be angry? This house is yours as long as you want it, remember.

ERMENGARDE

I don't see why the rest of you dislike it. I like it more than I can say.

LEONORA

I won't be long. I'll be back in no time and we can have some more of our readings-aloud in the evening.

(*She kisses her and goes into the hall.* ERMENGARDE *left alone, eats slowly and talks to Mary.*)

ERMENGARDE

Really, Mary, I'll change my mind. If you'll ask Bertha to be good enough to make me a little eggnog. A dear little eggnog. —Such a nice letter this morning from Mrs. Bayard, Mary. Such a nice letter. They're having their first Christmas dinner in the new house. They must be very happy. They call her Mother Bayard, she says, as though she were an old lady. And she says she finds it more comfortable to come and go in a wheel chair.—Such a dear letter. . . . And Mary, I can tell you a secret. It's still a great secret, mind! They're expecting a grandchild. Isn't that good news! Now I'll read a little.

(*She props a book up before her, still dipping a spoon into a custard from time to time. She grows from very old to immensely old. She sighs. The book falls down. She finds a cane beside her, and soon totters into the dark portal, murmuring:*)

Dear little Roderick and little Lucia.

THE END

The Ping-Pong Players

BY WILLIAM SAROYAN

In contrast to Thornton Wilder's structural theatricalization of reality is the technique of William Saroyan, whose theatricalism is less structural than whimsical. In the buoyantly lyrical world of Saroyan's imagination, representations may at first appear to be realistic, but they are soon broken through with non-realistic inventions of character and (especially) plot. These occurrences are consistent with his central theme, which is that were it not for circumstances, imagination would equal freedom, both in the play and in the world. ("My first impulse was simple," he noted in his essay "Why I Write," "I wanted to cause the impossible to happen . . . Thus, death would not be death, if anybody wanted it not to be.") The socially peripheral characters to whom he usually turns (actors, poets, children, dancers, prostitutes, wanderers, and inspired old men) are his "Beautiful People," gifted with an inscrutable, life-mastering force. In *The Ping-Pong Players,* a relatively early work, Saroyan sets up what might stand as an emblem of his personal aesthetic reality: Two ping-pong players/lovers struggle to maintain conventional and rather uninspired surfaces (represented by the tyrannical ping-pong table that lies between them) while attempting to resolve happily the intricacies of their romance. They conclude the play and remove the obstacles to their deeper feelings by smashing the ping-pong table and exiting. The comparison of the requirements of conventional existence with a meaningless ping-pong contest is curiously similar to the basic idea of a major "Absurd" drama of some decades later: Arthur Adamov's *Ping-Pong,* whose final scene seems like a pessimist's paraphrase of the Saroyan work. One might also note that, played properly, the choreographic actions of the characters around the table would provide an absorbing gestural, visual counterpoint to the text.

The Ping-Pong Players

SCENE: *A room.*
TIME: *After supper.*
A YOUNG MAN *and a* YOUNG WOMAN *are playing a game of ping-pong.*

YOUNG MAN
(*Making a point*)

I'm sorry.

YOUNG WOMAN

You've won again.

YOUNG MAN

No, that isn't game. That's 20–19.

YOUNG WOMAN

But you *will* win.

YOUNG MAN

You've got to try.

YOUNG WOMAN

Oh, I do. But you always win just the same. You're so much better than I am.

YOUNG MAN

The games are all close.

YOUNG WOMAN

That only makes it worse. I come so close to winning every game. And then I lose.

YOUNG MAN

I'm sorry I'm such a fool.

YOUNG WOMAN

You are not.

YOUNG MAN

I could let you win a game, you know.

YOUNG WOMAN

I should be hurt.

YOUNG MAN

I was *afraid* you would be. You're not the way most women are, you know.

YOUNG WOMAN

What do you mean?

YOUNG MAN

I mean you don't expect advantages. In fact you *give* advantages.

YOUNG WOMAN

No, I don't.

YOUNG MAN

You *do*. I'm sure you could beat me every game. You're a much better player.

YOUNG WOMAN

No. You are. You're steady and patient. That's why you *can't* lose.

YOUNG MAN

No. You are kind. It's very deep in you. So deep that you yourself don't realize it.

YOUNG WOMAN

Oh, really! I don't want you to imagine things about me.

YOUNG MAN

I'm not *imagining*.

YOUNG WOMAN

I'm sure you are.

YOUNG MAN

But why?

YOUNG WOMAN

I've wanted more than anything else in the world to beat you once—just once—at this silly little game. But I've never been able to do it.

YOUNG MAN

It's perfectly natural to want to win. The game wouldn't be worth playing if one didn't want to win.

YOUNG WOMAN

But I've wanted to *so* badly.

YOUNG MAN

As if I haven't.

YOUNG WOMAN

No, you haven't. You just play as if it were nothing. Nothing at all. That's the reason you win, too. Because you don't really care. Because it wouldn't hurt you if you lost. Even if you lost *all* the games.

YOUNG MAN

Oh, I *have* been a fool. I'm sorry.

YOUNG WOMAN

I've wanted terribly to beat you. I'm really quite ashamed.

(YOUNG MAN *looks at her*)

Let's not finish this game. And let's not play again.

YOUNG MAN

Really?

YOUNG WOMAN

Please.

YOUNG MAN

Oh, I'm delighted. I've always *hated* this game. I thought *you* liked it.

YOUNG WOMAN

No, I've hated it, too.

YOUNG MAN

Oh, how wonderful. Then we needn't bother any more?

YOUNG WOMAN

This is our last game.

YOUNG MAN

Let's break the table, and hit the silly little balls all over the place.

YOUNG WOMAN

Oh, let's.

YOUNG MAN

(*Hitting the ball*)

I must tell you something.

YOUNG WOMAN

(*Hitting another ball*)

Please tell me.

YOUNG MAN

I used to *think* I loved you. Now, I know I do.

(*He goes to her and looks at her*)

Where have you been?

YOUNG WOMAN

Oh, Lord, I wonder. I really don't know. I want to say something horrible. I really must.

YOUNG MAN

Oh, please do.

YOUNG WOMAN

I've hated you so much.

YOUNG MAN

Oh, this is wonderful. You're so lovely now. Do you know what?

YOUNG WOMAN

Yes?

YOUNG MAN

Now, I love your mother, too.

YOUNG WOMAN

Not *her!*

YOUNG MAN

Oh, yes. For doing me such a splendid kindness.

YOUNG WOMAN

What kindness could that be?

YOUNG MAN

Being your mother.

YOUNG WOMAN

Anybody's liable to be anybody's mother.

YOUNG MAN

Well, anybody who's been *your* mother, I love. And your father. Your father's mother, and father. Your mother's mother and father. I love them all. I never did before, you know. (*He hits a ball*) They're wretched people, you know.

YOUNG WOMAN

It's so silly not to be horrible, too, isn't it?

YOUNG MAN

It's absurd not to be everything one ought to be. Shall we quarrel? You know we never have. You know we've always been so polite and ridiculous, standing across from one another at a ping-pong table, batting a stupid little ball back and forth very carefully so that it wouldn't go out of bounds and would be a point in our favor. A stupid point in a stupid game. Let's really quarrel.

YOUNG WOMAN

All right. Let's shout at one another and strike one another and be perfectly beastly and wonderful.

YOUNG MAN

Darling, you are a bitch! Now, I feel wonderful.

YOUNG WOMAN

Darling, how dare you speak to me in that kind of language?

YOUNG MAN

(*Lifting his voice*)

I'll tell you what I please. I'll speak to you in any kind of language I please.

YOUNG WOMAN
(*Acidly*)

How dare you?

YOUNG MAN

You *are* a bitch, you know.

YOUNG WOMAN

You horrible, stupid, disgusting monkey.

YOUNG MAN

This is wonderful. You spoiled, overfed, hollow, sterile bitch.

YOUNG WOMAN

I'm going home to mother.

YOUNG MAN

Go to *hell,* and take your mother with you, too.

YOUNG WOMAN

Sterile? Why did you say that?

YOUNG MAN

We're quarreling. Let's not stop half-way, darling. You're not—

YOUNG WOMAN

I am.

YOUNG MAN

Don't be female and stupid. You're *not.*

YOUNG WOMAN

I am.

YOUNG MAN

You're a dirty liar.

YOUNG WOMAN

No. It's true. I was going to—

YOUNG MAN

You're lying.

YOUNG WOMAN

Really. I didn't want it. I hated it. I couldn't stand the thought of someone else like you.

YOUNG MAN

Oh, this is beautiful, all this wonderful lying. Let's really make a disgusting fight of it. Shall I hit you? I'll be careful.

YOUNG WOMAN

If you like, darling, and *don't* be careful.

YOUNG MAN

Oh, this is fun.

(*He goes to the* GIRL *and gets ready to strike her. Swings and intentionally misses*)

YOUNG WOMAN

Oh, but, darling, you can do better than *that.*

YOUNG MAN

I couldn't hit you.

YOUNG WOMAN

You said you would. You *said* you would. Please don't be a coward.

YOUNG MAN

I'll feel so disgusted with myself.

YOUNG WOMAN

Oh, please don't break your promise.

YOUNG MAN

(*Trying*)

I can't. Honest, I can't. I love you.

YOUNG WOMAN

If you love me, you must.

YOUNG MAN

You've got to give me a reason.

YOUNG WOMAN

I've been untrue to you.

YOUNG MAN

Oh, you *are* wonderful.

YOUNG WOMAN

No, really. I have.

YOUNG MAN

Oh, how exciting. Who?

YOUNG WOMAN

Oh, the awfulest people. Oh, ghastly people. You must keep your promise.

YOUNG MAN

I never imagined you could be so wonderful.

YOUNG WOMAN

You must hit me and be disgusted with yourself.

YOUNG MAN
(*Trying again*)

I can't. Honest, I can't.

YOUNG WOMAN

It's not yours. Now, will you do it?

YOUNG MAN

What's not mine?

YOUNG WOMAN

It's not yours, do you hear?

YOUNG MAN

Oh, this is wonderful. I almost believe you.

YOUNG WOMAN

I'm telling the truth.

YOUNG MAN

I swear it sounds as if you are. You really are a rich person.

YOUNG WOMAN

Please believe me.

YOUNG MAN

Aren't we quarreling?

YOUNG WOMAN

Yes, but I'm telling the truth. You will have to divorce me, or beat me, and I will have to have it destroyed. It's not yours.

YOUNG MAN

What are you saying?

YOUNG WOMAN

It's not yours.

YOUNG MAN

Why isn't it mine?

YOUNG WOMAN

It's another's. You must strike me, if you love me.

YOUNG MAN

I can't strike you. You do frighten a person, you know.

YOUNG WOMAN
(*Slaps his face*)
I'm with child. It's not yours. How many times do I have to tell you that?

YOUNG MAN
(*Shaking her*)
I heard you. Well, go ahead and have your wretched baby. This *is* dramatic, isn't it?

YOUNG WOMAN
Oh, heavens.

YOUNG MAN
Shall I really be angry with you?

YOUNG WOMAN
You might kill me.

YOUNG MAN
Shall we stop pretending?

YOUNG WOMAN
If you like.

YOUNG MAN
It was fun, though, wasn't it?

YOUNG WOMAN
The best I've ever had.
(*The* YOUNG WOMAN'S MOTHER *enters*)

MOTHER
I heard shouting. What *is* the matter?

YOUNG WOMAN
We've been quarreling.

MOTHER

What in the world about?

YOUNG WOMAN

I'm with child and it isn't (*Looking at* YOUNG MAN) my husband's.

MOTHER

My God, what are you saying?

YOUNG WOMAN

It's true.

YOUNG MAN

Isn't it wonderful?

MOTHER

Wonderful? Are you crazy?

YOUNG MAN

We decided to have an honest impolite quarrel. It's doing us so much good. I'll go get some beer, and we'll get drunk and really have a time. (*He goes*)

MOTHER

Now, what *is* this? You really frightened me.

YOUNG WOMAN
(*Sternly*)

I am with child, and it's not his.

MOTHER

Whose is it?

YOUNG WOMAN

I don't know.

MOTHER

What?

YOUNG WOMAN

Yes. There have been several. Four. The most wretched men in the world.

MOTHER

You *are* lying, aren't you?

YOUNG WOMAN

No. I'm telling the truth. *He* doesn't believe me either.

MOTHER

Oh, this is tiresome. What are you going to do?

YOUNG WOMAN

I don't know. Whatever he wishes, I suppose.

MOTHER

Please don't be a fool. He doesn't believe you.

YOUNG WOMAN

He must.

MOTHER

No.

YOUNG WOMAN

I love him. I *really* love him. I've never really loved him before. I've been perfectly ugly. He must understand what's happened. I'll do anything he says.

MOTHER

He mustn't know.

YOUNG WOMAN

I want him to want me to have it destroyed. Then we can really begin to be married. I didn't know until just now how much I love him.

MOTHER

If you tell him, I shall never speak to you again. I shall go home immediately.

YOUNG WOMAN

Please do, Mother. Go home and never speak to me again. Never.

MOTHER

Oh, you *are* horrible. (*She goes*)

(*The* YOUNG WOMAN *whacks a ball in the direction of her mother, who turns icily, stares at her, and goes.* YOUNG WOMAN *stares at the table a moment, then tips it over and kicks it several times, as* YOUNG MAN *returns with a* SERVANT *rolling a wagon with many bottles of beer.* SERVANT *goes*)

YOUNG MAN

We *are* having fun.

YOUNG WOMAN

Darling?

YOUNG MAN

Yes.

YOUNG WOMAN

Mother—

YOUNG MAN

What about her?

YOUNG WOMAN

She's gone home.

YOUNG MAN

Why? Just when I'm beginning to like her.

YOUNG WOMAN

I told her.

YOUNG MAN

You told her what?

YOUNG WOMAN

The truth.

YOUNG MAN

You mean, that I like her?

YOUNG WOMAN

No. That I'm with child, and it's not yours.

YOUNG MAN

You must have shocked her. You shouldn't have.

YOUNG WOMAN

Please.

YOUNG MAN

What is it?

YOUNG WOMAN

It's all true. I'm not lying.

YOUNG MAN

We've been having fun. Let's not spoil it. Let's get drunk on beer and be really disgusting. Let's not spoil it.

YOUNG WOMAN

I'm afraid we must.

YOUNG MAN

Why?

YOUNG WOMAN

It's true.

YOUNG MAN

Aren't we having fun?

YOUNG WOMAN

No.

YOUNG MAN

Oh.

(*Pause. He puts up the ping-pong table. Finds a ball. The* YOUNG WOMAN *takes a bat, gets ready*)

Ready?

YOUNG WOMAN

Ready.

YOUNG MAN

(*Serving*)

Whose is it?

YOUNG WOMAN

I don't know.

(*The point is the* YOUNG WOMAN'S)

YOUNG MAN

I'm quite hurt, you know.

YOUNG WOMAN

I know. I'm sorry.

YOUNG MAN

What do you want me to do?

YOUNG WOMAN

I really don't know.

YOUNG MAN

I'll not divorce you, you know. I *do* love you. I do love you still.

YOUNG WOMAN

You *must* divorce me. It's ghastly.

YOUNG MAN

No, really. I couldn't.

(*His point*)

YOUNG WOMAN

It wouldn't do at all.

YOUNG MAN

I'm not doing it for *you*. For me. I love you.

YOUNG WOMAN

Oh, you must divorce me.

YOUNG MAN

No.

YOUNG WOMAN

Oh, darling, let's stop playing this stupid game.

YOUNG MAN

Yes. (*Somberly*) It isn't going to be easy to—

YOUNG WOMAN

It's *mine*—at least.

YOUNG MAN

Oh, yes.—But I do wish it were partly mine, too.

(*He whacks a ball*)

YOUNG WOMAN

I wish it were, too. More than anything in the world.

(*She pushes over table and kicks it. They look at one another in silence*)

YOUNG MAN

Well.

YOUNG WOMAN

Darling?

YOUNG MAN

Yes.

YOUNG WOMAN

It's yours.

YOUNG MAN

Mine?

YOUNG WOMAN

Yes. I've never been untrue.

YOUNG MAN

You wonderful bitch.

YOUNG WOMAN

Oh, darling.

YOUNG MAN
(*Beer*)

From now on we're going to have all kinds of fun.

YOUNG WOMAN
(*Beer*)

Yes.

YOUNG MAN

First we're going to wreck this ping-pong table.

YOUNG WOMAN
(*Wrecking a leg*)

Oh, darling.

YOUNG MAN

Then we're going to get cockeyed. If you're lying, or if you're telling the truth, I love you, because you're mine and whatever is yours is mine, and nothing in the world can ever change that. Come on, let's go to a honky-tonk and get drunk and stay out all night.

(*He takes her arm. They go*)

The Tridget of Greva and *Abend di Anni Nouveau*

BY RING LARDNER

In a series of short plays he wrote at the peak of his career, the great humorist Ring Lardner's wit sails beyond the outrageously whimsical and into the completely black (one might note here that "Black Humor" is a term coined in the 1920s by André Breton, French Surrealism's chief spokesman). There are certain general resemblances to certain short European skits and dramas of the period—those by Daumal and Lecomte for example—but it seems doubtful that Lardner could have known their privately circulated writings. The spirit of Dada and Surrealism is, at any rate, certainly present. There is even a curious parallelism: instead of a fourth act, Breton's and Phillippe Soupault's drama *If You Please* (1920) presented the statement: "The authors of this play do not want the fourth act printed"; *Abend di Anni Nouveau* concludes with a section identified as Acts 3, 4, and 5. The first of the plays here is *The Tridget of Greva,* a work actually presented as part of a revue called *The Forty-Niners,* given by several members of the famous Algonquin Round Table of New York writers and critics. Whether or not, like so many French *pièces à lire* (plays for reading) of the period, the *Tridget* is actually performable (some of its humor lies in its stage directions) it, too, possesses rare qualities of freedom and charm.

The Tridget of Greva
TRANSLATED FROM THE SQUINCH

CHARACTERS

LOUIS BARHOOTER, *the Tridget*
DESIRE CORBY, *a Corn Vitter*
BASIL LAFFLER, *a Wham Salesman*

At the rise of the curtain, BARHOOTER, CORBY *and* LAFFLER *are seated in three small flat-bottomed boats. They are fishing.*

LAFFLER

Well, boys, any luck?

(*He looks from one to the other. Neither pays any attention*)

CORBY

(*After a pause, to* BARHOOTER)

How's your wife, Louis?

BARHOOTER

She in pretty bad shape.

CORBY

(*Who has paid no attention to the reply*)

That's fine.

BARHOOTER

By the way, what was *your* mother's name before she was married?

CORBY

I didn't know her then.

LAFFLER

Do they allow people to fish at the Aquarium?

(BARHOOTER *and* CORBY *ignore him*)

BARHOOTER

You must know her first name.

CORBY

I don't. I always called her Mother.

BARHOOTER

But your father must have called her something.

CORBY

Everything he could think of.

(LAFFLER'S *and* BARHOOTER'S *fishlines become entangled.* BARHOOTER *gets out of his boat, untangles the lines, and resumes his place in the boat*)

BARHOOTER

(*To* CORBY)

I wanted to ask you something about your sister, too.

CORBY

What about her?

BARHOOTER

Just anything. For instance, what's the matter with her?

CORBY

Who?

BARHOOTER

Your sister.

CORBY

I'm not married.

(*After a pause,* BARHOOTER *and* CORBY *both laugh.*)

BARHOOTER
(*To* LAFFLER)
Do you know what we were laughing at?

LAFFLER
I have no idea.

BARHOOTER
I wish I knew who to ask.

CORBY
(*To* BARHOOTER)
Which way is the wind from?

BARHOOTER
(*Moistens his finger and holds it up*)
It's from off-stage. (*He draws in his line, discovers the bait is gone*) That fellow got my bait. (*He throws his line out again without rebaiting it.*)

CORBY
(*To* BARHOOTER)
I understand you're an uncle.

BARHOOTER
Yes, but do you want to know what happened?

CORBY
No.

BARHOOTER
Well, two days before the baby was born, Bertha and her husband were out driving.

LAFFLER
Who's Bertha?

BARHOOTER

(*Paying no attention*)

They were going up a steep hill and Harry tried to change into second speed.

LAFFLER

Who's Harry?

BARHOOTER

But he made a mistake and shifted into reverse and the car went clear to the bottom of the hill.

CORBY

In reverse?

BARHOOTER

Yes. And the baby is very backward.

CORBY

It seems to me there is something wrong with all your sister's children. Look at Julia!

(BARHOOTER *and* LAFFLER *look in all directions, as if trying to locate Julia*)

BARHOOTER

(*To* CORBY)

Can you imitate birds?

CORBY

No. Why?

BARHOOTER

I'm always afraid I'll be near somebody that can imitate birds.

CORBY

(*To* BARHOOTER)

That reminds me, Louis—Do you shave yourself?

BARHOOTER

Who would I shave?

CORBY

Well, when you shave, what do you do with your old whiskers?

BARHOOTER

I don't do anything with them.

CORBY

Will you save them for me?

BARHOOTER

What do you do with them?

CORBY

I play with them.

BARHOOTER

(*With no apparent interest*)

You're a scream, Corby.

LAFFLER

(*To* BARHOOTER)

Is your first wife still living?

BARHOOTER

I'm not sure. I haven't been home for a long while. But I heard she was dead.

LAFFLER

What did she die of?

BARHOOTER

I think she got her throat caught between my fingers.

LAFFLER

Mr. Corby—

CORBY

Well?

LAFFLER

I often wonder how you spell your name.

CORBY

A great many people have asked me that. The answer is, I don't even try. I just let it go.

LAFFLER

I think that's kind of risky.

CORBY

I'm getting hungry. I wish we could catch some fish.

BARHOOTER

I'm hungry, too, but not for fish.

LAFFLER

I can't eat fish either. I've got no teeth. (*Opens his mouth and shows his teeth*) About all I can eat is broth.

BARHOOTER

Well, let's go to a brothel.

BLACK OUT

Abend di Anni Nouveau

A PLAY IN FIVE ACTS

CHARACTERS

ST. JOHN ERVINE, *an immigrant.*
WALTER WINCHELL, *a nun.*
HEYWOOD BROUN, *an usher at Roxy's.*
DOROTHY THOMPSON, *a tackle.*
THEODORE DREISER, *a former Follies girl.*
H. L. MENCKEN, *a kleagle in the Moose.*
MABEL WILLEBRANDT, *secretary of the League of American Wheelmen.*
BEN HECHT, *a taxi starter.*
JOHN ROACH STRATON, *a tap dancer.*
CARL LAEMMLE, *toys and games, sporting goods, outing flannels.*
ANNE NICHOLS, *a six-day bicyclist.*

ACT 1

A hired hall. It is twenty-five minutes of nine on New Year's Eve. A party, to which all the members of the cast were invited, is supposed to have begun at thirty-four minutes after eight. A WAITER *enters on a horse and finds all the guests dead, their bodies riddled with bullets and frightfully garbled. He goes to the telephone.*

WAITER
(*telephoning*)

I want a policeman. I want to report a fire. I want an ambulance. (*He tethers his mount and lies down on the hors d'oeuvres. The curtain is lowered and partially destroyed to denote the passage of four days.* TWO POLICEMEN *enter, neither having had any idea that the other would come. They find the* WAITER *asleep and shake him. He wakes and smilingly points at the havoc.*)

WAITER

Look at the havoc.

FIRST POLICEMAN

This is the first time I ever seen a havoc.

SECOND POLICEMAN

It's an inside job, I think.

FIRST POLICEMAN

You WHAT?

WAITER

The trouble now is that we'll have to recast the entire play. Every member of the cast is dead.

FIRST POLICEMAN

Is that unusual?

SECOND POLICEMAN

When did it happen?

WAITER

When did what happen?

SECOND POLICEMAN

I've forgotten.

(END OF ACT 1)

ACT 2

The interior of an ambulance. Three men named LOUIE BREESE *are playing bridge with an* INTERNE. *The* INTERNE *is* LOUIE BREESE'S *partner.* LOUIE *leads a club. The* INTERNE *trumps it.*

BREESE

Kindly play interne.

INTERNE

I get you men confused.

BREESE

I'm not confused.

THE OTHER TWO BREESES

Neither of us is confused.

(*They throw the* INTERNE *onto Seventh Avenue. An East Side* GANGSTER, *who was being used as a card table, gets up and stretches.*)

GANGSTER

Where are we at?

BREESE

Was you the stretcher we was playing on?

GANGSTER

Yes.

BREESE

There's only three of us now. Will you make a fourt'?

GANGSTER

There's no snow.

(END OF ACT 2)

ACTS 3, 4 AND 5

A one-way street in Jeopardy. Two SNAIL-GUNDERS *enter from the right, riding a tricycle. They shout their wares.*

FIRST SNAIL-GUNDER

Wares! Wares!

A NEWSBOY

Wares who?

FIRST SNAIL-GUNDER

Anybody. That is, anybody who wants their snails gunded.

(*Three men suddenly begin to giggle. It is a secret, but they give the impression that one of them's mother runs a waffle parlor. They go off the stage still giggling. Two Broadway* THEATRICAL PRODUCERS, *riding pelicans, enter almost nude.*)

FIRST PRODUCER

Have you got a dime?

SECOND PRODUCER

What do you think I am, a stage hand?

FIRST PRODUCER

Have you seen my new farce?

SECOND PRODUCER

No. I was out of town that night.

(END OF ACTS 3, 4 AND 5)

Three Travelers Watch a Sunrise

BY WALLACE STEVENS

It is by no means unprecedented that several of the most theatrically inventive of American plays should have been written by poets. In Europe, particularly in France, in the early years of the twentieth century, such writers as Apollinaire, Cocteau, Breton, Tzara and others were creating a completely new kind of non-naturalistic theatre, as well as poetry. Stevens' aesthetic as both playwright and poet was similarly uncommon. Following the roughish and realistic, or sometimes the merely picturesque and outdoorsy verse that dominated American poetry in the first decade of the century, Stevens proposed in his first book (*Harmonium,* 1923) that "poetry is the supreme fiction." Stevens' first play, composed about the same time as was his first book, is informed by the same sense of the role of artifice in art that shaped his poetry. There is the same tenuous, decorous style of verbal movement; the same attention to exquisiteness of decor, seen in numerous references to porcelains, jars, baskets, and various examples of *chinoiserie.* (There may even be a hint of actual familiarity with oriental theatre—a quality already introduced into English-speaking drama in the plays of W. B. Yeats, and the translations of Ezra Pound, both of whom explored the form of the Japanese Noh play.) Obviously, the frank acknowledgment and cultivation of artifice in poetry is not far from the stressing of theatricalism in the theatre. Though the plot of *Three Travelers Watch a Sunrise* involves love, the passions, and a mysterious crime, all these are accompanied by strummings of instruments on stage, the formalized serving of tea, and other ceremonial events. The whole has the quality of a delicate, stylized, self-contained ritual.

Three Travelers Watch a Sunrise

The characters are THREE CHINESE, TWO NEGROES *and* A GIRL.

The scene represents a forest of heavy trees on a hilltop in eastern Pennsylvania. To the right is a road, obscured by bushes. It is about four o'clock of a morning in August, at the present time.

When the curtain rises, the stage is dark. The limb of a tree creaks. A NEGRO *carrying a lantern passes along the road. The sound is repeated. The* NEGRO *comes through the bushes, raises his lantern and looks through the trees. Discerning a dark object among the branches, he shrinks back, crosses stage, and goes out through the woods to the left.*

A SECOND NEGRO *comes through the bushes to the right. He carries two large baskets, which he places on the ground just inside of the bushes. Enter* THREE CHINESE, *one of whom carries a lantern. They pause on the road.*

SECOND CHINESE

All you need,
To find poetry,
Is to look for it with a lantern.

(*The* CHINESE *laugh.*)

THIRD CHINESE

I could find it without,
On an August night,
If I saw no more
Than the dew on the barns.

(*The* SECOND NEGRO *makes a sound to attract their attention. The* THREE CHINESE *come through the bushes. The first is short, fat, quizzical, and of middle age. The second is of middle height, thin and turning gray; a man of sense and sympathy. The third is a young man, intent, detached. They wear European clothes.*)

SECOND CHINESE
(*glancing at the baskets*)

Dew is water to see,
Not water to drink:
We have forgotten water to drink.
Yet I am content
Just to see sunrise again.
I have not seen it
Since the day we left Pekin.
It filled my doorway,
Like whispering women.

FIRST CHINESE

And I have never seen it.
If we have no water,
Do find a melon for me
In the baskets.

(*The* SECOND NEGRO, *who has been opening the baskets, hands the* FIRST CHINESE *a melon.*)

FIRST CHINESE

Is there no spring?

(*The* NEGRO *takes a water bottle of red porcelain from one of the baskets and places it near the* THIRD CHINESE.)

SECOND CHINESE
(*to* THIRD CHINESE)

Your porcelain water bottle.

(*One of the baskets contains costumes of silk, red, blue, and green. During the following speeches, the* CHINESE *put on these costumes, with the assistance of the* NEGRO, *and seat themselves on the ground.*)

THIRD CHINESE

This fetches its own water.

(*Takes the bottle and places it on the ground in the center of the stage.*)

I drink from it, dry as it is,
As you from maxims, (*to* SECOND CHINESE)
Or you from melons. (*to* FIRST CHINESE)

FIRST CHINESE

Not as I, from melons.
Be sure of that.

SECOND CHINESE

Well, it is true of maxims.

(*He finds a book in the pocket of his costume, and reads from it.*)

"The court had known poverty and wretchedness; humanity had invaded its seclusion, with its suffering and its pity."

(*The limb of the tree creaks.*)

Yes: it is true of maxims,
Just as it is true of poets,
Or wise men, or nobles,
Or jade.

FIRST CHINESE

Drink from wise men? From jade?
Is there no spring?

(*Turning to the* NEGRO, *who has taken a jug from one of the baskets.*)

Fill it and return.

(*The* NEGRO *removes a large candle from one of the baskets and hands it to the* FIRST CHINESE; *then takes the jug and the lantern and enters the trees to the left. The* FIRST CHINESE *lights the candle and places it on the ground near the water bottle.*)

THIRD CHINESE

There is a seclusion of porcelain
That humanity never invades.

FIRST CHINESE
(*with sarcasm*)

Porcelain!

THIRD CHINESE

It is like the seclusion of sunrise,
Before it shines on any house.

FIRST CHINESE

Pooh!

SECOND CHINESE

This candle is the sun;
This bottle is earth:
It is an illustration
Used by generations of hermits.
The point of difference from reality
Is this:
That, in this illustration,
The earth remains of one color—
It remains red,
It remains what it is.
But when the sun shines on the earth,
In reality
It does not shine on a thing that remains
What it was yesterday.
The sun rises
On whatever the earth happens to be.

THIRD CHINESE

And there are indeterminate moments
Before it rises,
Like this,
(*with a backward gesture*)
Before one can tell
What the bottle is going to be—
Porcelain, Venetian glass,
Egyptian . . .

Well, there are moments
When the candle, sputtering up,
Finds itself in seclusion,
(*He raises the candle in the air.*)
And shines, perhaps, for the beauty of shining.
That is the seclusion of sunrise
Before it shines on any house.
(*replacing the candle*)

FIRST CHINESE
(*wagging his head*)
As abstract as porcelain.

SECOND CHINESE
Such seclusion knows beauty
As the court knew it.
The court woke
In its windless pavilions,
And gazed on chosen mornings,
As it gazed
On chosen porcelain.
What the court saw was always of the same color,
And well shaped,
And seen in a clear light.
(*He points to the candle.*)
It never woke to see,
And never knew,
The flawed jars,
The weak colors,
The contorted glass.
It never knew
The poor lights.
(*He opens his book significantly.*)
When the court knew beauty only,
And in seclusion,
It had neither love nor wisdom.
These came through poverty
And wretchedness,
Through suffering and pity.

(*He pauses.*)

It is the invasion of humanity
That counts.

(*The limb of the tree creaks. The* FIRST CHINESE *turns, for a moment, in the direction of the sound.*)

FIRST CHINESE
(*thoughtfully*)

The light of the most tranquil candle
Would shudder on a bloody salver.

SECOND CHINESE
(*with a gesture of disregard*)

It is the invasion
That counts.
If it be supposed that we are three figures
Painted on porcelain
As we sit here,
That we are painted on this very bottle,
The hermit of the place,
Holding this candle to us,
Would wonder;
But if it be supposed
That we are painted as warriors,
The candle would tremble in his hands;
Or if it be supposed, for example,
That we are painted as three dead men,
He could not see the steadiest light
For sorrow.
It would be true
If the emperor himself
Held the candle.
He would forget the porcelain
For the figures painted on it.

THIRD CHINESE
(*shrugging his shoulders*)

Let the candle shine for the beauty of shining.
I dislike the invasion

And long for the windless pavilions.
And yet it may be true
That nothing is beautiful
Except with reference to ourselves,
Nor ugly,
Nor high,

(*pointing to the sky*)

Nor low.

(*pointing to the candle*)

No: not even sunrise.
Can you play of this

(*mockingly to* FIRST CHINESE)

For us?

(*He stands up.*)

FIRST CHINESE
(*hesitatingly*)

I have a song
Called *Mistress and Maid.*
It is of no interest to hermits
Or emperors,
Yet it has a bearing;
For if we affect sunrise,
We affect all things.

THIRD CHINESE

It is a pity it is of women.
Sing it.

(*He takes an instrument from one of the baskets and hands it to the* FIRST CHINESE, *who sings the following song, accompanying himself, somewhat tunelessly, on the instrument. The* THIRD CHINESE *takes various things out of the basket for tea. He arranges fruit. The* FIRST CHINESE *watches him while he plays. The* SECOND CHINESE *gazes at the ground. The sky shows the first signs of morning.*)

FIRST CHINESE

The mistress says, in a harsh voice,
"He will be thinking in strange countries
Of the white stones near my door,
And I—I am tired of him."
She says sharply, to her maid,
"Sing to yourself no more."

Then the maid says, to herself,
"He will be thinking in strange countries
Of the white stones near her door;
But it is me he will see
At the window, as before.

"He will be thinking in strange countries
Of the green gown I wore.
He was saying good-by to her."
The maid drops her eyes and says to her mistress,
"I shall sing to myself no more."

THIRD CHINESE

That affects the white stones,
To be sure.

(*They laugh.*)

FIRST CHINESE

And it affects the green gown.

SECOND CHINESE

Here comes our black man.

(*The* SECOND NEGRO *returns, somewhat agitated, with water but without his lantern. He hands the jug to the* THIRD CHINESE. *The* FIRST CHINESE *from time to time strikes the instrument. The* THIRD CHINESE, *who faces the left, peers in the direction from which the* NEGRO *has come.*)

THIRD CHINESE

You have left your lantern behind you.
It shines, among the trees,
Like evening Venus in a cloud-top.

(*The* SECOND NEGRO *grins but makes no explanation. He seats himself behind the* CHINESE *to the right.*)

FIRST CHINESE

Or like a ripe strawberry
Among its leaves.

(*They laugh.*)

I heard tonight
That they are searching the hill
For an Italian.
He disappeared with his neighbor's daughter.

SECOND CHINESE
(*confidingly*)

I am sure you heard
The first eloping footfall
And the drum
Of pursuing feet.

FIRST CHINESE
(*amusedly*)

It was not an elopement.
The young gentleman was seen
To climb the hill
In the manner of a tragedian
Who sweats.
Such things happen in the evening.
He was
Un miserable.

SECOND CHINESE

Reach the lady quickly.

(*The* FIRST CHINESE *strikes the instrument twice as a prelude to his narrative.*)

FIRST CHINESE

There are as many points of view
From which to regard her
As there are sides to a round bottle.
(*pointing to the water bottle*)
She was represented to me
As beautiful.

(*They laugh. The* FIRST CHINESE *strikes the instrument, and looks at the* THIRD CHINESE, *who yawns.*)

FIRST CHINESE
(*reciting*)

She was as beautiful as a porcelain water bottle.
(*He strikes the instrument in an insinuating manner.*)

FIRST CHINESE

She was represented to me
As young.
Therefore my song should go
Of the color of blood.

(*He strikes the instrument. The limb of the tree creaks. The* FIRST CHINESE *notices it and puts his hand on the knee of the* SECOND CHINESE, *who is seated between him and the* THIRD CHINESE, *to call attention to the sound. They are all seated so that they do not face the spot from which the sound comes. A dark object, hanging to the limb of the tree, becomes a dim silhouette. The sky grows constantly brighter. No color is to be seen until the end of the play.*)

SECOND CHINESE
(*to* FIRST CHINESE)

It is only a tree
Creaking in the night wind.

THIRD CHINESE
(*shrugging his shoulders*)

There would be no creaking
In the windless pavilions.

FIRST CHINESE
(*resuming*)

So far the lady of the present ballad
Would have been studied
By the hermit and his candle
With much philosophy;
And possibly the emperor would have cried,
"More light!"
But it is a way with ballads
That the more pleasing they are
The worse end they come to;
For here it was also represented
That the lady was poor—
The hermit's candle would have thrown
Alarming shadows,
And the emperor would have held
The porcelain in one hand . . .
She was represented as clinging
To that sweaty tragedian,
And weeping up the hill.

SECOND CHINESE
(*with a grimace*)

It does not sound like an elopement.

FIRST CHINESE

It is a doleful ballad,
Fit for keyholes.

THIRD CHINESE

Shall we hear more?

SECOND CHINESE

Why not?

THIRD CHINESE

We came for isolation,
To rest in sunrise.

SECOND CHINESE

(*raising his book slightly*)

But this will be a part of sunrise,
And can you tell how it will end?—
Venetian,
Egyptian,
Contorted glass . . .

(*He turns toward the light in the sky to the right, darkening the candle with his hands.*)

In the meantime, the candle shines,

(*indicating the sunrise*)

As you say,

(*to the* THIRD CHINESE)

For the beauty of shining.

FIRST CHINESE

(*sympathetically*)

Oh! it will end badly.
The lady's father
Came clapping behind them
To the foot of the hill.
He came crying,
"Anna, Anna, Anna!"

(*imitating*)

He was alone without her,
Just as the young gentleman
Was alone without her:
Three beggars, you see,
Begging for one another.

(*The* FIRST NEGRO, *carrying two lanterns, approaches cautiously through the trees. At the sight of him, the* SECOND NEGRO, *seated near the* CHINESE, *jumps to his feet. The* CHINESE *get up in alarm. The* SECOND NEGRO *goes around the* CHINESE *toward the* FIRST NEGRO. *All see the body of a man hanging to the limb of the tree. They gather together, keeping their eyes fixed on it. The* FIRST NEGRO *comes out of the trees and places the lanterns on the ground. He looks at the group and then at the body.*)

FIRST CHINESE
(*moved*)
The young gentleman of the ballad.

THIRD CHINESE
(*slowly, approaching the body*)
And the end of the ballad.
Take away the bushes.
(*The* NEGROES *commence to pull away the bushes.*)

SECOND CHINESE
Death, the hermit,
Needs no candle
In his hermitage.
(*The* SECOND CHINESE *snuffs out the candle. The* FIRST CHINESE *puts out the lanterns. As the bushes are pulled away, the figure of* A GIRL, *sitting half stupefied under the tree, suddenly becomes apparent to the* SECOND CHINESE *and then to the* THIRD CHINESE. *They step back. The* NEGROES *move to the left. When the* FIRST CHINESE *sees the* GIRL, *the instrument slips from his hands and falls noisily to the ground. The* GIRL *stirs.*)

SECOND CHINESE
(*to the* GIRL)
Is that you, Anna?
(*The* GIRL *starts. She raises her head, looks around slowly, leaps to her feet and screams.*)

SECOND CHINESE
(*gently*)
Is that you, Anna?
(*She turns quickly toward the body, looks at it fixedly and totters up the stage.*)

ANNA
(*bitterly*)

Go.
Tell my father:
He is dead.

(*The* SECOND *and* THIRD CHINESE *support her. The* FIRST NEGRO *whispers to the* FIRST CHINESE, *then takes the lanterns and goes through the opening to the road, where he disappears in the direction of the valley.*)

FIRST CHINESE
(*to* SECOND NEGRO)

Bring us fresh water
From the spring.

(*The* SECOND NEGRO *takes the jug and enters the trees to the left. The* GIRL *comes gradually to herself. She looks at the* CHINESE *and at the sky. She turns her back toward the body, shuddering, and does not look at it again.*)

ANNA

It will soon be sunrise.

SECOND CHINESE

One candle replaces
Another.

(*The* FIRST CHINESE *walks toward the bushes to the right. He stands by the roadside, as if to attract the attention of anyone passing.*)

ANNA
(*simply*)

When he was in his fields,
I worked in ours—
Wore purple to see;
And when I was in his garden
I wore gold ear-rings.
Last evening I met him on the road.

He asked me to walk with him
To the top of the hill.
I felt the evil,
But he wanted nothing.
He hanged himself in front of me.

(*She looks for support. The* SECOND *and* THIRD CHINESE *help her toward the road. At the roadside, the* FIRST CHINESE *takes the place of the* THIRD CHINESE. *The girl and the two* CHINESE *go through the bushes and disappear down the road. The stage is empty except for the* THIRD CHINESE. *He walks slowly across the stage, pushing the instrument out of his way with his foot. It reverberates. He looks at the water bottle.*)

THIRD CHINESE

Of the color of blood . . .
Seclusion of porcelain . . .
Seclusion of sunrise . . .
(*He picks up the water bottle.*)
The candle of the sun
Will shine soon
On this hermit earth
(*indicating the bottle*)
It will shine soon
Upon the trees,
And find a new thing
(*indicating the body*)
Painted on this porcelain,
(*indicating the trees*)
But not on this.
(*indicating the bottle*)

(*He places the bottle on the ground. A narrow cloud over the valley becomes red. He turns toward it, then walks to the right. He finds the book of the Second Chinese lying on the ground, picks it up and turns over the leaves.*)

Red is not only
The color of blood,
Or

(*indicating the body*)

Of a man's eyes,
Or

(*pointedly*)

Of a girl's.
And as the red of the sun
Is one thing to me
And one thing to another,
So it is the green of one tree

(*indicating*)

And the green of another,
Without which it would all be black.
Sunrise is multiplied,
Like the earth on which it shines,
By the eyes that open on it,
Even dead eyes,
As red is multiplied by the leaves of trees.

(*Toward the end of this speech, the* SECOND NEGRO *comes from the trees to the left, without being seen. The* THIRD CHINESE, *whose back is turned toward the* NEGRO, *walks through the bushes to the right and disappears on the road. The* NEGRO *looks around at the objects on the stage. He sees the instrument, seats himself before it and strikes it several times, listening to the sound. One or two birds twitter. A voice, urging a horse, is heard at a distance. There is the crack of a whip. The* NEGRO *stands up, walks to the right and remains at the side of the road. The curtain falls slowly.*)

Santa Claus

BY E. E. CUMMINGS

E. E. Cummings' view of theatrical as well as other aesthetic phenomena was in every way uncommon for his day; and some of his views of popular American culture were prophetic of attitudes which were to make themselves widely felt only decades later. In a review, he asserted that ". . . the daily comic strip of George Herriman ("Krazy Kat") is easily the most amusing and fantastic and satisfactory work of art produced in America today; Ring Lardner and Mr. Dooley in their best work are more entertaining and more important than James Branch Cabell and Joseph Hergesheimer; . . . Florenz Ziegfeld is a better producer than David Belasco; . . . the circus can be and often is more artistic than the Metropolitan Opera House in New York." As a theatre critic in the mid-twenties, Cummings seems to have developed an unconventional sense of theatre as event; once he reviewed a boxing-match. He is the author of two full-length plays. *him,* a product of the twenties, is unusual both for its excellence and because it was influenced less by the Nordic psychological dramas of Ibsen and Strindberg, which dominated the psychologically realistic theatre of the period, than by the more distinctly anti-realistic style of French Surrealism. *Santa Claus,* published two decades after *him,* explores a prenaturalistic approach. It is a modern morality play. Its characters may casually suggest the outlines of "real people," but at the same time they most trenchantly represent such abstract forces as Evil, Good, and Mankind itself. Cummings' fascination with the pageant aspect of the morality genre is augmented by hints of other kinds of spectacle, not only the circus, but the burlesque and vaudeville halls as well. For all its gravity, *Santa Claus* has a breathtakingly brisk, revue-like pace. As in most spectacles, there is a key use of masks and other apparel; the play revolves around an exchange of character, effected simply by a quick shift of costumes.

Santa Claus
A MORALITY

for Fritz Wittels

CHARACTERS

DEATH
SANTA CLAUS
MOB
CHILD
WOMAN

SCENE ONE

DEATH, *strolling—he wears black tights on which the bones of his skeleton are vividly suggested by daubs of white paint, and his mask imitates crudely the face of a fleshless human skull. Enter, slowly and despondently, a prodigiously paunchy figure in faded red motheaten Santa Claus costume, with the familiar Santa Claus mask-face of a bewhiskered jolly old man.*

DEATH: Something wrong, brother?
SANTA CLAUS: Yes.
DEATH: Sick?
SANTA CLAUS: Sick at heart.
DEATH: What seems to be the trouble? Come—speak out.
SANTA CLAUS: I have so much to give; and nobody will take.
DEATH: My problem is also one of distribution,
only it happens to be the other way round.
SANTA CLAUS: The other way round?
DEATH: Quite.
SANTA CLAUS: What do you mean?

DEATH: I mean
I have so much to take; and nobody will give.
SANTA CLAUS: Strange.
DEATH: Strange, indeed. But this is even stranger:
I'm certain I can help you.
SANTA CLAUS: Very kind—
DEATH: Tut, tut; who helps another helps himself.
Now if I may be allowed to analyze your case—
SANTA CLAUS: Analyze?
DEATH: Listen. You're trying to give people something—right?
SANTA CLAUS: Right.
DEATH: And people won't take it?
SANTA CLAUS: Right.
DEATH: Why not?
SANTA CLAUS: Why not, indeed; I wish I knew.
DEATH: Because, my poor misguided friend, they can't.
SANTA CLAUS: Can't?
DEATH: Cannot.
SANTA CLAUS: But surely nothing could be simpler than taking something which is freely offered?
DEATH: You're speaking of a true or actual world.
Imagine, if you can, a world so blurred
that its inhabitants are one another
—an idiotic monster of negation:
so timid, it would rather starve itself
eternally than run the risk of choking;
so greedy, nothing satisfies its hunger
but always huger quantities of nothing—
a world so lazy that it cannot dream;
so blind, it worships its own ugliness:
a world so false, so trivial, so unso,
phantoms are solid by comparison.
But no—you can't imagine such a world.
SANTA CLAUS: Any more than such a world could imagine me.
DEATH: Very good. Now as to this ungivable something you're trying to give, this gift which nobody can take—what, just exactly, is it?

SANTA CLAUS: I don't know.
DEATH: I do.
SANTA CLAUS: Do you?
DEATH: Yes. It is understanding.
SANTA CLAUS: Understanding?
DEATH: Yes.
SANTA CLAUS: Tell me, how do you know?
DEATH: You told me, when you answered "I don't know."
And when you said you had something to give, you told me;
for isn't understanding the only gift?
Well, there's precisely your predicament.
We are not living in an age of gifts:
this is an age of salesmanship, my friend;
and you are heavy with the only thing
which simply can't be sold.
SANTA CLAUS: May I ask you a question?
DEATH: Go right ahead.
SANTA CLAUS: What's the easiest thing to sell?
DEATH: Knowledge.
SANTA CLAUS: Knowledge—without understanding?
DEATH: Correct.
SANTA CLAUS: No.
DEATH: Absolutely.
SANTA CLAUS: But that's absurd!
DEATH: Absurd—and also tragic; yet a fact.
In this empty un-understanding world
anyone can sell knowledge; everybody wants knowledge,
and there's no price people won't pay to get it.
—Become a Scientist and your fortune's made.
SANTA CLAUS: Scientist—?
DEATH: Or, in plain English, a knowledge-salesman.
SANTA CLAUS: I have no knowledge . . . only understanding—
DEATH: Forget your understanding for a while,
(*he plucks off* SANTA CLAUS' *mask, revealing a young man's face*)
and as for knowledge, why, don't let that worry you:
(*he slips off his own mask, revealing a fleshless human skull,*

and crams the skull mask over the young face of SANTA CLAUS)

once people hear the magic name of "Science"

(*slipping the* SANTA CLAUS *mask over his own skull face*)

you can sell people anything—except understanding.

SANTA CLAUS: Yes?

DEATH: Anything at all.

SANTA CLAUS: You mean, provided—

DEATH: Provided nothing!

SANTA CLAUS: You don't mean to tell me

I could sell people something which didn't exist?

DEATH: Why not? You don't suppose people exist, do you?

SANTA CLAUS: Don't people exist?

DEATH: People?—I'll say they don't!

I wish to heaven they did exist; in that case

I shouldn't be the skeleton I am.

No—in this "Science" game, this "knowledge" racket,

infinity's your limit; but remember:

the less something exists, the more people want it.

SANTA CLAUS: I can't seem to think of anything which doesn't exist.

—perhaps you could help me.

DEATH: How about a wheelmine?

SANTA CLAUS: A wheelmine?

DEATH: Surely a wheelmine doesn't exist

and never will, and never has existed.

SANTA CLAUS: A wheelmine . . . but that's perfectly fantastic!

DEATH: Why say "fantastic" when you mean "Scientific"?

—Well, I'll be strolling. So long, Mister Scientist!

Scene Two

(SANTA CLAUS, *masked as* DEATH, *haranguing a Mob*)

SANTA CLAUS: Hear ye! Hear ye! I am a Scientist!

And just to prove it, ladies and gentlemen,

I'll tell you anything you want to know.
—Go ahead: ask me something; anything.

VOICE: Mister.

SANTA CLAUS: Yes?

VOICE: How can I make a million dollars?

SANTA CLAUS: A million dollars—is that all you want?

VOICE: Well, I could use a couple, if you've got 'em.

SANTA CLAUS: Could you use ten or twelve?

VOICE: Ten or twelve million dollars?
—O, boy!

SANTA CLAUS: You're kidding.

VOICE: Kidding! Why, you can't tell me anything I wouldn't do for ten or twelve million.

SANTA CLAUS: I'll bet you I can.

VOICE: O yeah? How much'll you bet?

SANTA CLAUS: I'll bet a dollar.

VOICE: You're on! What wouldn't I do?

SANTA CLAUS: You wouldn't spend five hundred measly dollars for a share of preferred stock in a giltedged wheelmine.

VOICE: Wheelmine?

SANTA CLAUS: Don't tell me you never heard of a wheelmine!

VOICE: Well, maybe—

SANTA CLAUS: Maybe you don't even know what wheels are.

VOICE: Wheels?

SANTA CLAUS: They're the things that make the world go round.

VOICE: Sure, I know wheels—why, wheels are everywhere.

SANTA CLAUS: I'll say they are: including people's heads
—now can you tell me what a mine is?

VOICE: A mine?
Why, a mine is a hole in the ground.

SANTA CLAUS: Now can you tell me what one and one make?

VOICE: One and one?

SANTA CLAUS: Yes.

VOICE: Two.

SANTA CLAUS: You're wonderful! My boy, with a brain like that

you ought to be President of the United States
—now listen carefully: one and one make two;
but what do wheel and mine make?
VOICE: They make wheelmine.
SANTA CLAUS: Congratulations! You know everything—
VOICE: But people don't dig wheels out of the ground.
SANTA CLAUS: I'll say people don't!
VOICE: Well, who does?
SANTA CLAUS: Can't you guess?
VOICE: Science?
SANTA CLAUS: By Jove, you're just another Einstein!
I certainly was a fool to bet with you
—here's your certificate of preferred stock.
VOICE: Here's your five hundred dollars—
SANTA CLAUS: Five hundred? Listen:
you may have been dealing with conmen all your life,
but I'm a Scientist: here's the dollar you won.
VOICE: Thanks, mister.
SANTA CLAUS: You're quite welcome.—Anybody else?
VOICES: Me! Me, too! Gimme!
SANTA CLAUS: —Just a moment. Friends,
it never shall be said that Science favored
or slighted anyone. Remember: Science
is no mere individual. Individuals
are, after all, nothing but human beings;
and human beings are corruptible:
for (as you doubtless know) to err is human.
Think—only think! for untold centuries
this earth was overrun by human beings!
Think: it was not so many years ago
that individuals could be found among us!
O those dark ages! What a darkness, friends!
But now that hideous darkness turns to light;
the flame of Science blazes far and wide:
Science, impartial and omnipotent,
before whose superhuman radiance
all dark prescientific instincts vanish.
Think—only think! at last the monster, man,

is freed from his obscene humanity!
—While men were merely men, and nothing more,
what was equality? A word. A dream.
Men never could be equal—why? Because
equality's the attribute of supermen
like you, and you, and you, and you. And therefore
(superladies and supergentlemen)
when the impartial ear of Science hears
your superhuman voices crying "gimme,"
Science responds in Its omnipotence
"let there be enough wheelmine stock for all."

VOICES: Adda baby! Long live Science! Hooray for wheelmines!

SCENE THREE

(DEATH, *masked as* SANTA CLAUS, *strolling: angry voices offstage*)

DEATH: I've got him now!
(*Enter* SANTA CLAUS, *masked as* DEATH, *running*)
—Hello there: what's your hurry?

SANTA CLAUS: Help—quick—for mercy's sake—they're after me—

DEATH: After you?

SANTA CLAUS: After me, yes! They're coming!

DEATH: Who's coming?

SANTA CLAUS: Everybody!

DEATH: Why?

SANTA CLAUS: It's the accident—

DEATH: Accident?

SANTA CLAUS: To the miners in the mine—

DEATH: Miners?

SANTA CLAUS: Wheelminers!

DEATH: Are you crazy?

SANTA CLAUS: I don't know—will you tell me something?

DEATH: Tell you what.

SANTA CLAUS: Does a wheelmine exist, or doesn't it?
DEATH: A wheelmine?
SANTA CLAUS: Yes.
DEATH: Don't be ridiculous.
SANTA CLAUS: You mean it doesn't exist?
DEATH: Exist? Of course not!
SANTA CLAUS: In other words, a wheelmine is nonexistent isn't it?
DEATH: Perfectly.
SANTA CLAUS: O, then tell me; tell me:
how can it maim, how can it mutilate;
how can it turn mere people into monsters:
answer me—how!
DEATH: My friend, you've forgotten something:
namely, that people, like wheelmines, don't exist
—two negatives, you know, make an affirmative.
Now if I may be allowed to analyze—
SANTA CLAUS: Do you want to die?
DEATH: I die? Ha-ha-ha-ha! How could Death die?
SANTA CLAUS: —Death?
DEATH: Didn't you know?
SANTA CLAUS: I'm going mad. You: tell me,
whatever you are, Death or the Devil, tell me:
how can I prove I'm not to blame for the damage
caused by an accident which never happened
to people who are nonexistent?
DEATH: You can't.
SANTA CLAUS: My God—but what am I going to do, then?
DEATH: Do?
why, my dear fellow, it looks to me as if
you'd have to prove you don't exist yourself.
SANTA CLAUS: But that's absurd!
DEATH: —And tragic; yet a fact.
So make it snappy, Mister Santa Claus!
(*Exit. From the opposite direction enter Mob, furious: a little girl follows*)
VOICES: There he is! Grab him! Listen, Mister Science
—you're going to hang for this!

SANTA CLAUS: What do you mean?
A VOICE: You know what we mean!
SANTA CLAUS: Why, who do you think I am?
ANOTHER: Think? We don't think; we know! You're Science!
SANTA CLAUS: Science?
ANOTHER: Science—the crook who sold us stock in a wheelmine!
ANOTHER: Science—the beast who buries men alive!
SANTA CLAUS: —Stop!
Ladies and gentlemen, this is all a mistake:
I am not Science; wheelmines don't exist,
and as for burying people alive—that's nonsense.
VOICES: We say you're Science! Down with Science!
SANTA CLAUS: —Wait!
Ladies and gentlemen: if you all have been
deceived by some impostor—so have I.
If you all have been tricked and ruined—so have I.
And so has every man and woman, I say.
I say it, and you feel it in your hearts:
we are all of us no longer glad and whole,
we have all of us sold our spirits into death,
we are all of us the sick parts of a sick thing,
we have all of us lost our living honesty,
and so we are all of us not any more ourselves.
—Who can tell truth from falsehood any more?
I say it, and you feel it in your hearts:
No man or woman on this big small earth.
—How should our sages miss the mark of life,
and our most skillful players lose the game?
your hearts will tell you, as my heart has told me:
because all know, and no one understands.
—O, we are all so very full of knowing
that we are empty: empty of understanding;
but, by that emptiness, I swear to you
(and if I lie, ladies and gentlemen,
hang me a little higher than the sky)
all men and every woman may be wrong;
but nobody who lives can fool a child.

—Now I'll abide the verdict of that little girl
over there, with the yellow hair and the blue eyes.
I'll simply ask her who I am; and whoever
she says I am, I am: is that fair enough?

VOICES: Okay! Sure! Why not? Fine! A swell idea!
The kid will tell him who he is, all right!
Everybody knows!

SANTA CLAUS: —Silence! (*To* CHILD) Don't be afraid:
who am I?

CHILD: You are Santa Claus.

VOICES: . . . Santa Claus?

CHORUS: Ha-ha-ha-ha—there ain't no Santa Claus!

SANTA CLAUS: Then, ladies and gentlemen, I don't exist.
And since I don't exist, I am not guilty.
And since I am not guilty, I am innocent.
—Goodbye! And, next time, look before you leap.

(*Exit. Mob disintegrates slowly, muttering*)

SCENE FOUR

(SANTA CLAUS, *masked as* DEATH, *strolling*)

SANTA CLAUS: That was a beautiful child . . . If only I were
sure—

(*Enter* DEATH, *masked as* SANTA CLAUS)

Hello there!

DEATH: O—hello. You're looking better.

SANTA CLAUS: Better? Why not?

DEATH: I take it, my advice
proved efficacious?

SANTA CLAUS: Death, you've saved my life!

DEATH: You don't say so.

SANTA CLAUS: Absolutely!

DEATH: Well, my friend,
I'm going to ask you to do me a favor now.

SANTA CLAUS: Go right ahead!

DEATH: I've got a heavy date
with a swell jane up the street a little way,
but something tells me she prefers plump fellows.
Will you give me your fat and take my skeleton?

SANTA CLAUS: With all the pleasure in the world, old-timer;
and I'll throw in a wheelmine, just for luck!

DEATH: No wheelmines, thank you.

(*They undress*)

SANTA CLAUS: That was a beautiful child.

DEATH: —Child?

SANTA CLAUS: I was . . .

DEATH: Thinking of the old days, eh?
Well, children are your specialty.

SANTA CLAUS: I love them.
I have always loved them, and I shall love them always.

(*They exchange costumes, and dress as each other*)

DEATH: De gustibus non disputandum est;
or, in good American: I prefer women.

SANTA CLAUS: Have you ever loved a woman?

DEATH: Pardon me,
did you say "loved"?

SANTA CLAUS: I said "loved."

DEATH: No. Have you?

SANTA CLAUS: Once.

DEATH: Well, everybody makes mistakes
—I'll see you later. So long, Mister Death!

(*Exit* DEATH *as* SANTA CLAUS, *paunchily swaggering. From the opposite direction enter, on tiptoe,* CHILD)

CHILD: Hello.

SANTA CLAUS: —Well, hello!

CHILD: You remember me?

SANTA CLAUS: Of course I do.

CHILD: You're different, aren't you.

SANTA CLAUS: Yes;
I am.

CHILD: Much thinner.

SANTA CLAUS: Do you like me this way?

[1] *What Happened*. The piano as sculpture. (Al Carmines, Joan Baker.) Photo by Peter Moore.

[2] *What Happened.* The pianist as dancer; the singing dancers; the portable chorus. Left to right: Masato Kawasaki, John Quinn, Lucinda Childs, Arlene Rothlein, Aileen Pasloff, Burton Supree, Joan Baker, Al Carmines, Yvonne Rainer. Photo by Peter Moore.

[3] *What Happened.* The dancers as actors. (Lucinda Childs, Joan Baker, Aileen Pasloff, Arlene Rothlein, Yvonne Rainer.) Photo by Peter Moore.

[4] *What Happened*. "What is the occasion for all that." Photo by Peter Moore.

[5] *Flower*. The Ball-Girls of Part One. The man is pulling out the newspaper from one. Photo by Robert McElroy.

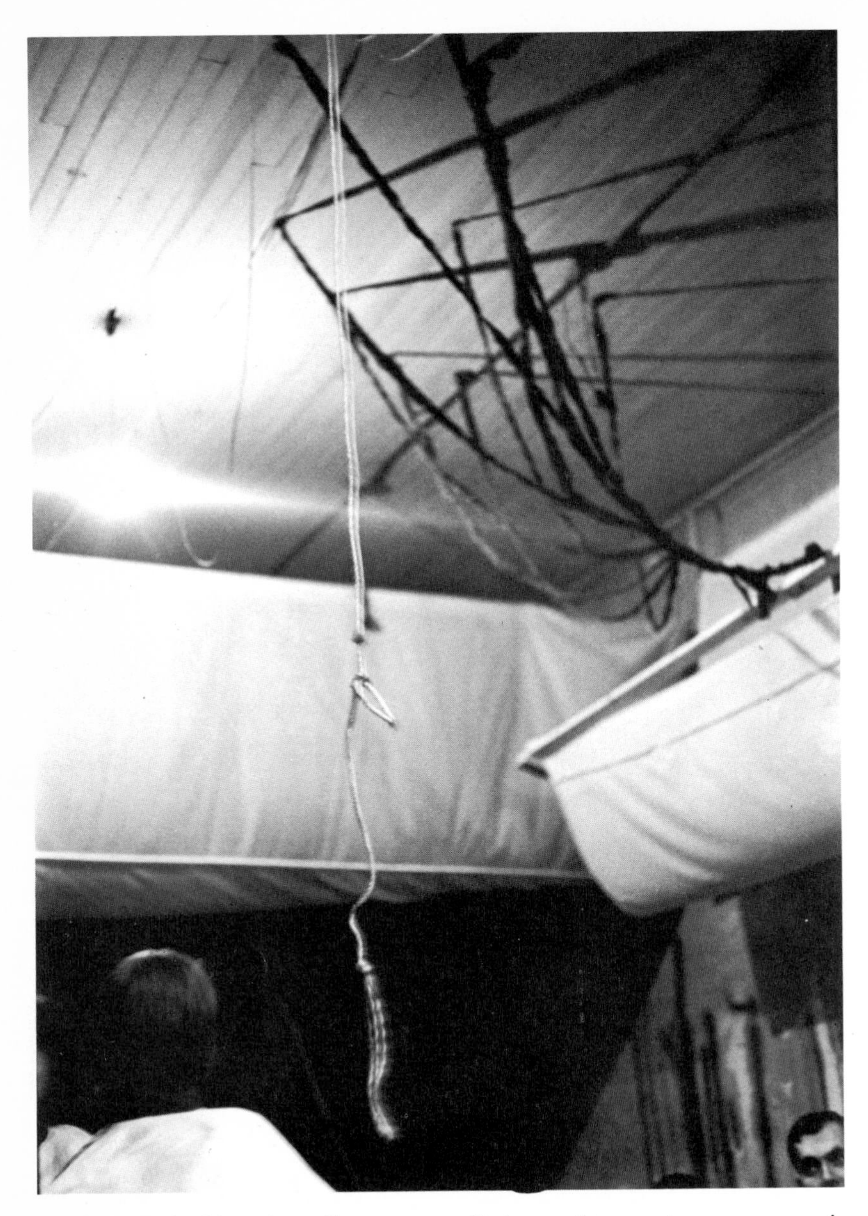

[6] *Flower*. The hinged muslin canopy-walls lowered to create a new space in Part Two. Photo by Peter Moore.

[7] *Flower*. The Sugar Cube at the start of Part Two. Photo by Robert McElroy.

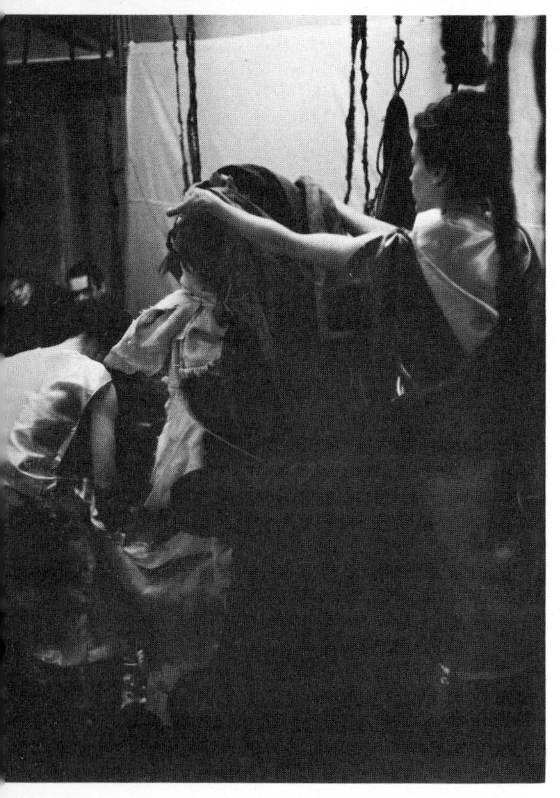

[8] *Flower*. The Costume-Changing. As the girls finish adjusting their costumes, the man begins to empty one of the hanging sacks. At left, large flower-emblem backdrop; at top, hanging vines. Photo by Robert McElroy.

[9] *Flower*. The girl from the sack is covered with rags. Photo by Robert McElroy.

[10] *Flower*. The red silk flower petals are opened; fresh materials grow from the center. Photo by Robert McElroy.

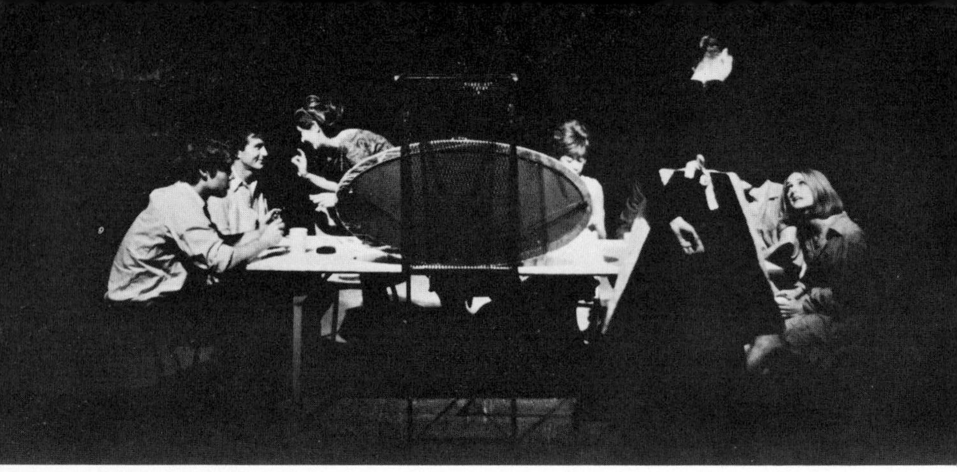

[11] *Meat Joy*. Prelude: The Make-up Table. Photo by Tony Ray-Jones.

[12] *Meat Joy*. The rolling Body Package; the Undressing Walk. Photo by Al Giese.

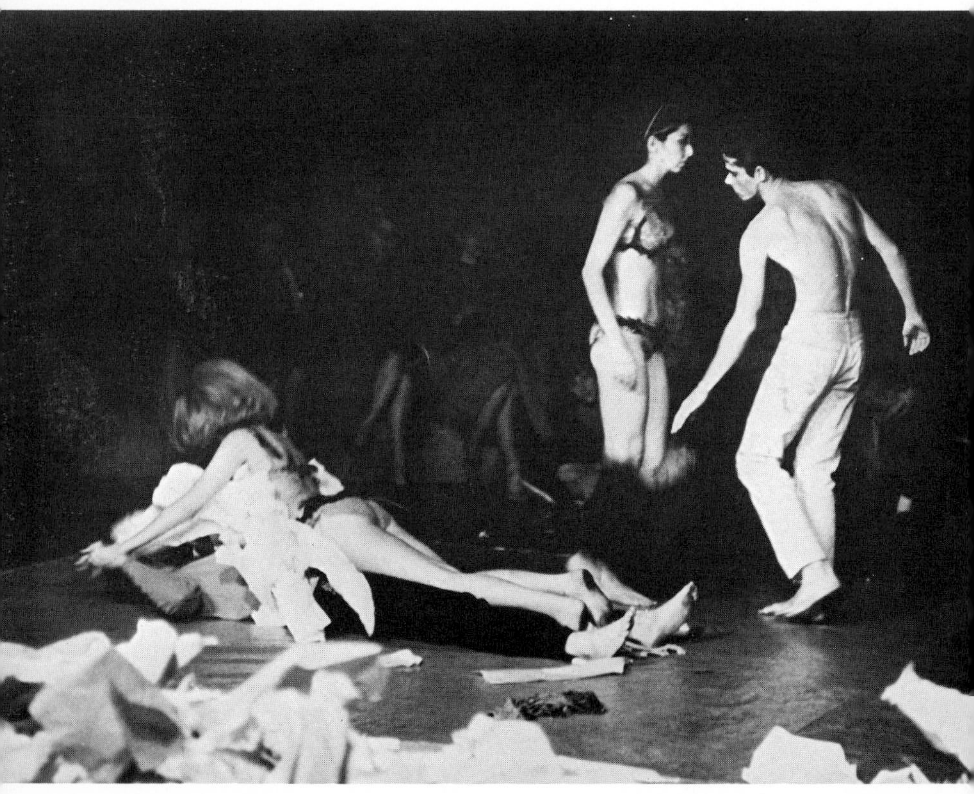

CHILD: I guess . . . I like you any way—if you're you.
SANTA CLAUS: I guess that makes me very happy.
CHILD: But I guess . . .
SANTA CLAUS: What do you guess?
CHILD: You could be happier,
couldn't you?
SANTA CLAUS: Perhaps I could.
CHILD: —Because you're looking
for somebody?
SANTA CLAUS: I am.
CHILD: And I'm looking for somebody, too.
SANTA CLAUS: Somebody very beautiful?
CHILD: O, yes;
she's very beautiful. And very sad.
SANTA CLAUS: Very beautiful and very sad.
Tell me: is she sad because she lost you?
CHILD: Because we lost each other—and somebody else.
(*Confused voices, far offstage*)
Goodbye—
SANTA CLAUS: Why are you going?
CHILD: Don't be afraid:
we'll find her.
SANTA CLAUS: I should never be afraid
of anything in the sky and on the earth
and anywhere and everywhere and nowhere,
if I were only sure of one thing.
CHILD: What.
SANTA CLAUS: Who was that somebody else?
CHILD: That somebody
we lost?
SANTA CLAUS: Yes.
CHILD: Can't you guess who?
SANTA CLAUS: Can I?
CHILD: You.
(*She dances away*)

Scene Five

(*Enter* WOMAN, *weeping*)

WOMAN: Knowledge has taken love out of the world
and all the world is empty empty empty:
men are not men any more in all the world
for a man who cannot love is not a man,
and only a woman in love can be a woman;
and, from their love alone, joy is born—joy!
Knowledge has taken love out of the world
and all the world is joyless joyless joyless.
Come, death! for I have lost my joy and I
have lost my love and I have lost myself.
(*Enter* SANTA CLAUS, *as* DEATH)
You have wanted me. Now take me.
SANTA CLAUS: Now and forever.
WOMAN: How fortunate is dying, since I seem
to hear his voice again.
VOICE: (*offstage*) Dead! Dead!
WOMAN: Could the world be emptier?
(*Tumult offstage. She cringes*)
SANTA CLAUS: Don't be afraid.
WOMAN: O voice of him I loved more than my life,
protect me from that deathless lifelessness—.
(*Enter Mob in procession, reeling and capering: the last Mobsters carry a pole, from which dangles the capering and reeling corpse of* DEATH *disguised as* SANTA CLAUS)
CHORUS: Dead. Dead. Dead. Dead. Dead.
VOICES: Hooray! Dead; yes, dead: dead. Hooray!
Science is dead! Dead. Science is dead!
VOICE: He'll never sell another wheelmine—never!
VOICES: Dead! Hooray! Dead! Hooray! Dead!
VOICE: The filthy lousy stinking son of a bitch.
CHORUS: Hooray hooray hooray hooray hooray!
A VOICE: He fooled us once, and once was once too much!
ANOTHER: He never fooled us, pal: it was the kid.
(WOMAN *starts*)

ANOTHER: Yeah, but the second time—boy, was that good!

ANOTHER: I'll say it was!

ANOTHER: Did you see the look she gave him?

ANOTHER: Did you hear her say "*that* isn't Santa Claus"?

(WOMAN *turns: sees the dangling effigy—recoils from the real* SANTA CLAUS)

CHORUS: Ha-ha-ha-ha—there ain't no Santa Claus!

(*Exit Mob, reeling and capering, booing whistling screeching*)

WOMAN: Yes, the world could be emptier.

SANTA CLAUS: Now and—

WOMAN: Never.

I had remembered love—but who am I?
Thanks, Death, for making love remember me.

(*Enter dancing* CHILD: *sees* WOMAN, *and rushes to her arms*)

WOMAN: Joy—yes! My (yes; O yes) my life my love
my soul myself . . . —Not yours, Death!

SANTA CLAUS (*unmasking*): No.

WOMAN (*kneeling to* SANTA CLAUS): Ours.

The Birthday

BY PAUL GOODMAN

In his poem, "Song of the Playwright," Bertolt Brecht touched upon an important anti-naturalistic technique of playwrighting in our time—although at the time he wrote the poem, he meant it to apply only to his own theatrical practice. This approach, which both European and American playwrights have found attractive, involves the adaptation of the theatricalist modes and styles of other countries and periods to contemporary purposes. Brecht wrote:

So that I can show what I see
I read the plays of other times and other people.
A few of my plays are copied from them, minutely
Testing their technique to find out
What of theirs I can make use of.
I studied the plays of the feudal
Englishmen, giant figures
For whom the world existed only that they might shine.
I studied the moralizing Spaniards,
The Indians, masters of the beautiful sentiment,
And the Chinese, who show us families,
And the colorful lives of the cities.

In his first plays, Paul Goodman set out quite deliberately and "minutely" (to use Brecht's word) to imitate an Asiatic non-naturalistic style. *The Birthday* is taken from a volume entitled *Stop-Light: Noh*. An actual character is the poet's own birthday; there are sudden but structurally important modulations into passages of singing and dancing; and a chorus gives (good) advice. It is not at all atypical of Anti-Naturalist theatre that, while Goodman's technique is "artificial" and theatrical in the extreme, and the play is pointedly an experiment, the impression it creates is directly moving.

Thanks are due Paul Goodman for revising this play especially for this volume.

The Birthday

Protagonist: a BIRTHDAY
Second Actor: PAUL
Scene: Amber Lake, New York

PAUL

To such a height of pleasure
the night-ride has raised me!
our headlights on and off
like thoughts on a face
flashed among the thick leafage;
we sang the song-hits, and the songs
swallowed by the wind, came and went;
and laughing pierced my heart;—till now
my legs are weak, my ankles fold,
I cannot stand but lean against this tree
until I gain a second wind of joy!

How quiet is it in this cedar wood:
hear the others thru the forest, honking.
This is Amber Lake, here we propose
again to drink and foxtrot, starting over,
beginning over! pleasure without end;
I too . . . just for a moment I have come
apart to taste the joy, and get my strength back.

CHORUS

Look, he can hardly stand.

PAUL

I'm *not* drunk,
it's with laughing that my legs are weak.

CHORUS

Your moonlit face is pink.

PAUL

That's excitement.

CHORUS

Brutal noises tear the night—

PAUL

Silence is nothing until formed by sound—

CHORUS

We hardly hear the Time.

PAUL

Beginning over!
blessed be all things comparable to waves,
that return to their childhood again and again!
Hurrah for the boys of 8 or 10!
and 12! and 13! and 11!

CHORUS

I see that all this has a gloomy finish:
such noises are indecorous by moonlight.

PAUL

How sharp, how clear they ring across the lake!
See, on the rippling water
the moon is an accordion of silver:
hi! hi! *"Jada jada jing jing jing"*—
(*singing and dancing*)
The noises of the night are loud and soft,
shrilling crickets, bullfrogs raucous, and
my friends; and hark! across from Kauneonga
(how far the sound travels across flat water!)
a tolling bell—1, 2, Bong! bong!
it tolls—bong! bong!—9, 10,

it must be 12 o'clock—across the lake—
tolling, tolling—a new day!
beginning over! didn't I tell you?
There fades away the last of the 12 strokes.
(*enter* BIRTHDAY)

BIRTHDAY

What day is it?

PAUL

It is the end of summer—
September—it's my birthday!

BIRTHDAY

I am he.

PAUL

Who are you, stranger, sprung out of the night?
I thought I was alone and with friends.

BIRTHDAY

Paul,—I am no enemy of yours.

PAUL

O do not call my name: you make me freeze,
you unmake me by calling out my name,
for none of us is merry as himself
but only by forgetting who he is.

BIRTHDAY

I am your birthday. Only wild men omit
to mark the year with days memorial,—
and so the careless flight of time is stayed.
Feasts and fast-days and commemorations
point beyond their own sliding existence
to some past absence that is present still;
and so we are not wholly lost in change,
every day shall come again forever.

We are immortal. Birthdays also call back
to each one in his history (always aging)
what he is really—if indeed he is.

PAUL

Immortal? like the Emperor of China
who never died because he never lived!
Don't mention it! Oh, I am ill at ease,
my joy is marred by this midnight encounter.

CHORUS

Don't be alarmed, one day is like another,
even the Fourth of July is like the fifth.

PAUL

Why has *he* come—black monk in the moonlight?
couldn't he see that I was well enough?
laughing so hard that, fainting away, I cling
to this friendly tree beside the shining water?

BIRTHDAY

Paul—what place is this?

PAUL

Why, Amber Lake.

BIRTHDAY

Last year, where were you?

PAUL

I was at Schroon Lake.

BIRTHDAY

Before that?

PAUL

I was on the Delaware.
I spent the summer of 1931
visiting the Princess Delaware.

BIRTHDAY

Have you no home to spend your birthday, Paul?

PAUL

Home? did you say? why shall I have a home?
what home particular should a poet have?

CHORUS

That's a shallow answer to a profound question!

PAUL

What do you want of me? Tell me, how old
am I?

BIRTHDAY

Now 22.

PAUL

I seem to be
a child.

BIRTHDAY

Yes, I agree—a kind of child.

PAUL

Being a child, let me stand apart.
(*he goes apart*)
Standing apart:
on the water glassy black
is rising mist through which
the moon is round and dead;

rowboats at the shore
huddle, their noses together,
like horses in the cold.

My confused soul
haunted by memories
is like an orchestra tuning up,—

how joyous are the recollections
of my eighth to tenth years!
what a happy sound had they!

CHORUS

One poet said: "In future time,
even these hardships may be sweet to recall!"[1]

Another said, "There is no greater grief
than to think of a happy past in a time of misery!"[2]

But we say, "There is no greater pain
than recalling innocent joys in a riot of pleasure."

PAUL

(*weeps; he notices his* BIRTHDAY *beside him*)
What! are you here still? black monk.
how long? how long? when will you go away?

BIRTHDAY

Twenty-four hours—say, you're a grown boy,
you know how long a day is, certainly!

PAUL

I *have* remembered; what do you want more?

BIRTHDAY

I? I want nothing.
Observe me only, I shall dance for you.
Attend closely, many things are learned
by closely looking at a dance, or face,
or flower, or anything.

[1] Aeneid, I, 203
[2] *Commedia,* Inferno v, 21

PAUL

I am all eyes.

BIRTHDAY

(*dancing*)

Chuga chuga graa!
dayvanash toodle-doo
boom! boom!
hi! lo! chuga chuga chuga
ribiri dayvanash. Selah.

kalgefori sagwenoo
  daymetori aradoo
    pesteneeri petenti
      sikador endio-pareesis.

Chuga chuga chuga, without doubt.
lougabashis petenti—
slightly susceptible,
O doodledoo! boom boom.

PAUL

It has sound, but I see no meaning in it.
Why are *you* weeping? did you catch his drift?

CHORUS

(*weeping in his sleeve*)

Not I—but spontaneously the tears
rise in me, thinking of the past.

PAUL

From the outset you were a hostile Chorus!
you hated me even before he came.
It is unjust.

CHORUS

I did not, but I thought
your loud mirth was indecorous in the moonlight.

PAUL

Now we have lost the mirth and the moonlight both.
The mist is rising around us everywhere.
Hear my friends, calling across the water—
Paul! Paul!—they are out there in boats
looking for me, they will be alarmed,
the voices are as foghorns—*Paul!*
their lights are slowly blinking in the fog.
Paul! Paul!—yet how can I cry out
and join them, with him always at my side?

Benito Cereno

BY ROBERT LOWELL

Ever since Jean Cocteau made his celebrated distinction between poetry *in* the theatre (which he, as a poet, completely rejected), and poetry *of* the theatre (which he recommended), poets have been attempting to create a stage language that would be appropriately yet not excessively eloquent, while at the same time aiming for the true theatrical poetry that Cocteau urged. In his trilogy *The Old Glory,* from which *Benito Cereno* is taken, Robert Lowell managed not only to create a distinctly effective stage verse, a verse suggestive of exceptionally lucid and precise prose, but also produced a series of structurally potent, truly "poetic" plays.

Benito Cereno is based on a novella by Herman Melville, but Lowell has rendered it more than just stageworthy. He has infused it with qualities of theatricalism, of motion, gesture, and vision which are not merely those of theatre, but of inventive theatre indeed. In his remarks on the play, the original director, Jonathan Miller, speaks of the deliberateness of his efforts to produce a special theatrical world here, a deliberateness intended to complement the inventiveness of Lowell's basic script:

> . . . As regards staging and diction, it seemed to me that Lowell had written an opera without music and the four principal actors were directed to move and speak as if they were soloists in an oratorio and they should be placed on the stage as if they were delivering Mozartian quartets and duets—very formal with no restless modern naturalism. This play seemed to me to be like a new Tempest with the Spanish captain playing a sort of drugged Prospero held captive by his Negro Babu. This idea turns the Spanish boat into a black magic island where all the normal laws of nature and society are relaxed and paralysed. The vision of the American captain is blurred by the heat, the lethargy and the exotic languor of the Negro slaves. . . . The entertainment should be

baroque and courtly with no concession made to modern nightclub negritude.

Many of the play's most intense moments are in fact products of Lowell's textually complementing, non-verbal sense of the theatrical; the play has great visual eloquence. One of its most unforgettable aspects is the formal, stylized contrasting of crowd scenes and "solos"; the play's sudden yet apt resolutions into dance, mime, and ceremony. Despite the almost Elizabethan elegance of Lowell's verse, the meaning of the play is contained as much in its spectacle-like qualities; it is the tragically exotic visual life of Lowell's slave-world that sets it off permanently from the understanding of the conventionally rationalistic Captain Delano—a limitation that nearly costs Delano his life. And it is consistent with the style of the play that a summary of the work's "meaning"—in which a glass ball representing the earth is shattered by a "slave"—is expressed not by a final speech or peroration, but in an eloquent event.

Benito Cereno

CHARACTERS
(In order of appearance)

CAPTAIN AMASA DELANO
JOHN PERKINS
DON BENITO CERENO
BABU
ATUFAL
FRANCESCO
AMERICAN SAILORS
SPANISH SAILORS
NEGRO SLAVES

About the year 1800, an American sealing vessel, the President Adams, *at anchor in an island harbor off the coast of Trinidad. The stage is part of the ship's deck. Everything is unnaturally clean, bare and ship-shape. To one side, a polished, coal-black cannon. The American captain,* AMASA DELANO *from Duxbury, Massachusetts, sits in a cane chair. He is a strong, comfortable looking man in his early thirties who wears a spotless blue coat and white trousers. Incongruously, he has on a straw hat and smokes a corncob pipe. Beside him stands* JOHN PERKINS, *his bosun, a very stiff, green young man, a relative of* DELANO'S. THREE SAILORS, *one carrying an American flag, enter.* EVERYONE *stands at attention and salutes with machinelike exactitude. Then the* THREE SAILORS *march off-stage.* DELANO *and* PERKINS *are alone.*

DELANO
There goes the most beautiful woman in South America.

PERKINS

We never see any women, Sir;
just this smothering, overcast Equator,
a seal or two,
the flat dull sea,
and a sky like a gray wasp's nest.

DELANO

I wasn't talking about women,
I was calling your attention to the American flag.

PERKINS

Yes, Sir! I wish we were home in Duxbury.

DELANO

We are home. America is wherever her flag flies.
My own deck is the only place in the world
where I feel at home.

PERKINS

That's too much for me, Captain Delano.
I mean I wish I were at home with my wife;
these world cruises are only for bachelors.

DELANO

Your wife will keep. You should smoke, Perkins.
Smoking turns men into philosophers
and swabs away their worries.
I can see my wife and children or not see them
in each puff of blue smoke.

PERKINS

You are always tempting me, Sir!
I try to keep fit,
I want to return to my wife as fit as I left her.

DELANO

You're much too nervous, Perkins.
Travel will shake you up. You should let

a little foreign dirt rub off on you.
I've taught myself to speak Spanish like a Spaniard.
At each South American port, they mistake me for a
Castilian Don.

PERKINS

Aren't you lowering yourself a little, Captain?
Excuse me, Sir, I have been wanting to ask you a question,
Don't you think our President, Mr. Jefferson, is
    lowering himself
by being so close to the French?
I'd feel a lot safer in this unprotected place
if we'd elected Mr. Adams instead of Mr. Jefferson.

DELANO

The better man ran second!
Come to think of it, he rather let us down
by losing the election just after we had named this ship,
the *President Adams*. Adams is a nervous dry fellow.
When you've travelled as much as I have,
you'll learn that that sort doesn't export, Perkins.
Adams didn't get a vote outside New England!

PERKINS

He carried every New England state;
that was better than winning the election.
I'm afraid I'm a dry fellow, too, Sir.

DELANO

Not when I've educated you!
When I am through with you, Perkins,
you'll be as worldly as the Prince Regent of England,
only you'll be a first class American officer.
I'm all for Jefferson, he has the popular touch.
Of course he's read too many books,
but I've always said an idea or two won't sink
    our Republic.
I'll tell you this, Perkins,
Mr. Jefferson is a gentleman and an American.

PERKINS

They say he has two illegitimate Negro children.

DELANO

The more the better! That's the quickest way
to raise the blacks to our level.
I'm surprised you swallow such Federalist bilge, Perkins!
I told you Mr. Jefferson is a gentleman and an American;
when a man's in office, Sir, we all pull behind him!

PERKINS

Thank God our Revolution ended where the French
one began.

DELANO

Oh the French! They're like the rest of the Latins,
they're hardly white people,
they start with a paper republic
and end with a toy soldier, like Bonaparte.

PERKINS

Yes, Sir. I see a strange sail making for the harbor.
They don't know how to sail her.

DELANO

Hand me my telescope.

PERKINS

Aye, aye, Sir!

DELANO

(*With telescope*)

I see an ocean undulating in long scoops of swells;
it's set like the beheaded French Queen's high wig;
the sleek surface is like waved lead,
cooled and pressed in the smelter's mould.
I see flights of hurried gray fowl,
patches of fluffy fog.
They skim low and fitfully above the decks,

like swallows sabering flies before a storm.
This gray boat foreshadows something wrong.

PERKINS

It does, Sir!
They don't know how to sail her!

DELANO

I see a sulphurous haze above her cabin,
the new sun hangs like a silver dollar to her stern;
low creeping clouds blow on from them to us.

PERKINS

What else, Sir?

DELANO

The yards are woolly
the ship is furred with fog.
On the cracked and rotten head-boards,
the tarnished, gilded letters say, the *San Domingo.*
A rat's-nest messing up the deck,
black faces in white sheets are fussing with the ropes.
I think it's a cargo of Dominican monks.

PERKINS

Dominican monks, Sir! God help us,
I thought they were outlawed in the new world.

DELANO

No, it's nothing. I see they're only slaves.
The boat's transporting slaves.

PERKINS

Do you believe in slavery, Captain Delano?

DELANO

In a civilized country, Perkins,
everyone disbelieves in slavery,
everyone disbelieves in slavery and wants slaves.

We have the perfect uneasy answer;
in the North, we don't have them and want them;
Mr. Jefferson has them and fears them.

PERKINS

Is that how you answer, Sir,
when a little foreign dirt has rubbed off on you?

DELANO

Don't ask me such intense questions.
You should take up smoking, Perkins.
There was a beautiful, dumb English actress—
I saw her myself once in London.
They wanted her to look profound,
so she read Plato and the Bible and Benjamin Franklin,
and thought about them every minute.
She still looked like a moron.
Then they told her to think about nothing.
She thought about nothing, and looked like Socrates.
That's smoking, Perkins, you think about nothing and
look deep.

PERKINS

I don't believe in slavery, Sir.

DELANO

You don't believe in slavery or Spaniards
or smoking or long cruises or monks or Mr. Jefferson!
You are a Puritan, all faith and fire.

PERKINS

Yes, Sir.

DELANO

God save America from Americans!
(*Takes up the telescope*)
I see octagonal network bagging out
from her heavy top like decayed beehives.

The battered forecastle looks like a raped Versailles.
On the stern-piece, I see the fading arms of Spain.
There's a masked satyr, or something
with its foot on a big white goddess.
She has quite a figure.

PERKINS

They oughtn't to be allowed on the ocean!

DELANO

Who oughtn't? Goddesses?

PERKINS

I mean Spaniards, who cannot handle a ship,
and mess up its hull with immoral statues.

DELANO

You're out of step. You're much too dry.
Bring me my three-cornered hat.
Order some men to clear a whaleboat.
I am going to bring water and fresh fish to the
    San Domingo.
These people have had some misfortune, Perkins!

PERKINS

Aye, aye, Sir.

DELANO

Spaniards? The name gets you down,
you think their sultry faces and language
make them Zulus.
You take the name *Delano*—
I've always thought it had some saving
Italian or Spanish virtue in it.

PERKINS

Yes, Sir.

DELANO

A Spaniard isn't a negro under the skin,
particularly a Spaniard from Spain—
these South American ones mix too much with the Indians.
Once you get inside a Spaniard,
he talks about as well as your wife in Duxbury.

PERKINS

(*Shouting*)

A boat for the captain! A whaleboat for Captain Delano!

(*A bosun's whistle is heard, the lights dim. When they come up, we are on the deck of the* San Domingo, *the same set, identical except for litter and disorder.* THREE AMERICAN SAILORS *climb on board. They are followed by* PERKINS *and* DELANO, *now wearing a three-cornered hat. Once on board, the* AMERICAN SAILORS *salute* DELANO *and stand stiffly at attention like toys.* NEGROES *from the* San Domingo *drift silently and furtively forward*)

DELANO

I see a wen of barnacles hanging to the waterline of
this ship.
It sticks out like the belly of a pregnant woman.
Have a look at our dory Bosun.

PERKINS

Aye, aye, Sir!

(*By now, about twenty blacks and two Spanish sailors have drifted in. They look like some gaudy, shabby, unnautical charade, and pay no attention to the Americans, until an unseen figure in the rigging calls out a single sharp warning in an unknown tongue. Then they all rush forward, shouting, waving their arms and making inarticulate cries like birds. Three shrill warnings come from the rigging. Dead silence. The men from the* San Domingo *press back in a dense semicircle. One by one, individuals come forward, make showy bows to* DELANO, *and speak*)

FIRST NEGRO

Scurvy, Master Yankee!

SECOND NEGRO

Yellow fever, Master Yankee!

THIRD NEGRO

Two men knocked overboard rounding Cape Horn,
Master Yankee!

FOURTH NEGRO

Nothing to eat, Master Yankee!

NEGRO WOMAN

Nothing to drink, Master Yankee!

SECOND NEGRO WOMAN

Our mouths are dead wood, Master Yankee!

DELANO

You see, Perkins,
these people have had some misfortune.

(*General hubbub, muttering, shouts, gestures, ritual and dumbshow of distress. The rigging, hitherto dark, lightens, as the sun comes out of a cloud, and shows* THREE OLD NEGROES, *identical down to their shabby patches. They perch on cat's-heads; their heads are grizzled like dying willow tops; each is picking bits of unstranded rope for oakum. It is they who have been giving the warnings that control the people below. Everyone,* DELANO *along with the rest, looks up.* DELANO *turns aside and speaks to* PERKINS)

It is like a Turkish bazaar.

PERKINS

They are like gypsies showing themselves for money
at a county fair, Sir.

DELANO

This is enchanting after the blank gray roll of the ocean!
Go tell the Spanish captain I am waiting for him.

(PERKINS *goes off. Sharp warnings from the* OAKUM-PICKERS. *A big black spread of canvas is pulled creakingly and ceremoniously aside.* SIX FIGURES *stand huddled on a platform about four feet from the deck. They look like weak old invalids in bathrobes and nightcaps until they strip to the waist and turn out to be huge, shining young negroes. Saying nothing, they set to work cleaning piles of rusted hatchets. From time to time, they turn and clash their hatchets together with a rhythmic shout.* PERKINS *returns*)

PERKINS

Their captain's name is Don Benito Cereno,
he sends you his compliments, Sir.
He looks more like a Mexican planter than a seaman.
He's put his fortune on his back:
he doesn't look as if he had washed since they left port.

DELANO

Did you tell him I was waiting for him?
A captain should be welcomed by his fellow-captain.
I can't understand this discourtesy.

PERKINS

He's coming, but there's something wrong with him.

(BENITO CERENO, *led by his negro servant,* BABU, *enters.* BENITO, *looking sick and dazed, is wearing a sombrero and is dressed with a singular but shabby richness. Head bent to one side, he leans in a stately coma against the rail, and stares unseeingly at* DELANO. BABU, *all in scarlet, and small and quick, keeps whispering, pointing and pulling at* BENITO'S *sleeve.* DELANO *walks over to them*)

DELANO

Your hand, Sir. I am Amasa Delano,
captain of the *President Adams,*

a sealing ship from the United States.
This is your lucky day,
the sun is out of hiding for the first time in two weeks,
and here I am aboard your ship
like the Good Samaritan with fresh food and water.

BENITO

The Good Samaritan? Yes, yes,
we mustn't use the Scriptures lightly.
Welcome, Captain. It is the end of the day.

DELANO

The end? It's only morning.
I loaded and lowered a whaleboat
as soon as I saw how awkwardly your ship was making for the harbor.

BENITO

Your whaleboat's welcome, Captain.
I am afraid I am still stunned by the storm.

DELANO

Buck up. Each day is a new beginning.
Assign some sailors to help me dole out my provisions.

BENITO

I have no sailors.

BABU

(*In a quick sing-song:*)

Scurvy, yellow fever,
ten men knocked off on the Horn,
doldrums, nothing to eat, nothing to drink!
By feeding us, you are feeding the King of Spain.

DELANO

Sir, your slave has a pretty way of talking.
What do you need?

(DELANO *waits for* BENITO *to speak. When nothing more is said, he shifts awkwardly from foot to foot, then turns to his* SAILORS)

Stand to, men!

(*The* AMERICAN SAILORS, *who have been lounging and gaping, stand in a row, as if a button had been pressed*)

Lay our fish and water by the cabin!

(*The* SAILORS *arrange the watercans and baskets of fish by the cabin. A sharp whistle comes from the* OAKUM-PICKERS. *Almost instantly, the provisions disappear*)

Captain Cereno, you are surely going to taste my water!

BENITO

A captain is a servant, almost a slave, Sir.

DELANO

No, a captain's a captain.
I am sending for more provisions.
Stand to!

(*The* AMERICAN SAILORS *stand to*)

Row back to the ship. When you get there,
take on five hogsheads of fresh water,
and fifty pounds of soft bread.

(FIRST SAILOR *salutes and goes down the ladder*)

Bring all our remaining pumpkins!

(SECOND *and* THIRD SAILORS *salute and go down the ladder*)

My bosun and I will stay on board,
until our boat returns.
I imagine you can use us.

BENITO

Are you going to stay here alone?
Won't your ship be lost without you?
Won't you be lost without your ship?

BABU

Listen to Master!
He is the incarnation of courtesy, Yankee Captain.
Your ship doesn't need you as much as we do.

DELANO

Oh, I've trained my crew.
I can sail my ship in my sleep.

(*Leaning over the railing and calling*)

Men, bring me a box of lump sugar,
and six bottles of my best cider.

(*Turning to* BENITO)

Cider isn't my favorite drink, Don Benito,
but it's a New England specialty;
I'm ordering six bottles for your table.

(BABU *whispers and gestures to* DON BENITO, *who is exhausted and silent*)

BABU

Une bouteille du vin (*to* NEGROES)
My master wishes to give you a bottle
of the oldest wine in Seville.

(*He whistles. A negro woman rushes into the cabin and returns with a dusty beribboned bottle, which she holds like a baby*)

(BABU *ties a rope around the bottle*)

BABU

I am sending this bottle of wine to your cabin.
When you drink it, you will remember us.
Do you see these ribbons? The crown of Spain is tied
to one.
Forgive me for tying a rope around the King of
Spain's neck.

(*Lowers the wine on the rope to the whaleboat*)

DELANO

(*Shouting to his* SAILORS)

Pick up your oars!

SAILORS

Aye, aye, Sir!

DELANO

We're New England Federalists;
we can drink the King of Spain's health.

(BENITO *stumbles off-stage on* BABU'S *arm*)

PERKINS

Captain Cereno hasn't travelled as much as you have;
I don't think he knew what you meant by the New England Federalists.

DELANO

(*Leaning comfortably on the rail; half to himself and half to* PERKINS)

The wind is dead. We drift away.
We will be left alone all day,
here in this absentee empire.
Thank God, I know my Spanish!

PERKINS

You'll have to watch them, Sir.
Brown men in charge of black men—
it doesn't add up to much!
This Babu, I don't trust him!
Why doesn't he talk with a Southern accent,
Like Mr. Jefferson? They're out of hand, Sir!

DELANO

Nothing relaxes order more than misery.
They need severe superior officers.
They haven't one.
Now, if this Benito were a man of energy . . .
a Yankee . . .

PERKINS

How can a Spaniard sail?

DELANO

Some can. There was Vasco da Gama and Columbus . . .
No, I guess they were Italians. Some can,
but this captain is tubercular.

PERKINS

Spaniards and Negroes have no business on a ship.

DELANO

Why is this captain so indifferent to me?
If only I could stomach his foreign reserve!
This absolute dictator of his ship
only gives orders through his slaves!
He is like some Jesuit-haunted Hapsburg king
about to leave the world and hope the world will end.

PERKINS

He said he was lost in the storm.

DELANO

Perhaps it's only policy,
a captain's icy dignity
obliterating all democracy—

PERKINS

He's like someone walking in his sleep.

DELANO

Ah, slumbering dominion!
He is so self-conscious in his imbecility . . .
No, he's sick. He sees his men no more than me.
This ship is like a crowded immigration boat;
it needs severe superior officers,
the friendly arm of a strong mate.
Perhaps, I ought to take it over by force.
No, they're sick, they've been through the plague.
I'll go and speak and comfort my fellow captain.
I think you can help me, Captain. I'm feeling useless.

My own thoughts oppress me, there's so much to do.
I wonder if you would tell me the whole sad story of
your voyage.
Talk to me as captain to captain.
We have sailed the same waters.
Please tell me your story.

BENITO

A story? A story! That's out of place.
When I was a child, I used to beg for stories back in Lima.
Now my tongue's tied and my heart is bleeding.
(*Stops talking, as if his breath were gone. He stares for a few moments, then looks up at the rigging, as if he were counting the ropes one by one.* DELANO *turns abruptly to* PERKINS)

DELANO

Go through the ship, Perkins,
and see if you can find me a Spaniard who can talk.

BENITO

You must be patient, Captain Delano;
if we only see with our eyes,
sometimes we cannot see at all.

DELANO

I stand corrected, Captain;
tell me about your voyage.

BENITO

It's now a hundred and ninety days . . .
This ship, well manned, well officered, with several
cabin passengers,
carrying a cargo of Paraguay tea and Spanish cutlery.
That parcel of Negro slaves, less than four score now,
was once three hundred souls.
Ten sailors and three officers fell from the mainyard off
the Horn;

part of our rigging fell overboard with them,
as they were beating down the icy sail.
We threw away all our cargo,
Broke our waterpipes,
Lashed them on deck
this was the chief cause of our suffering.

DELANO

I must interrupt you, Captain.
How did you happen to have three officers on
the mainyard?
I never heard of such a disposal,
it goes against all seamanship.

BABU

Our officers never spared themselves;
if there was any danger, they rushed in
to save us without thinking.

DELANO

I can't understand such an oversight.

BABU

There was no oversight. My master had a hundred eyes.
He had an eye for everything.
Sometimes the world falls on a man.
The sea wouldn't let Master act like a master,
yet he saved himself and many lives.
He is still a rich man, and he saved the ship.

BENITO

Oh my God, I wish the world had fallen on me,
and the terrible cold sea had drowned me;
that would have been better than living through what I've
lived through!

BABU

He is a good man, but his mind is off;
he's thinking about the fever when the wind stopped—

poor, poor Master!
Be patient, Yankee Captain, these fits are short,
Master will be the master once again.

BENITO

The scurvy was raging through us.
We were on the Pacific. We were invalids
and couldn't man our mangled spars.
A hurricane blew us northeast through the fog.
Then the wind died.
We lay in irons fourteen days in unknown waters,
our black tongues stuck through our mouths,
but we couldn't mend our broken waterpipes.

BABU

Always those waterpipes,
he dreams about them like a pile of snakes!

BENITO

Yellow fever followed the scurvy,
the long heat thickened in the calm,
my Spaniards turned black and died like slaves,
The blacks died too. I am my only officer left.

BABU

Poor, poor Master! He had a hundred eyes,
he lived our lives for us.
He is still a rich man.

BENITO

In the smart winds beating us northward,
our torn sails dropped like sinkers in the sea;
each day we dropped more bodies.
Almost without a crew, canvas, water, or a wind,
we were bounced about by the opposing waves
through cross-currents and the weedy calms,
and dropped our dead.

Often we doubled and redoubled on our track
like children lost in jungle. The thick fog
hid the Continent and our only port from us.

BABU

We were poor kidnapped jungle creatures.
We only lived on what he could give us.
He had a hundred eyes, he was the master.

BENITO

These Negroes saved me, Captain.
Through the long calamity,
they were as gentle as their owner, Don Aranda, promised.
Don Aranda took away their chains before he died.

BABU

Don Aranda saved our lives, but we couldn't save his.
Even in Africa I was a slave.
He took away my chains.

BENITO

I gave them the freedom of my ship.
I did not think they were crates or cargo or cannibals.
But it was Babu—under God, I swear I owe my life
to Babu!
He calmed his ignorant, wild brothers,
never left me, saved the *San Domingo*.

BABU

Poor, poor Master. He is still a rich man.
Don't speak of Babu. Babu is the dirt under your feet.
He did his best.

DELANO

You are a good fellow, Babu.
You are the salt of the earth. I envy you, Don Benito;
he is no slave, Sir, but your friend.

BENITO

Yes, he is salt in my wounds.
I can never repay him, I mean.
Excuse me, Captain, my strength is gone.
I have done too much talking. I want to rest.
(BABU *leads* BENITO *to a shabby straw chair at the side.* BENITO *sits.* BABU *fans him with his sombrero*)

PERKINS

He's a fine gentleman, but no seaman.
A cabin boy would have known better
than to send his three officers on the mainyard.

DELANO

(*Paying no attention*)
A terrible story. I would have been unhinged myself.
(*Looking over toward* BABU *and* BENITO)
There's a true servant. They do things better
in the South and in South America—
trust in return for trust!
The beauty of that relationship is unknown
in New England. We're too much alone
in Massachusetts, Perkins.
How do our captains and our merchants live,
each a republic to himself.
Even Sam Adams had no friends and only loved the mob.

PERKINS

Sir, you are forgetting that
New England seamanship brought them their slaves.

DELANO

Oh, just our Southern slaves;
we had nothing to do with these fellows.

PERKINS

The ocean would be a different place

if every Spaniard served an apprenticeship on an
American ship
before he got his captain's papers.

DELANO

This captain's a gentleman, not a sailor.
His little yellow hands
got their command before they held a rope—
in by the cabin-window, not the hawse-hole!
Do you want to know why
they drifted hog-tied in those easy calms—
inexperience, sickness, impotence and aristocracy!

PERKINS

Here comes Robinson Crusoe and his good man Friday.

DELANO

We don't beat a man when he's down.
(BENITO *advances uncertainly on* BABU'S *arm*)
I am glad to see you on your feet again,
That's the only place for a Captain, sir!
I have the cure for you, I have decided
to bring you medicine and a sufficient supply of water.
A first class deck officer, a man from Salem,
shall be stationed on your quarter deck,
a temporary present from my owners.
We shall refit your ship and clear this mess.

BENITO

You will have to clear away the dead.

BABU

This excitement is bad for him, Yankee Master.
He's lived with death. He lives on death still;
this sudden joy will kill him. You've heard
how thirsty men die from overdrinking!
His heart is with his friend, our owner, Don Aranda.

BENITO

I am the only owner.

(*He looks confused and shaken*)

(BABU *scurries off and brings up the straw chair.* BENITO *sits*)

DELANO

Your friend is dead? He died of fever?

BENITO

He died very slowly and in torture.
He was the finest man in Lima.
We were brought up together,
I am lost here.

DELANO

Pardon me, Sir. You are young at sea.
My experience tells me what your trouble is:
this is the first body you have buried in the ocean.
I had a friend like yours, a warm honest fellow,
who would look you in the eye—
we had to throw him to the sharks.
Since then I've brought embalming gear on board.
Each man of mine shall have a Christian grave on land.
You wouldn't shake so, if Don Aranda were on board,
I mean, if you'd preserved the body.

BENITO

If he were on board this ship?
If I had preserved his body?

BABU

Be patient, Master!
We still have the figurehead.

DELANO

You have the figurehead?

BABU

You see that thing wrapped up in black cloth?
It's a figurehead Don Aranda bought us in Spain.
It was hurt in the storm. It's very precious.
Master takes comfort in it,
he is going to give it to Don Aranda's widow.
It's time for the pardon ceremony, Master.
(*Sound of clashing hatchets*)

DELANO

I am all for these hatchet-cleaners.
They are saving cargo. They make
an awful lot of pomp and racket though
about a few old, rusty knives.

BENITO

They think steel is worth its weight in gold.
(*A slow solemn march is sounded on the gongs and other instruments. A gigantic coal-black* NEGRO *comes up the steps. He wears a spiked iron collar to which a chain is attached that goes twice around his arms and ends padlocked to a broad band of iron. The* NEGRO *comes clanking forward and stands dumbly and like a dignitary in front of* BENITO. *Two small black boys bring* BENITO *a frail rattan cane and a silver ball, which they support on a velvet cushion.* BENITO *springs up, holds the ball, and raises the cane rigidly above the head of the negro in chains. For a moment, he shows no trace of sickness. The assembled blacks sing, "Evviva, Benito!" three times*)

BABU

(*At one side with the Americans, but keeping an eye on* BENITO)
You are watching the humiliation of King Atufal,
once a ruler in Africa. He ruled as much land there
as your President.
Poor Babu was a slave even in Africa,
a black man's slave, and now a white man's.

BENITO

(*In a loud, firm voice*)

Former King Atufal, I call on you to kneel!
Say, "My sins are black as night,
I ask the King of Spain's pardon
through his servant, Don Benito."

(*Pause.* ATUFAL *doesn't move*)

NEGROES

Your sins are black as night, King Atufal!
Your sins are black as night, King Atufal!

BENITO

What has King Atufal done?

BABU

I will tell you later, Yankee Captain.

BENITO

Ask pardon, King Atufal.
If you will kneel,
I will strike away your chains.

(ATUFAL *slowly raises his chained arms and lets them drop*)

Ask pardon!

WOMAN SLAVE

Ask pardon, King Atufal.

BENITO

Go!

(*Sound of instruments. The* BLACK BOYS *take* BENITO'S *ball and cane. The straw chair is brought up.* BENITO *sits.* FRANCESCO *then leads him off-stage*)

BABU

Francesco!
I will be with you in a moment, Master.

You mustn't be afraid,
Francesco will serve you like a second Babu.

BENITO

Everyone serves me alike here,
but no one can serve me as you have.

BABU

I will be with you in a moment.
The Yankee master is at sea on our ship.
He wants me to explain our customs.
(BENITO *is carried off-stage*)
You would think Master's afraid of dying,
if Babu leaves him!

DELANO

I can imagine your tenderness during his sickness.
You were part of him,
you were almost a wife.

BABU

You say such beautiful things,
the United States must be a paradise for people like Babu.

DELANO

I don't know.
We have our faults. We have many states,
some of them could stand improvement.

BABU

The United States must be heaven.

DELANO

I suppose we have fewer faults than other countries.
What did King Atufal do?

BABU

He used the Spanish flag for toilet paper.

DELANO

That's treason.
Did Atufal know what he was doing?
Perhaps the flag was left somewhere it shouldn't have been.
Things aren't very strict here.

BABU

I never thought of that.
I will go and tell Master.

DELANO

Oh, no, you mustn't do that!
I never interfere with another man's ship.
Don Benito is your lord and dictator.
How long has this business with King Atufal been
going on?

BABU

Ever since the yellow fever,
and twice a day.

DELANO

He did a terrible thing, but he looks like a royal fellow.
You shouldn't call him a king, though,
it puts ideas into his head.

BABU

Atufal had gold wedges in his ears in Africa;
now he wears a padlock and Master bears the key.

DELANO

I see you have a feeling for symbols of power.
You had better be going now,
Don Benito will be nervous about you.
(BABU *goes off*)
That was a terrible thing to do with a flag;
everything is untidy and unravelled here—
this sort of thing would never happen on the
President Adams.

PERKINS

Your ship is as shipshape as our country, Sir.

DELANO

I wish people wouldn't take me as representative of
our country:
America's one thing, I am another;
we shouldn't have to bear one another's burdens.

PERKINS

You are a true American for all your talk, Sir;
I can't believe you were mistaken for a Castilian Don.

DELANO

No one would take me for Don Benito.

PERKINS

I wonder if he isn't an impostor, some travelling actor from
a circus?

DELANO

No, Cereno is a great name in Peru, like Winthrop or
Adams with us.
I recognize the family features in our captain.
(*An* OLD SPANISH SAILOR, *grizzled and dirty, is seen crawling on all fours with an armful of knots toward the Americans. He points to where* BENITO *and* BABU *have disappeared and whistles. He holds up the knots as though he were in chains, then throws them out loosely on the deck in front of him. A* GROUP OF NEGROES *forms a circle around him, holding hands and singing childishly. Then, laughing, they carry the* SPANIARD *off-stage on their shoulders*)
These blacks are too familiar!
We are never alone!
(*Sound of gongs. Full minute's pause, as if time were passing.* DELANO *leans on the railing. The sun grows brighter*)
This ship is strange.
These people are too spontaneous—all noise and show,

no character!
Real life is a simple monotonous thing.
I wonder about that story about the calms;
it doesn't stick.
Don Benito hesitated himself in telling it.
No one could run a ship so stupidly,
and place three officers on one yard.

(BENITO *and* BABU *return*)

A captain has unpleasant duties;
I am sorry for you, Don Benito.

BENITO

You find my ship unenviable, Sir?

DELANO

I was talking about punishing Atufal;
he acted like an animal!

BENITO

Oh, yes, I was forgetting . . .
He was a King,
How long have you lain in at this island, Sir?

DELANO

Oh, a week today.

BENITO

What was your last port, Sir?

DELANO

Canton.

BENITO

You traded seal-skins and American muskets
for Chinese tea and silks, perhaps?

DELANO

We took in some silks.

BENITO

A little gold and silver too?

DELANO

Just a little silver. We are only merchants.
We take in a dollar here and there. We have no Peru,
or a Pizarro who can sweat gold out of the natives.

BENITO

You'll find things have changed
a little in Peru since Pizarro, Captain.
(*Starts to move away.* BABU *whispers to him, and he comes back abruptly, as if he had forgotten something important*)
How many men have you on board, Sir?

DELANO

Some twenty-five, Sir. Each man is at his post.

BENITO

They're all on board, Sir, now?

DELANO

They're all on board. Each man is working.

BENITO

They'll be on board tonight, Sir?

DELANO

Tonight? Why do you ask, Don Benito?

BENITO

Will they all be on board tonight, Captain?

DELANO

They'll be on board for all I know.
(PERKINS *makes a sign to* DELANO)
Well, no, to tell the truth, today's our Independence Day.
A gang is going ashore to see the village.

A little diversion improves their efficiency,
a little regulated corruption.

BENITO

You North Americans take no chances. Generally,
I suppose,
even your merchant ships go more or less armed?

DELANO

A rack of muskets, sealing spears and cutlasses.
Oh, and a six-pounder or two; we are a sealing ship,
but with us each merchant is a privateer—
only in case of oppression, of course.
You've heard about how we shoot pirates.

BABU

Boom, boom, come Master.

(BENITO *walks away on* BABU'S *arm and sits down, almost off-stage in his straw chair. They whisper. Meanwhile, a* SPANISH SAILOR *climbs the rigging furtively, spread-eagles his arms and shows a lace shirt under his shabby jacket. He points to* BENITO *and* BABU *and winks. At a cry from* ONE OF THE OAKUM-PICKERS, THREE NEGROES *help the* SPANIARD *down with servile, ceremonious attentions*)

PERKINS

Did you see that sailor's lace shirt, Sir?
He must have robbed one of the cabin passengers.
I hear that people strip the dead
in these religious countries.

DELANO

No, you don't understand the Spaniards.
In these old Latin countries,
each man's a beggar or a noble, often both;
they have no middle class. With them it's customary
to sew a mess of gold and pearls on rags—
that's how an aristocracy that's going to the dogs
keeps up its nerve.

DELANO

It's odd though,
that Spanish sailor seemed to want to tell me something.
He ought to dress himself properly and speak his mind.
That's what we do. That's why we're strong:
everybody trusts us. Nothing gets done
when every man's a noble. I wonder why
the captain asked me all those questions?

PERKINS

He was passing the time of day, Sir;
It's a Latin idleness.

DELANO

It's strange. Did you notice how Benito stopped rambling?
He was conventional . . . consecutive for the first time
 since we met him.
Something's wrong. Perhaps, they've men below the decks,
a sleeping volcano of Spanish infantry. The Malays do it,
play sick and cut your throat.
A drifting boat, a dozen doped beggars on deck,
two hundred sweating murderers packed below
 like sardines—
that's rot! Anyone can see these people are really sick,
sicker than usual. Our countries are at peace.
I wonder why he asked me all those questions?

PERKINS

Just idle curiosity. I hear
the gentlemen of Lima sit at coffee-tables from sun to sun
and gossip. They don't even have women to look at;
they're all locked up with their aunts.

DELANO

Their sun is going down. These old empires go.
They are much too familiar with their blacks.
I envy them though, they have no character,
they feel no need to stand alone.

We stand alone too much,
that's why no one can touch us for sailing a ship;
When a country loses heart, it's easier to live.
Ah, Babu! I suppose Don Benito's indisposed again!
Tell him I want to talk to his people;
there's nothing like a well man to help the sick.

BABU

Master is taking his siesta, Yankee Master.
His siesta is sacred, I am afraid to disturb it.
Instead, let me show you our little entertainment.

DELANO

Let's have your entertainment;
if you know a man's pleasure
you know his measure.

BABU

We are a childish people. Our pleasures are childish.
No one helped us, we know nothing
about your important amusements,
such as killing seals and pirates.

DELANO

I'm game. Let's have your entertainment.

(BABU *signals. The gong sounds ten times and the canvas is pulled from the circular structure. Enclosed in a triangular compartment, an* OLD SPANISH SAILOR *is dipping naked white dolls in a tar-pot*)

BABU

This little amusement keeps him alive, Yankee Master.
He is especially fond of cleaning the dolls
after he has dirtied them.

(*The* OLD SPANISH SAILOR *laughs hysterically, and then smears his whole face with tar*)

OLD SPANISH SAILOR

My soul is white!

BABU

The yellow fever destroyed his mind.

DELANO

Let's move on. This man's brain,
as well as his face, is defiled with pitch!

BABU

He says his soul is white.

(*The structure is pushed around and another triangular compartment appears. A* NEGRO BOY *is playing chess against a splendid Spanish doll with a crown on its head. He stops and holds two empty wine bottles to his ears*)

This boy is deaf.
The yellow fever destroyed his mind.

DELANO

Why is he holding those bottles to his ears?

BABU

He is trying to be a rabbit,
or listening to the ocean, his mother—
who knows?

DELANO

If he's deaf, how can he hear the ocean?
Anyway, he can't hear me.
I pass, let's move on.

(*The structure is pushed around to a third compartment. A* SPANISH SAILOR *is holding a big armful of rope*)

What are you knotting there, my man?

SPANISH SAILOR

The knot.

DELANO

So I see, but what's it for?

SPANISH SAILOR

For someone to untie. Catch!

(*Throws the knot to* DELANO)

BABU

(*Snatching the knot from* DELANO)

It's dirty, it will dirty your uniform.

DELANO

Let's move on. Your entertainment
is rather lacking in invention, Babu.

BABU

We have to do what we can
We are just beginners at acting.
This next one will be better.

(*The structure is pushed around and shows a beautiful* NEGRO WOMAN. *She is dressed and posed as the Virgin Mary. A Christmas crèche is arranged around her. A* VERY WHITE SPANIARD *dressed as Saint Joseph stands behind her. She holds a Christ-child, the same crowned doll, only black, the* NEGRO BOY *was playing chess against*)

She is the Virgin Mary. That man is not the father.

DELANO

I see. I suppose her son is the King of Spain.

BABU

The Spaniards taught us everything,
there's nothing we can learn from you, Yankee Master.
When they took away our country, they gave us a
better world.
Things do not happen in that world as they do here.

DELANO

That's a very beautiful,
though unusual Virgin Mary.

BABU

Yes, the Bible says, "I am black not white."
When Don Aranda was dying,
we wanted to give him the Queen of Heaven
because he took away our chains.

PERKINS

The Spaniards must have taught them everything;
they're all mixed up, they don't even know their religion.

DELANO

No, no! The Catholic Church doesn't just teach,
it knows how to take from its converts.

BABU

Do you want to shake hands with the Queen of Heaven,
Yankee Master?

DELANO

No, I'm not used to royalty.
Tell her I believe in freedom of religion,
if people don't take liberties.
Let's move on.

BABU

(*Kneeling to the Virgin Mary*)

I present something Your Majesty has never seen,
a white man who doesn't believe in taking liberties,
Your Majesty.

(*The structure is pushed around and shows* ATUFAL *in chains but with a crown on his head*)

BABU

This is the life we believe in.

THE NEGROES ALL TOGETHER

Ask pardon, King Atufal!
Kiss the Spanish flag!

DELANO

Please don't ask me to shake hands with King Atufal!
(*The canvas is put back on the structure*)

BABU

You look tired and serious, Yankee Master.
We have to have what fun we can.
We never would have lived through the deadly calms
without a little amusement.
(*Bows and goes off*)

(*The* NEGROES *gradually drift away.* DELANO *sighs with relief*)

DELANO

Well, that wasn't much!
I suppose Shakespeare started that way.

PERKINS

Who cares?
I see a speck on the blue sea, Sir,
our whaleboat is coming.

DELANO

A speck? My eyes are speckled.
I seem to have been dreaming. What's solid?
(*Touches the ornate railing; a piece falls onto the deck*)
This ship is nothing, Perkins!
I dreamed someone was trying to kill me!
How could he? Jack-of-the-beach,
they used to call me on the Duxbury shore.
Carrying a duck-satchel in my hand, I used to paddle
along the waterfront from a hulk to school.
I didn't learn much there. I was always shooting duck

or gathering huckleberries along the marsh with
  Cousin Nat!
I like nothing better than breaking myself on the surf.
I used to track the seagulls down the five-mile stretch
  of beach for eggs.
How can I be killed now at the ends of the earth
by this insane Spaniard?
Who could want to murder Amasa Delano?
My conscience is clean. God is good.
What am I doing on board this nigger-pirate ship?

PERKINS

You're not talking like a skipper, Sir.
Our boat's a larger spot now.

DELANO

I am childish.
I am doddering and drooling into my second childhood.
God help me, nothing's solid!

PERKINS

Don Benito, Sir. Touch him,
he's as solid as his ship.

DELANO

Don Benito? He's a walking ghost!
(BENITO *comes up to* DELANO. BABU *is a few steps behind him*)

BENITO

I am the ghost of myself, Captain.
Excuse me, I heard you talking about dreams
  and childhood.
I was a child, too, once, I have dreams about it.

DELANO
(*Starting*)

I'm sorry.
This jumping's just a nervous habit.
I thought you were part of my dreams.

BENITO

I was taking my siesta,
I dreamed I was a boy back in Lima.
I was with my brothers and sisters,
and we were dressed for the festival of Corpus Christi
like people at our Bourbon court.
We were simple children, but something went wrong;
little black men came on us with beetle backs.
They had caterpillar heads and munched away on our
fine clothes.
They made us lick their horned and varnished insect legs.
Our faces turned brown from their spit,
we looked like bugs, but nothing could save our lives!

DELANO

Ha, ha, Captain. We are like two dreams meeting head-on.
My whaleboat's coming,
we'll both feel better over a bottle of cider.

(BABU *blows a bosun's whistle. The gongs are sounded with descending notes. The* NEGROES *assemble in ranks*)

BABU

It's twelve noon, Master Yankee.
Master wants his midday shave.

ALL THE NEGROES

Master wants his shave! Master wants his shave!

BENITO

Ah, yes, the razor! I have been talking too much.
You can see how badly I need a razor.
I must leave you, Captain.

BABU

No, Don Amasa wants to talk.
Come to the cabin, Don Amasa.
Don Amasa will talk, Master will listen.
Babu will lather and strop.

DELANO

I want to talk to you about navigation.
I am new to these waters.

BENITO

Doubtless, doubtless, Captain Delano.

PERKINS

I think I'll take my siesta, Sir.

(*He walks off*)

(BENITO, BABU, *and* DELANO *walk toward the back of the stage. A scrim curtain lifts, showing a light deck cabin that forms a sort of attic. The floor is matted, partitions that still leave splintered traces have been knocked out. To one side, a small table screwed to the floor; on it, a dirty missal; above it, a small crucifix, rusty crossed muskets on one side, rusty crossed cutlasses on the other.* BENITO *sits down in a broken thronelike and gilded chair.* BABU *begins to lather. A magnificent array of razors, bottles and other shaving equipment lies on a table beside him. Behind him; a hammock with a pole in it and a dirty pillow*)

DELANO

So this is where you took your siesta.

BENITO

Yes, Captain, I rest here when my fate will let me.

DELANO

This seems like a sort of dormitory, sitting-room,
sail-loft, chapel, armory, and private bedroom all together.

BENITO

Yes, Captain: events have not been favorable
to much order in my personal arrangements.

(BABU *moves back and opens a locker. A lot of flags, torn shirts and socks tumble out. He takes one of the flags, shakes it with a flourish, and ties it around* BENITO'S *neck*)

BABU

Master needs more protection.
I do everything I can to save his clothes.

DELANO

The Castle and the Lion of Spain.
Why, Don Benito, this is the flag of Spain you're using!
It's well it's only I and not the King of Spain who sees this!
All's one, though, I guess, in this carnival world.
I see you like gay colors as much as Babu.

BABU

(*Giggling*)

The bright colors draw the yellow fever
from Master's mind.

(*Raises the razor*)

(BENITO *begins to shake*)

Now, Master, now, Master!

BENITO

You are talking while you hold the razor.

BABU

You mustn't shake so, Master.
Look, Don Amasa, Master always shakes when I shave him,
though he is braver than a lion and stronger than a castle.
Master knows Babu has never yet drawn blood.
I may, though, sometime, if he shakes so much.
Now, Master!
Come, Don Amasa, talk to Master about the gales
and calms,
he'll answer and forget to shake.

DELANO

Those calms, the more I think of them the more I wonder.
You say you were two months sailing here;
I made that stretch in less than a week.
We never met with any calms.

If I'd not heard your story from your lips,
and seen your ruined ship,
I would have said something was missing,
I would have said this was a mystery ship.

BENITO

For some men the whole world is a mystery;
they cannot believe their senses.
(BENITO *shakes, the razor gets out of hand and cuts his cheek*)
Santa Maria!

BABU

Poor, poor Master, see, you shook so;
this is Babu's first blood.
Please answer Don Amasa, while I wipe
this ugly blood from the razor and strop it again.

BENITO

The sea was like the final calm of the world
On, on it went. It sat on us and drank our strength,
cross-currents eased us out to sea,
the yellow fever changed our blood to poison.

BABU

You stood by us. Some of us stood by you!

BENITO

Yes, my Spanish crew was weak and surly, but the blacks,
the blacks were angels. Babu has kept me in this world.
I wonder what he is keeping me for?
You belong to me. I belong to you forever.

BABU

Ah, Master, spare yourself.
Forever is a very long time;
nothing's forever.
(*With great expertness, delicacy and gentleness,* BABU *mas-*

sages BENITO'S *cheeks, shakes out the flag, pours lotion from five bottles on* BENITO'S *hair, cleans the shaving materials, and stands off admiring his work*)

Master looks just like a statue.
He's like a figurehead, Don Amasa!

(DELANO *looks, then starts to walk out leaving* BENITO *and* BABU. *The curtain drops upon them.* DELANO *rejoins* PERKINS, *lounging at the rail*)

PERKINS

Our boat is coming.

DELANO
(*Gaily*)

I know!
I don't know how I'll explain this pomp
and squalor to my own comfortable family of a crew.
Even shaving here is like a High Mass.
There's something in a Negro, something
that makes him fit to have around your person.
His comb and brush are castanets.
What tact Babu had!
What noiseless, gliding briskness!

PERKINS

Our boat's about along side, Sir.

DELANO

What's more, the Negro has a sense of humor.
I don't mean their boorish giggling and teeth-showing,
I mean his easy cheerfulness in every glance and gesture.
You should have seen Babu toss that Spanish flag like
a juggler,
and change it to a shaving napkin!

PERKINS

The boat's here, Sir.

DELANO

We need inferiors, Perkins,
more manners, more docility, no one has an inferior mind
in America.

PERKINS

Here is your crew, Sir.
(BABU *runs out from the cabin. His cheek is bleeding*)

DELANO

Why, Babu, what has happened?

BABU

Master will never get better from his sickness.
His bad nerves and evil fever made him use me so.
I gave him one small scratch by accident,
the only time I've nicked him, Don Amasa.
He cut me with his razor. Do you think I will die?
I'd rather die than bleed to death!

DELANO

It's just a pinprick, Babu. You'll live.

BABU

I must attend my master.
(*Runs back into cabin*)

DELANO

Just a pinprick, but I wouldn't have thought
Don Benito had the stuff to swing a razor.
Up north we use our fists instead of knives.
I hope Benito's not dodging around some old grindstone
in the hold, and sharpening a knife for me.
Here, Perkins, help our men up the ladder.
(*Two immaculate* AMERICAN SAILORS *appear carrying great casks of water. Two more follow carrying net baskets of wilted pumpkins. The* NEGROES *begin to crowd forward, shouting, "We want Yankee food, we want Yankee drink!"*

DELANO *grandiosely holds up a pumpkin; an* OLD NEGRO *rushes forward, snatches at the pumpkin, and knocks* DELANO *off-balance into* PERKINS'S *arms.* DELANO *gets up and knocks the* NEGRO *down with his fist. All is tense and quiet. The* SIX HATCHET-CLEANERS *lift their hatchets above their heads*)

DELANO

(*Furious*)

Americans, stand by me! Stand by your captain!

(*Like lightning, the* AMERICANS *unsling their muskets, fix bayonets, and kneel with their guns pointing at the* NEGROES)

Don Benito, Sir, call your men to order!

BABU

We're starving, Yankee Master. We mean no harm;
we've never been so scared.

DELANO

You try my patience, Babu.
I am talking to Captain Cereno;
call your men to order, Sir.

BENITO

Make them laugh, Babu. The Americans aren't going
to shoot.

(BABU *airily waves a hand. The* NEGROES *smile.* DELANO *turns to* BENITO)

You mustn't blame them too much; they're sick
and hungry.
We have kept them cooped up for ages.

DELANO

(*As the* NEGROES *relax*)

Form them in lines, Perkins!
Each man shall have his share.
That's how we run things in the States—
to each man equally, no matter what his claims.

NEGROES

(*Standing back, bleating like sheep*)
Feed me, Master Yankee! Feed me, Master Yankee!

DELANO

You are much too close.
Here, Perkins, take the provisions aft.
You'll save lives by giving each as little as you can,
Be sure to keep a tally.
(FRANCESCO, *a majestic, yellow-colored mulatto, comes up to* DELANO)

FRANCESCO

My master requests your presence at dinner, Don Amasa.

DELANO

Tell him I have indigestion.
Tell him to keep better order on his ship.
It's always the man of good will that gets hurt;
my fist still aches from hitting that old darky.

FRANCESCO

My master has his own methods of discipline
that are suitable for our unfortunate circumstances.
Will you come to dinner, Don Amasa?

DELANO

I'll come. When in Rome, do as the Romans.
Excuse my quick temper, Sir.
It's better to blow up than to smoulder.
(*The scrim curtain is raised. In the cabin, a long table loaded with silver has been laid out. The locker has been closed and the Spanish flag hangs on the wall.* DON BENITO *is seated,* BABU *stands behind him. As soon as* DELANO *sits down,* FRANCESCO *begins serving with great dignity and agility*)

FRANCESCO

A finger bowl, Don Amasa.
(*After each statement, he moves about the table*)
A napkin, Don Amasa.
A glass of American water, Don Amasa.
A slice of American pumpkin, Don Amasa.
A goblet of American cider, Don Amasa.
(DELANO *drinks a great deal of cider,* BENITO *hardly touches his*)

DELANO

This is very courtly for a sick ship, Don Benito.
The Spanish Empire will never go down, if she keeps
her chin up.

BENITO

I'm afraid I shan't live long enough to enjoy
your prophecy.

DELANO

I propose a toast to the Spanish Empire
on which the sun never sets;
may you find her still standing, when you land, Sir!

BENITO

Our Empire has lasted three hundred years,
I suppose she will last another month.
I wish I could say the same for myself. My sun is setting,
I hear the voices of the dead in this calm.

DELANO

You hear the wind lifting;
it's bringing our two vessels together.
We are going to take you into port, Don Benito.

BENITO

You are either too late or too early with your good works.
Our yellow fever may break out again.
You aren't going to put your men in danger, Don Amasa?

DELANO

My boys are all healthy, Sir.

BENITO

Health isn't God, I wouldn't trust it.

FRANCESCO

May I fill your glass, Don Amasa?

BABU

New wine in new bottles,
that's the American spirit, Yankee Master.
They say all men are created equal in North America.

DELANO

We prefer merit to birth, boy.
(BABU *motions imperiously for* FRANCESCO *to leave. As he goes, bowing to the* CAPTAINS, FOUR NEGROES *play the Marseillaise*)
Why are they playing the *Marseillaise?*

BABU

His uncle is supposed to have been in the
French Convention,
and voted for the death of the French King.

DELANO

This polite and royal fellow is no anarchist!

BABU

Francesco is very *ancien regime,*
he is even frightened of the Americans.
He doesn't like the way you treated King George.
Babu is more liberal.

DELANO

A royal fellow,
this usher of yours, Don Benito!

He is as yellow as a goldenrod.
He is a king, a king of kind hearts.
What a pleasant voice he has!

BENITO

(*Glumly*)

Francesco is a good man.

DELANO

As long as you've known him,
he's been a worthy fellow, hasn't he?
Tell me, I am particularly curious to know.

BENITO

Francesco is a good man.

DELANO

I'm glad to hear it, I am glad to hear it!
You refute the saying of a planter friend of mine.
He said, "When a mulatto has a regular European face,
look out for him, he is a devil."

BENITO

I've heard your planter's remark applied
to intermixtures of Spaniards and Indians;
I know nothing about mulattoes.

DELANO

No, no, my friend's refuted;
if we're so proud of our white blood,
surely a little added to the blacks improves their breed.
I congratulate you on your servants, Sir.

BABU

We've heard that Jefferson, the King of your Republic,
would like to free his slaves.

DELANO

Jefferson has read too many books, boy,
but you can trust him. He's a gentleman and an American!
He's not lifting a finger to free his slaves.

BABU

We hear you have a new capital modelled on Paris,
and that your President is going to set up
a guillotine on the Capitol steps.

DELANO

Oh, Paris! I told you you could trust Mr. Jefferson, boy,
he stands for law and order like your mulatto.
Have you been to Paris, Don Benito?

BENITO

I'm afraid I'm just a provincial Spaniard, Captain.

DELANO

Let me tell you about Paris.
You know what French women are like—
nine parts sex and one part logic.
Well, one of them in Paris heard
that my ship was the *President Adams*. She said,
"You are descended from Adam, Captain,
you must know everything,
tell me how Adam and Eve learned to sleep together."
Do you know what I said?

BENITO

No, Captain.

DELANO

I said, "I guess Eve was a Frenchwoman,
the first Frenchwoman."
Do you know what she answered?

BENITO

No, Captain Delano.

DELANO

She said, "I was trying to provoke a philosophical
discussion, Sir."
A philosophical discussion, ha, ha!
You look serious, Sir. You know, something troubles me.

BENITO

Something troubles you, Captain Delano?

DELANO

I still can't understand those calms,
but let that go. The scurvy,
why did it kill off three Spaniards in every four,
and only half the blacks?
Negroes are human, but surely you couldn't have
favored them
before your own flesh and blood!

BENITO

This is like the Inquisition, Captain Delano.
I have done the best I could.

(BABU *dabs* BENITO'S *forehead with cider*)

BABU

Poor, poor Master; since Don Aranda died,
he trusts no one except Babu.

DELANO

Your Babu is an uncommonly intelligent fellow;
you are right to trust him, Sir.
Sometimes I think we overdo our talk of freedom.
If you looked into our hearts, we all want slaves.

BENITO

Disease is a mysterious thing;

it takes one man, and leaves his friend.
Only the unfortunate can understand misfortune.

DELANO

I must return to my bosun;
he's pretty green to be left alone here.
Before I go I want to propose a last toast to you!
A good master deserves good servants!
(*He gets up. As he walks back to* PERKINS, *the scrim curtain falls, concealing* BENITO *and* BABU)
That captain must have jaundice,
I wish he kept better order.
I don't like hitting menials.

PERKINS

I've done some looking around, Sir. I've used my eyes.

DELANO

That's what they're for, I guess. You have to watch your step,
this hulk, this rotten piece of finery,
will fall apart. This old world needs new blood
and Yankee gunnery to hold it up.
You shouldn't mess around, though, it's their ship;
you're breaking all the laws of the sea.

PERKINS

Do you see that man-shaped thing in canvas?

DELANO

I see it.

PERKINS

Behind the cloth, there's a real skeleton,
a man dressed up like Don Benito.

DELANO

They're Catholics, and worship bones.

PERKINS

There's writing on its coat. It says,
"I am Don Aranda," and, "Follow your leader."

DELANO

Follow your leader?

PERKINS

I saw two blacks unfurling a flag,
a black skull and crossbones on white silk.

DELANO

That's piracy. We've been ordered
to sink any ship that flies that flag.
Perhaps they were playing.

PERKINS

I saw King Atufal throw away his chains,
He called for food, the Spaniards served him two pieces
 of pumpkin,
and a whole bottle of your cider.

DELANO

Don Benito has the only key to Atufal's padlock.
My cider was for the captain's table.

PERKINS

Atufal pointed to the cabin where you were dining,
and drew a finger across his throat.

DELANO

Who could want to kill Amasa Delano?

PERKINS

I warned our men to be ready for an emergency.

DELANO

You're a mind reader,

I couldn't have said better myself;
but we're at peace with Spain.

PERKINS

I told them to return with loaded muskets
and fixed bayonets.

DELANO

Here comes Benito. Watch how I'll humor him
and sound him out.
(BABU *brings out* BENITO'S *chair.* BENITO *sits in it*)
It's good to have you back on deck, Captain.
Feel the breeze! It holds and will increase.
My ship is moving nearer. Soon we will be together.
We have seen you through your troubles.

BENITO

Remember, I warned you about the yellow fever.
I am surprised you haven't felt afraid.

DELANO

Oh, that will blow away.
Everything is going to go better and better;
the wind's increasing, soon you'll have no cares.
After the long voyage, the anchor drops into the harbor.
It's a great weight lifted from the captain's heart.
We are getting to be friends, Don Benito.
My ship's in sight, the *President Adams!*
How the wind braces a man up!
I have a small invitation to issue to you.

BENITO

An invitation?

DELANO

I want you to take a cup of coffee
with me on my quarter deck tonight.
The Sultan of Turkey never tasted such coffee
as my old steward makes. What do you say, Don Benito?

BENITO

I cannot leave my ship.

DELANO

Come, come, you need a change of climate.
The sky is suddenly blue, Sir,
my coffee will make a man of you.

BENITO

I cannot leave my ship.
Even now, I don't think you understand my position here.

DELANO

I want to speak to you alone.

BENITO

I am alone, as much as I ever am.

DELANO

In America, we don't talk about money
in front of servants and children.

BENITO

Babu is not my servant.
You spoke of money—since the yellow fever,
he has had a better head for figures than I have.

DELANO

You embarrass me, Captain,
but since circumstances are rather special here,
I will proceed.

BENITO

Babu takes an interest in all our expenses.

DELANO

Yes, I am going to talk to you about your expenses.
I am responsible to my owners for all

the sails, ropes, food and carpentry I give you.
You will need a complete rerigging, almost a new ship,
in fact,
You shall have our services at cost.

BENITO

I know, you are a merchant.
I suppose I ought to pay you for our lives.

DELANO

I envy you, Captain. You are the only owner
of the *San Domingo,* since Don Aranda died.
I am just an employee. Our owners would sack me,
if I followed my better instincts.

BENITO

You can give your figures to Babu, Captain.

DELANO

You are very offhand about money, Sir;
I don't think you realize the damage that has been done
to your ship.
Ah, you smile. I'm glad you're loosening up.
Look, the water gurgles merrily, the wind is high,
a mild light is shining. I sometimes think
such a tropical light as this must have shone
on the tents of Abraham and Isaac.
It seems as if Providence were watching over us.

PERKINS

There are things that need explaining here, Sir.

DELANO

Yes, Captain, Perkins saw some of your men
unfurling an unlawful flag,
a black skull and crossbones.

BENITO

You know my only flag is the Lion and Castle of Spain.

DELANO

No, Perkins says he saw a skull and crossbones.
That's piracy. I trust Perkins.
You've heard about how my government blew
the bowels out of the pirates at Tripoli?

BENITO

Perhaps my Negroes . . .

DELANO

My government doesn't intend
to let you play at piracy!

BENITO

Perhaps my Negroes were playing.
When you take away their chains . . .

DELANO

I'll see that you are all put back in chains,
if you start playing pirates!

PERKINS

There's something else he can explain, Sir.

DELANO

Yes, Perkins saw Atufal throw off his chains
and order dinner.

BABU

Master has the key, Yankee Master.

BENITO

I have the key.
You can't imagine how my position exhausts me, Captain.

DELANO

I can imagine. Atufal's chains are fakes.
You and he are in cahoots, Sir!

PERKINS

They don't intend to pay for our sails and service.
They think America is Santa Claus.

DELANO

The United States are death on pirates and debtors.

PERKINS

There's one more thing for him to explain, Sir.

DELANO

Do you see that man-shaped thing covered with black
cloth, Don Benito?

BENITO

I always see it.

DELANO

Take away the cloth. I order you to take away the cloth!

BENITO

I cannot. Oh, Santa Maria, have mercy!

DELANO

Of course, you can't. It's no Virgin Mary.
You have done something terrible to your friend,
Don Aranda.
Take away the cloth, Perkins!

(*As* PERKINS *moves forward,* ATUFAL *suddenly stands unchained and with folded arms, blocking his way*)

BABU

(*Dancing up and down and beside himself*)

Let them see it! Let them see it!
I can't stand any more of their insolence;
the Americans treat us like their slaves!

(BABU *and* PERKINS *meet at the man-shaped object and start pulling away the cloth.* BENITO *rushes between them, and throws them back and sprawling on the deck.* BABU *and* PERKINS *rise, and stand hunched like wrestlers, about to close in on* BENITO, *who draws his sword with a great gesture. It is only a hilt. He runs at* BABU *and knocks him down.* ATUFAL *throws off his chains and signals to the* HATCHET-CLEANERS. *They stand behind* BENITO *with raised hatchets. The Negroes shout ironically, "Evviva Benito!")*

You too, Yankee Captain!
If you shoot, we'll kill you.

DELANO

If a single American life is lost,
I will send this ship to the bottom,
and all Peru after it.
Do you hear me, Don Benito?

BENITO

Don't you understand? I am as powerless as you are!

BABU

He is as powerless as you are.

BENITO

Don't you understand? He has been holding a knife at my back.
I have been talking all day to save your life.

BABU

(*Holding a whip*)

Do you see this whip? When Don Aranda was out of temper,
he used to snap pieces of flesh off us with it.
Now I hold the whip.
When I snap it, Don Benito jumps!

(*Snaps the whip.* DON BENITO *flinches*)

DELANO

(*Beginning to understand*)

It's easy to terrorize the defenseless.

BABU

That's what we thought when Don Aranda held the whip.

DELANO

You'll find I am made of tougher stuff than your Spaniards.

ATUFAL

We want to kill you.

NEGROES

We want to kill you, Yankee Captain.

DELANO

Who could want to kill Amasa Delano?

BABU

Of course. We want to keep you alive.
We want you to sail us back to Africa.
Has anyone told you how much you are worth, Captain?

DELANO

I have another course in mind.

BENITO

Yes, there's another course if you don't like Africa, there's
another course.
King Atufal, show the Yankee captain
the crew that took the other course!
(*Three dead* SPANISH SAILORS *are brought on stage*)

ATUFAL

Look at Don Aranda?

DELANO

Yes, you are hot-tempered and discourteous, Captain.
I am going to introduce you to Don Aranda.
You have a new command, Captain. You must meet your
new owner.

(*The black cloth is taken from the man-shaped object and shows a chalk-white skeleton dressed like* DON BENITO)

Don Amasa, Don Aranda!
You can see that Don Aranda was a white man like you,
because his bones are white.

NEGROES

He is a white because his bones are white!
He is a white because his bones are white!

ATUFAL

(*Pointing to the ribbon on the skeleton's chest*)

Do you see that ribbon?
It says, "Follow the leader."
We wrote it in his blood.

BABU

He was a white man
even though his blood was red as ours.

NEGROES

He is white because his bones are white!

BABU

Don Aranda is our figurehead,
we are going to chain him to the bow of our ship
to scare off devils.

BABU

This is the day of Jubilee,
I am raising the flag of freedom!

NEGROES

Freedom! Freedom! Freedom!

(*The black skull and crossbones is raised on two poles. The* NEGROES *form two lines, leading up to the flag, and leave an aisle. Each man is armed with some sort of weapon*)

BABU

Spread out the Spanish flag!

(*The Lion and Castle of Spain is spread out on the deck in front of the skull and crossbones*)

The Spanish flag is the road to freedom.
Don Benito mustn't hurt his white feet on the splinters.

(*Kneeling in front of* BENITO)

Your foot, Master!

(BENITO *holds out his foot.* BABU *takes off* BENITO'S *shoes*)

Give Don Benito back his sword!

(*The sword-hilt is fastened back in* BENITO'S *scabbard*)

Load him with chains!

(*Two heavy chains are draped on* BENITO'S *neck. The cane and ball are handed to him*)

Former Captain Benito Cereno, kneel!
Ask pardon of man!

BENITO

(*Kneeling*)

I ask pardon for having been born a Spaniard.
I ask pardon for having enslaved my fellow man.

BABU

Strike off the oppressor's chain!

(*One of* BENITO'S *chains is knocked off, then handed to* ATUFAL, *who dashes it to the deck*)

Former Captain Benito Cereno,
you must kiss the flag of freedom.

(*Points to* DON ARANDA)

Kiss the mouth of the skull!

(BENITO *walks barefoot over the Spanish flag and kisses the mouth of* DON ARANDA)

NEGROES

Evviva Benito! Evviva Benito!

(*Sounds are heard from* PERKINS, *whose head is still covered with the sack*)

ATUFAL

The bosun wants to kiss the mouth of freedom.

BABU

March over the Spanish flag, Bosun.

(PERKINS *starts forward*)

DELANO

You are dishonoring your nation, Perkins!
Don't you stand for anything?

PERKINS

I only have one life, Sir.

(*Walks over the Spanish flag and kisses the mouth of the skull*)

NEGROES

Evviva Bosun! *Evviva* Bosun!

DELANO

You are no longer an American, Perkins!

BABU

He was free to choose freedom, Captain.

ATUFAL

Captain Delano wants to kiss the mouth of freedom.

BABU

He is jealous of the bosun.

ATUFAL

In the United States, all men are created equal.

BABU

Don't you want to kiss the mouth of freedom, Captain?

DELANO

(*Lifting his pocket and pointing the pistol*)

Do you see what I have in my hand?

BABU

A pistol.

DELANO

I am unable to miss at this distance.

BABU

You must take your time, Yankee Master.
You must take your time.

DELANO

I am unable to miss.

BABU

You can stand there like a block of wood
as long as you want to, Yankee Master.
You will drop asleep, then we will tie you up,
and make you sail us back to Africa.

(*General laughter. Suddenly, there's a roar of gunfire. Several* NEGROES, *mostly women, fall.* AMERICAN SEAMEN *in spotless blue and white throw themselves in a lying position on deck.* MORE *kneel above them, then* MORE *stand above these. All have muskets and fixed bayonets. The First Row fires. More* NEGROES *fall. They start to retreat. The Second Row fires. More* NEGROES *fall. They retreat further. The Third Row fires. The Three* AMERICAN LINES *march forward, but all the* NEGROES *are either dead or in retreat.* DON BENITO *has been wounded. He staggers over to* DELANO *and shakes his hand*)

BENITO

You have saved my life.
I thank you for my life.

DELANO

A man can only do what he can,
We have saved American lives.

PERKINS

(*Pointing to* ATUFAL'S *body*)
We have killed King Atufal,
we have killed their ringleader.
(BABU *jumps up. He is unwounded*)

BABU

I was the King. Babu, not Atufal
was the king, who planned, dared and carried out
the seizure of this ship, the *San Domingo.*
Untouched by blood myself, I had all
the most dangerous and useless Spaniards killed.
I freed my people from their Egyptian bondage.
The heartless Spaniards slaved for me like slaves.
(BABU *steps back, and quickly picks up a crown from the litter*)
This is my crown.
(*Puts crown on his head. He snatches* BENITO'S *rattan cane*)
This is my rod.
(*Picks up silver ball*)
This is the earth.
(*Holds the ball out with one hand and raises the cane*)
This is the arm of the angry God.
(*Smashes the ball*)

PERKINS

Let him surrender. Let him surrender.
We want to save someone.

BENITO

My God how little these people understand!

BABU

(*Holding a white handkerchief and raising both his hands*)
Yankee Master understand me. The future is with us.

DELANO

(*Raising his pistol*)
This is your future.

(BABU *falls and lies still.* DELANO *pauses, then slowly empties the five remaining barrels of his pistol into the body. Lights dim*)

CURTAIN

George Washington Crossing the Delaware

BY KENNETH KOCH

Although both Lowell's *Benito Cereno* and Koch's *George Washington Crossing the Delaware* are based on "actual historical events" and have certain common aspects of pageant (the climactic scene of *Washington* is an almost wordless *tableau vivante*), they nevertheless form a complete contrast. While an essential issue of the Lowell play is the problem of gaining a mature, full view of reality (the task at which its "hero," Delano, fails almost fatally), Koch's play attacks its familiar subject as if from a child's point of view—a point of view also evident in Koch's volume of verse, *Thank You*. Since it is in fact from a child's point of view that we first learn this essential American myth and perhaps unconsciously continue to think about it, Koch might be credited with the same aim as Wilder: reality, not verisimilitude—or, in this case, not historical accuracy. The point of Koch's approach is neither nostalgic, nor satirical; it is theatrical. His knowing adaptation of a youthful perspective produces effects that in their freshness are akin to children's paintings, but possess the great additional virtue of an over-all sophistication and control. The language, for example, has a seemingly innocent sublimity, full of archaisms and grand gestures, but it is constantly qualified by absurdity, most often in the form of reference to more recent myths than those that could have animated Washington (Cornwallis: "What tomfoolery is that you speak, George Washington? You are a general, and generals are supposed to have a college education."). Structurally, the play moves with a quick-paced, kaleidoscopically illustrational fervor that obviously refers to no known reality; the transparency of the attempt to organize the myth to show that the ideal of "Democracy in Action" governed every aspect of the Revolutionary War effort is particularly amusing. In the original production it seemed only proper that the sets, by Alex Katz, were constructed of that most obviously artificial of all stage materials, cardboard—down to an English-woman's teacups, the British and American troops, and the waves of the Delaware. Like the paintings of both Katz and Larry Rivers (to whom the play is dedicated, and of whose 1953 painting "George Washington Crossing the Delaware" its spirit is reminiscent), Koch's play is a witty approximation of reality for reality-subverting purposes, and in the interest of a new, unpredictable reality of the playwright's own.

George Washington Crossing the Delaware

To Larry Rivers

SCENE 1. *Alpine, New Jersey.*

GEORGE WASHINGTON

General Cornwallis, you cannot stay here in the trails of Alpine, New Jersey. The American army will drive you away, and away! Americans shall be masters of the American continent! then, perhaps, of the world!

CORNWALLIS

What tomfoolery is that you speak, George Washington? You are a general, and generals are supposed to have a college education. No man with any sense would see a victory in this conflict for any power but GREAT BRITAIN!

GEORGE WASHINGTON

General Cornwallis, I am a mild man, but you had better not say that kind of thing to me. I tell you, America shall win the Revolutionary War!

FIRST AIDE TO GEORGE WASHINGTON

Our general speaks the truth, Englishmen.

FIRST AIDE TO CORNWALLIS

Do you dare to speak to General Cornwallis, impudent Yankee?

FIRST AIDE TO GEORGE WASHINGTON

Aye, I am an American, and I fear to speak to no man.

GEORGE WASHINGTON

My aide is expressing the philosophy we all have. It is bound to triumph over your own British authoritarian and colonial system. My men all see eye to eye on this point.

CORNWALLIS

I caution you, General Washington, that many of them will never see eye to eye with anything again if you persist in this useless, cruel and wasteful battle.

GEORGE WASHINGTON

Come, my loyal men. We waste our time in entreaty with the English lord. He mocks us and all we believe.

FIRST AIDE TO GEORGE WASHINGTON

Aye, General. I follow you.

OTHER AIDES

Aye, General, we come. (*They leave*)

CORNWALLIS

There goes the greatest man who will ever live in America! If only he could come over to the English side, I could bring myself to give up my command to him. He is a perfect gentleman, excelling in manners as in speech. His dress is perfect, his buttoning neat, and his shoes of a high polish. He speaks frankly and freely, and will say straight out to his most bitter opponent that which is in his mind. There is nothing he could not accomplish, would he but set himself to it. What task, indeed, could ever challenge that general of the Revolutionary Army? He rides as he walks, with perfect grace; and when he reclines, one imagines one sees the stately bison taking its rest among the vast unexplored plains of this country, America, which now in foul and lawless revolt dares to lift its head against its English nurse and mother. What is more unnatural than that this man, Washington, who is one of God's gentlemen, should so defy the laws of right and wrong as to raise his hand against the breast that gave him suck, against the tender maternal care of England? O England, England! we who are your subjects are the most fortunate men on earth, and we shall struggle boldly to defend you, on land and at sea, no matter where we shall find ourselves, in whatever tempest or time of trouble that may come—we shall be, as we are, loyal to the end, and triumph we shall, for love makes our cause right . . . But that man Washington! (*Cornwallis leaves*)

FIRST AIDE TO CORNWALLIS

Our general is troubled.

SECOND AIDE TO CORNWALLIS

The sight of the Yankee general has quite o'erthrown him.

FIRST BRITISH SOLDIER
(*cockney accent*)

A did not think 'e was such a great man but I could 'ave ho'ertopped 'im wi' my little musket 'ere. 'Tis bare gaddiness that our general be disturbed.

SECOND BRITISH SOLDIER
(*cockney accent*)

Aye, but disturbed 'e is.

THIRD BRITISH SOLDIER
(*Irish brogue*)

Come off, now. What is it turns your heads so low, and the sun beatin' back against them, and your steps draggin', and no light of day in your eyes, and here it bein' God's own glorious time, when His Majesty walked in the Garden of Eden, in the cool of the day, and the glorious messenger of Zeus almighty and the eye of friendly Apollo ashinin' and aglistenin' in yonder famous West, where so many of our victories has been? What is there to make a man sad in a time of day such as this is, when all is gold as far as the eye can listen, and where the buzzin' of a thrillion insects shines through the ear? If a man were not happy at such a moment, he were but half a man, and that half not much good neither, but only for changin' and blackin' the pots while old Mother helps herself to some kidneys. It is a glad song I would be singin' but for some that would have it that all men must be sad in the time of the American War. Saw you not General Washington?

FIRST BRITISH SOLDIER
(*cockney accent*)

Sawr 'im plain, I did, just as big as your 'ead there. Troubled a bit, our general is, 'aving seen 'im 'isself. Gaive a nice speech habout Hengland though.

SECOND BRITISH SOLDIER
(*cockney accent*)

Aye, troubled 'e is, and deep, too. I see no good of this meetin'.

(*They all leave*)

SCENE 2. *The American Camp.*

FIRST AMERICAN SOLDIER

The general returns, and surely he will tell us much that he has seen.

SECOND AMERICAN SOLDIER

When the general goes abroad, he never fails to tell each private soldier, though he be lowest in station in the entire Revolutionary Army, what he, the general, has seen, and what his thoughts have been upon the subjects of his contemplation.

THIRD AMERICAN SOLDIER

Thus, each and every man in the Revolutionary Army shares in the secrets of the High Command, and every man knows exactly why he is fighting.

FOURTH AMERICAN SOLDIER

This is democracy in action, actually being practiced in a military situation. The method of our struggle exemplifies its end—freedom for every man from the English.

FIFTH AMERICAN SOLDIER

Here comes the general!

(*George Washington enters and mounts a podium*)

GEORGE WASHINGTON

Friends, soldiers, and Americans, lend me your ears! (*Laughter.*)
I have seen the British general, Cornwallis—
Brightly he shines in regal uniform,
And brightly shines his sword—but she will cut
No better, boys, than ours! (*Draws his sword, amid the thunderous cheers of the soldiers*). He said that we
Had not a chance at all to win the war . . . (*Laughter*)
Let's show that Englishman how wrong he is. (*Growls*)
And conquer them as quickly as we can! (*Cheers*)

A RAGGED SOLDIER

General Washington, how can we conquer the Englishmen when we have no guns, no ammunition, no clothing, and no food?

(*Loud murmurs from the soldiers of "Shhhhh shhh," "Strike him," "Why does he want to spoil everything?" "Kill him," etc.*)

GEORGE WASHINGTON

(*Unruffled*)

We must make raids—raids, raids,
Raids on the English supplies. We must make raids!
Raids for clothing and raids for food
To do the Revolutionary Army good;
Raids in the morning and raids at night,
Raids on our stomachs by candlelight,
Raids on the tea chest and raids on the mill,
Raids on the granary that stands by the hill;
Raids on the clothing tents, beautiful raids,
Raids on Cornwallis, and raids on his aides.
For stealing is licensed if for a good cause,
And in love and war, boys, you know there're no laws.
So pack up your shyness, your shame, and your fear,
And throw them away, and come meet me, all, here,

At twelve o'clock midnight, and off we shall go
To the camp of the English that lies down below!
And we shall return in their splendid attire,
And every man present shall have his desire.
So, come, get you ready—go blacken each face,
And meet me at midnight in this very place!

SCENE 3. *An English Home.*

ENGLISH GIRL

You mustn't cry, Mummy. There's absolutely nothing we can do. We are in England, and he is in America. Your tears are going to waste. Has he written?

MOTHER

The poor little fellow. I remember the first step he ever took. His father, may his soul rest in peace, was holding on to his tiny hands; and, when he began to step forward, all by his little self, his daddy let him go. And he took such a tumble! How I kissed him then—oh!

ENGLISH GIRL

I don't see why you keep having these morbid thoughts. Many soldiers return from wars unhurt, only to engage in some peaceful occupation in the pursuit of which they are killed by some unforeseeable accident.

MOTHER

Oh!

ENGLISH GIRL

Hugh is as safe in the army of General Cornwallis as he would be right back here at home. After all, General Washington's army is made up only of seedy criminals and starving bootblacks! They have neither food nor equipment, and everyone says it is not possible that they shall hold out for more than a few weeks against the skilled and well-equipped troops of our English army.

In all probability the war has already ended in our favor, and but for the slow and sluggish meanders of the ships bringing the news, we should be cognizant of it this day, this very hour in which I must know the pain of seeing tears fall from your deeply beloved and old friendly eyes, Mother.

MOTHER

Child, Artella, you are kind. But, dear, when a people fights for its freedom, even though its army be composed of little children bearing branches, that people will never stop until it has attained that freedom; so that it seems that, inevitably, that people will win, and Hugh, if he stay long enough, be, of necessity, wounded or killed, which is that at which I weep—for nothing touches more nearly a mother's heart than the death of her only son.

ENGLISH GIRL

But, Mother! the Americans cannot possibly win—they have no supplies!

SCENE 4. *The British Camp at Night. Complete Darkness.*

FIRST AMERICAN SOLDIER

Jim!

SECOND AMERICAN SOLDIER

Yes, Jack?

FIRST AMERICAN SOLDIER

Jim, are you there, Jim?

SECOND AMERICAN SOLDIER

Yes, Jack, I'm here, right here. What did you want, Jim?

FIRST AMERICAN SOLDIER

Have you got some tobacco?

SECOND AMERICAN SOLDIER

Yes. Here.

FIRST AMERICAN SOLDIER

Thanks, buddy. It sure tastes good.

SECOND AMERICAN SOLDIER

Isn't it delicious? I'm glad you like it.

FIRST AMERICAN SOLDIER

It really is good.

SECOND AMERICAN SOLDIER

I get a lot of satisfaction from hearing you say that. Why don't you take a little more so you'll have some for after the raid?

FIRST AMERICAN SOLDIER

Aw, I don't want to—

SECOND AMERICAN SOLDIER

No, go on, really, take it. I want you to have it.

FIRST AMERICAN SOLDIER

Well, if you insist.

SECOND AMERICAN SOLDIER

I do.

FIRST AMERICAN SOLDIER

Thanks, Jim. You're . . .

SECOND AMERICAN SOLDIER

Don't try to put it into words, Jack. Let's just forget it.

FIRST AMERICAN SOLDIER

No—I . . .

SERGEANT
(*cockney accent*)

Quiet up there! This is supposed to be a sneak raid.

GEORGE WASHINGTON

What's the trouble here, Sergeant?

SERGEANT

(*cockney accent*)

God save your honor, hit's a couple of men, sir, 'as been talking more than what they ought to 'ave, and I was for putting them in line, sir.

GEORGE WASHINGTON

How long have you been in this country, Sergeant?

SERGEANT

Two months, sir. Not long. But I feel hit's as much my own country as if I'd been 'ere fifty years, Your Lordship.

GEORGE WASHINGTON

You wouldn't be a spy, by any chance, would you, trying to tip the enemy off by making noise?

SERGEANT

Bless me, no, Your Lordship, by all that's sacred and 'oly. I am but a poor soldier would do 'is best to make this a land for free men to live and trade in.

GEORGE WASHINGTON

Very good. Continue with your work.

FIRST AIDE TO GEORGE WASHINGTON

General Washington?

GEORGE WASHINGTON

Is that you, Fitzdaniel? Haven't I told you not to use my name?

FIRST AIDE TO GEORGE WASHINGTON

Begging Your Worship's pardon, sir, but I think we may have come on something, sir. Here are many heads, arms, and legs, and if it is not the English camp, I know not what it might be.

GEORGE WASHINGTON

Excellent. Every man on his stomach. Get away with everything you can. Food is most important. Next, ammunition and clothing. Whatever you do, make no noise. Kill no man unless absolutely necessary. Is that understood?

ALL

(*whisper*)

Yes, General Washington.

(*Sounds of crawling about and scuffling*)

CORNWALLIS

(*in his sleep*)

What's that? Ho!

FIRST AIDE TO GEORGE WASHINGTON

What was that noise?

SECOND AIDE TO GEORGE WASHINGTON

The voice had a familiar ring.

FIRST AIDE TO GEORGE WASHINGTON

Yes! it was Cornwallis.

SECOND AIDE TO GEORGE WASHINGTON

Where does the English general lie?

FIRST AIDE TO GEORGE WASHINGTON

Near us, most likely, since we heard him so clearly.

SECOND AIDE TO GEORGE WASHINGTON

Let's go into his tent. It is likely to be rich in booty!

THIRD BRITISH SOLDIER

(*waking up; speaks with an Irish brogue*)

Ooo-oooooh me! (*pause*). Agh, it's little sleep I can be gettin', what with the cold wind blowin' against my head, and me all the time thinkin' of those that are near and those that are far away. And I did imagine as I lay thinkin' that I heard almost a rustlin', a kind of noise almost, as if the winds themselves had come to bring some news into our Irish camp. It's a little air I'll be needin', and out of my tent I'll be steppin' and lookin' at the fair face of the moon with all her tiny stars.

FIRST AMERICAN SOLDIER

What's this?

SECOND AMERICAN SOLDIER

It's a limey, Jack.

FIRST AMERICAN SOLDIER

Shall we drop him?

SECOND AMERICAN SOLDIER

The general said no.

FIRST AMERICAN SOLDIER

Then what shall we do?

SECOND AMERICAN SOLDIER

Wait, and listen.

THIRD BRITISH SOLDIER

Ah, 'tis a fair dark night, and such as it would be wrong to sleep through. There is beauty in the blackness of the sky, which bears not one tiny star. 'Twould be a fair night for a murder, and that's certain, for a man cannot see his hand before his face, even though he hold it up. A man could jump on another on a night such as this and sink a blade in his back without bein' noticed so much as a puff of smoke on a cloudy day. It's glad I am that the camp is guarded well by stalwart Irish soldiers and that we are safe from all harm.

SECOND AMERICAN SOLDIER

Quick, into his tent!

FIRST AMERICAN SOLDIER

Supposing he comes back?

SECOND AMERICAN SOLDIER

Then we'll have to—

FIRST AMERICAN SOLDIER

No!

SECOND AMERICAN SOLDIER

Yes! But he may not come. Come on, Jack!

FIRST AMERICAN SOLDIER

Lead the way!

GEORGE WASHINGTON

Sergeant, tell the men that the object of the raid has been accomplished. We have more than enough supplies for the campaign. Have them reassemble here, and we will then depart for our own camp.

SERGEANT

Yes, sir. Yes, sir. Oh, yes, sir!

(*Much crawling and scuffling*)

GEORGE WASHINGTON

Men, the raid has succeeded. We return to the American camp tonight!

ALL

Hurrah for General Washington!

SCENE 5. *The English Camp, Next Day.*

CORNWALLIS

(*running out of his tent*)

Help! I've been robbed! My guns, my clothes, my food supplies—everything is gone!

FIRST AIDE TO CORNWALLIS

And so have I! Everything is gone, everything!

[13] *Meat Joy*. On the Paint Table: the start of The Love-Paint Exchange between the Central Couple. (Paris performance.) Photo by Harold Chapman.

[14] *Meat Joy*. General View. The Independent Couple (right); continuation of the Love-Paint Exchange between the Central Couple (center); two Leg Mixtures (right and left). Photo by Peter Moore.

[15] *Meat Joy*. The Intractable Rosette: Wheel Formation. Photo by Al Giese.

[16] *Meat Joy*. The Intractable Rosette: Star Formation. Photo by Al Giese.

[17] *Meat Joy*. The Serving Maid distributes the chickens, fish, and hot dogs. Photo by Peter Moore.

[18] *Meat Joy*. Fish and Chickens (Paris performance). Photo by Harold Chapman.

[19] *Meat Joy*. Fish and Chickens. Carolee Schneemann, center. Photo by Peter Moore.

[20] *Meat Joy*. A characteristic pile-up during Fish and Chickens. Photo by Al Giese.

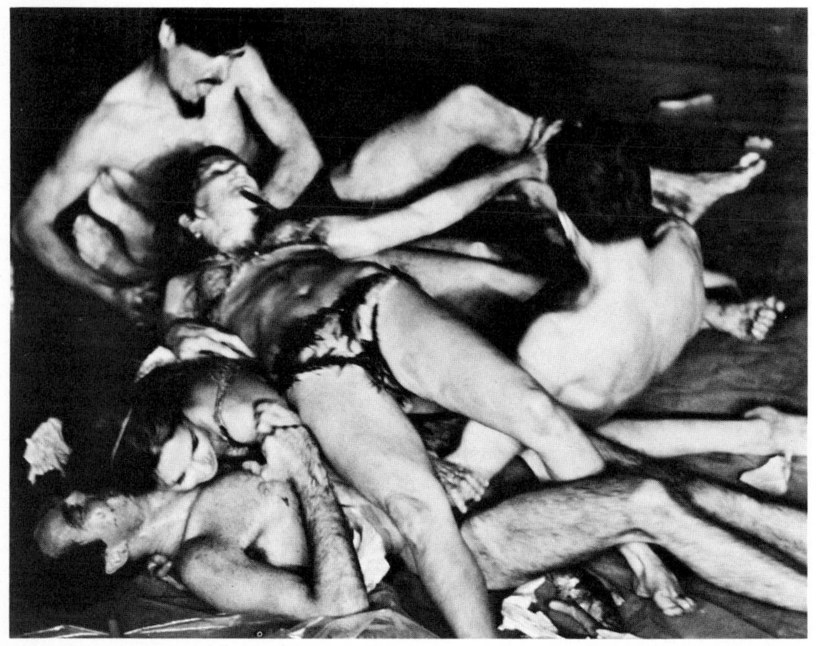

[21] *Meat Joy*. The building of The Tree. Photo by Peter Moore.

[22] *Meat Joy*. The collapsing of The Tree. Photo by Manfred Schroeder.

[23] *Meat Joy*. The Paint Attack (Editor, seated second from right). Photo by Charles Rotenberg.

[24] *Gas*. The Parade at Southampton. "The 'Neutron Kid' [Kaprow himself] ...swathed in black plastic, wearing dark glasses and a World War I aviator's helmet." Photo by Peter Moore.

SECOND AIDE TO CORNWALLIS

And I.

THIRD BRITISH SOLDIER
(*Irish brogue*)

And I.

COOK

The kitchen tent is completely emptied of supplies!

QUARTERMASTER

All our equipment and ammunition are gone!

ASSISTANT QUARTERMASTER

And our clothing!

FIRST AIDE TO CORNWALLIS

What shall we do?

SECOND AIDE TO CORNWALLIS

Who has done this deed? It is impossible—

CORNWALLIS
(*suddenly enlightened; is his calm self once more*)

Men, return to your quarters. Do not be alarmed. I shall issue instructions for your further conduct. Demoda and Bilgent, come with me.

(*All leave, save for* CORNWALLIS *and his* TWO AIDES)

FIRST AIDE TO CORNWALLIS

If it please Your Grace, how—?

SECOND AIDE TO CORNWALLIS

If Your Lordship knows—

CORNWALLIS

Precisely. It is very simple. The man Washington has duped us. In the dead of night, he and his soldiers must have crept into our camp and stripped us of supplies. It is the only possibility. The man is a genius! If only we could win him over to our side . . . I've got it! Bilgent, you were once on the stage. Go to my tent. There is one trunk there they did not steal, because it was anchored to the ground. Take this key and open it. Inside you will find the uniform of an American officer. Put on this uniform and present yourself to General Washington, saying you have been sent to him by General Stevens, in Haskell. Then, when you have won his confidence, convince him of the justness of our cause. Washington is a righteous man, and if he is convinced we are right he will join us without hesitation. The future of England may depend on your mission! Take this key, and go! (FIRST AIDE TO CORNWALLIS *leaves*). Now, Demoda, we must figure out a plan to obtain supplies. Our rear section is only three hours' march away, and we can easily reach them and resupply ourselves unless one thing happens—unless Washington is able to cut us off; and that he can do in one way only, by crossing a river —I forget its name. At any rate, there is little danger of his doing so, for he and his men are probably asleep after their strenuous night. Let's organize and march!

SECOND AIDE TO CORNWALLIS

Aye, Aye, General.

SCENE 6. *The American Camp. George Washington's Tent.*

GEORGE WASHINGTON

(*sitting on his bed*)

I am tired, and I need sleep. Good night, America. (*Lies down and sleeps.*)

(*A placard is now displayed, which reads* The Dream of George Washington. *Throughout the dream,* GEORGE WASHINGTON *the man remains sleeping on his bed.*)

GEORGE WASHINGTON

(*as a little boy*)

Where's Daddy, Mommy?

MOTHER

He'll be here in just a little while, dear. He's bringing you a present for your birthday.

GEORGE WASHINGTON

Oh, Mommy! a real present?

MOTHER

Yes, and you must thank him for it and be nice to your daddy, as he loves you very much. Here he is now!

(*Enter George Washington's* FATHER. *He is carrying a young cherry tree, which he gives to* GEORGE.)

FATHER

George, little George! Happy birthday to my little son!

GEORGE WASHINGTON

(*cries*)

MOTHER

Why, baby, what's the matter?

GEORGE WASHINGTON

Oh, Mommy, you said it was so nice, but it's all dirty and covered with roots!

FATHER

What's the matter with the little crybaby? Is he afraid of getting his hands dirty?

MOTHER

Oh, Elbert, you promised! Be nice to the child. It is a little one yet.

FATHER

Humph! He'll never amount to a hill of beans, I can guarantee you that. All right, sister, give me back the cherry tree! I'll give it to some other kid in the neighborhood, one who's a real man!

GEORGE WASHINGTON

Oh, Daddy, don't! Is it really a cherry tree?

FATHER

Come on, let go of it!

MOTHER

Let the child keep it, dear. He wants it. He was only frightened at first, because it was so dirty and covered with roots.

FATHER

All right, all right, he can have it. But give it to me! You don't think it's going to grow in your hands, do you, you little squirt? These things have to be planted, you know.

MOTHER

Elbert, don't be so sarcastic. George only wants to be sure that you will not give the tree to another child.

FATHER

No, of course I won't! I got it to give to him, didn't I? I only said that about another boy because he acted like he didn't want it before, like it was something that was no good, something dirty.

MOTHER

George, go with your daddy and help him plant the tree.

GEORGE WASHINGTON

Yes, Mommy.

(GEORGE WASHINGTON *and his* FATHER *plant the cherry tree, and both leave. Then* GEORGE WASHINGTON *comes back with a little ax and chops down the tree. The tree is carried offstage, and once again all three members of the family appear.*)

MOTHER

Oh, I'm so sorry to hear about that! I wonder who could have chopped it down?

GEORGE WASHINGTON

I did, Mother. I cannot tell a lie.

MOTHER

Oh, my darling! (*Hugs him.*)

FATHER

What? You chopped down the tree I slaved for, you little brat? I'm going to give you the beating of your life!

MOTHER

Elbert, please!

FATHER

I'm going to give you a thrashing such as the world has never seen before!

GEORGE WASHINGTON

I cannot tell a lie, but I can run! I can flee from injustice! The tree was mine, to chop down as I pleased!

FATHER

I'll give you such a beating . . . !

(GEORGE WASHINGTON *runs off, his* FATHER *following him.* MOTHER *remains.* FATHER *returns.*)

FATHER

He foxed me. He swam across the river. It was the only way he could have done it. The ONLY WAY!

(MOTHER *and* FATHER *vanish, as the "Dream" placard is removed.*)

GEORGE WASHINGTON

(*waking up suddenly*)

Father! you help me now! Quickly, assemble the men! We march at once for the Delaware River!

SCENE 7. *A grayish-blue, flat area in front of the Delaware; the river cannot be seen.*

(GEORGE WASHINGTON *enters at the head of his troops*)

FIRST AIDE TO GEORGE WASHINGTON

We have marched quickly, and we have marched well. But what is the general's plan?

SECOND AIDE TO GEORGE WASHINGTON

He has not confided it to me, but I have gathered from little things that he has said that it is to cross the Delaware and cut off Cornwallis' army in its search for supplies.

FIRST AIDE TO GEORGE WASHINGTON

Washington is a genius! The army with supplies is the army that wins the war. Washington has planned everything just right. First our night raid, which took away all of their supplies; and now this forced march, to cut them off in their attempt to renew their supplies.

SECOND AIDE TO GEORGE WASHINGTON

You speak well. Washington has planned our every step. See how nobly he marches at the head of our troops!

GEORGE WASHINGTON

Halt! Here let us stop and dismount and prepare the boats.

(*Busy activity—dismounting, boat-building, etc. Enter* FIRST AIDE TO CORNWALLIS, *disguised as an American officer.*)

FIRST AIDE TO CORNWALLIS

(*to George Washington*)

I come to you from General Haskell, sir, who is hard-pressed at Stevens. I mean Stevens, Stevens, Sir, Stevens who is hard-hask at pretzelled, hart had at Prexelled, sir, General Stevens, sir, hart-passed at Haxel—

GEORGE WASHINGTON

Tenwillet, remove this man at once to the medical tent, and place him under armed guard. He seems dangerous.

SECOND AIDE TO GEORGE WASHINGTON

Yes, Your Worship.

FIRST AIDE TO CORNWALLIS

(*being led away*)

The man is a genius! It is impossible to deceive him.

GEORGE WASHINGTON

Fitzdaniel, what news is there of Cornwallis' army?

FIRST AIDE TO GEORGE WASHINGTON

He advances quickly, sir, but by crossing at once, sir, we shall be ahead of him by half an hour.

GEORGE WASHINGTON

Then let us go! For only if we go swiftly shall we have victory! And only victory is sweet! Come, men, battalions, uniforms, weapons, come, across the Delaware—we have nothing to fear but death, and we have America to win!

(*They go. Two Old Men enter. Both stare in the direction in which George Washington and his army have gone.*)

FIRST OLD MAN

What do you see?

SECOND OLD MAN

I am old, and I see nothing.

FIRST OLD MAN

I hear something, as though the sound of splashing.

SECOND OLD MAN

I hear nothing. My ears are dead things.

FIRST OLD MAN

(*suddenly very excited*)

Why do I ask you what you hear and see, when now I hear and I see. Do you know what I hear and see?

SECOND OLD MAN

No.

FIRST OLD MAN

(*rapt*)

I see General George Washington crossing the Delaware, with all his troops and horsemen. I see him standing up in his boat, but I cannot make out the expression on his face. The men and horses on the other side of the river are shaking themselves free of water.

SECOND OLD MAN

Go on! Do you see anything else?

FIRST OLD MAN

No. Now everything is dark again.

SECOND OLD MAN

What you saw was enough.

(*Cannons boom*)

FIRST OLD MAN

The American army has crossed the Delaware.

Hot Buttered Roll
BY ROSALYN DREXLER

In addition to writing plays, the libretto for *Home Movies* which won the off-Broadway award known as the "Obie," and two successful novels, Rosalyn Drexler is a successful painter. This visual orientation may explain her highly untraditional view of theatrical language, a quality evident in all her plays. Like Koch, she conceives of language as most engaging when least eloquent, and closest to a state of pure "flatness." In *Hot Buttered Roll* the dialogue is in the prose style of the girlie magazine. The play is about a certain Mr. Corrupt Savage, whose most passionate wish is to go on spending his days in contemplation of the supposedly inspiring pictures and text characteristic of this genre. Corrupt's conversation, as well as that of the two female assistants who come to both comfort and swindle him, is a stylized amalgam of photo captions and popular clichés. Language here is not only flat, but so bare that it tends to become the raw material in terms of which the play is evolved. Entire scenes are language-triggered, the dominant role being played by puns both linguistic (as in Scene 4, revolving around witty puns on the words "will" and "wilt") and visual (as in Scene 2, involving, during a discussion of swindling practices, the eating and *pocketing* of lettuce leaves). The moral of the play is similarly fresh. "Hot buttered roll" is a phrase drawn from an I. L. Peretz story about one Bontche Schweig, a truly saintly man who, upon reaching heaven, cited as his concept of the ideal life "every day . . . a hot roll with fresh butter." In Drexler's reality, the eternally flesh-contemplating Corrupt Savage is the nearest thing to a true saint, or hero. It is the cold calculators who surround him, those contemptuous of human fantasies however odd or pathetic, who are the real villains of the piece.

Hot Buttered Roll
A PLAY IN ONE ACT

CAST

JAN, *a call girl*
JORDAN, *a purveyor of burly girls*
SAVAGE, *a weak old man, also a billionaire*
JEWEL, *a female bodyguard*
JAKE

SCENE 1

The scene opens in the bedroom of MR. CORRUPT SAVAGE. *He is in bed, reclining against three huge pillows. His hair is a gray bush resembling Colette's. He is wearing tinted eyeglasses. Strewn over his bed and on his pillow and in his lap are girlie magazines. He is perusing one intently and reads out loud.*

SAVAGE

Irish McCalla, incredible yardage. Yas, that gal is pretty fat linoleum. Money-back guarantee, wal I don't expect to not like! I expect to keep my big glossies, 39½, 25, 36, Irish dear—(*he kisses the magazine*) turn you upside down and do your eggs for you. (*calls loudly*) Jewel, my eggs! Nasty monster that woman, even a whale can play possum. (*calls again*) Jewel, I'm sloshing around again!

JEWEL *kicks open door since she is carrying a tray. On it is an open can of beans, two soft-boiled eggs, buttered toast, coffee, and one perfect rose.* JEWEL *is a huge, robust woman. She is obviously in charge*)

JEWEL

Stop thrashing about, you'll tire yourself out. (*Lays the tray on a bed table at the foot of the bed, and rolls it up to* SAVAGE'S *lap*) What're you lookin' at now?

SAVAGE

Her sensuous charms are available to me. Look, she's much too hot to be warm.

JEWEL

Men! Men! Men! You'd think I wasn't enough woman for any man.

SAVAGE

Want quick action? Butter my toast and crack my eggs, this offer will not be repeated.

JEWEL

You don't intend to eat first?

SAVAGE

First from what?

JEWEL

The sheets, Corrupt, they must be changed. Jan is coming to see you right after you eat.

SAVAGE

It's your fault you put the tray right under my nose.

JEWEL

I forgot, but I can't make thousands happy, the way your ladies do.

SAVAGE

I hired you through the private mailways, and I believed *Big Ten-in-One* was complete for one dollar.

JEWEL

Stingy retired gentleman. Someone would like to hear from you, but not me. Confidentially I don't desire contact, and intend to delay my happiness.

SAVAGE

Right you are, muscled maiden; your duty is to protect me, not to think of yourself. Lift me out of the damp and change the bedding. By the way, the rubber sheet underneath has slipped to one side; make sure you anchor it properly this time. Ready! (*He holds out his arms for her to lift him out*)

JEWEL

Say: "Into your arms."

SAVAGE

Into your arms, attractive member.

JEWEL

I give the finest personalized assistance to help you. (*She takes him in her arms and puts him in a chair. Goes to cupboard*)

SAVAGE

Stop what you're doing!

JEWEL

Why?

SAVAGE

Feed me my eggs first.

JEWEL

First from what?

SAVAGE

Let the sheets rot.

(JEWEL *sighs and cracks his eggs into the dish. She feeds him. He eats with relish. His face drips with yolk*)

Clean me up.

JEWEL

You have a very pretty napkin for your mouth.

SAVAGE

The egg's dried, and you're more thorough.

JEWEL

I'll dampen a washcloth.

SAVAGE

Someday you'll be sorry, sorry you weren't nicer to me, someday when I receive five hundred and twelve photos and find real love, then you'll be sorry.

JEWEL

Cupid's destiny seeks you in every mail, I don't suppose you've ever heard of self-introduction?

SAVAGE

Speak freely.

JEWEL

I am.

SAVAGE

Introduce yourself.

JEWEL

Kiss me and cry no more. I'm a glamazon, and anything goes. Power-packed and best in action is Jewel.

SAVAGE

That's why I hired you. Your department is beyond words; however, I wish I could go beyond—to do—

JEWEL

Try not to slide off that chair while I make everything nice.

SAVAGE

Jan is all business. (*Petulantly*)

JEWEL

You're playing with fire.

SAVAGE

She's naughty but nice.

JEWEL

An amateur! (*Removes sheet from bed*)

SAVAGE

Puts on a show you'll never forget. Say what's that?

JEWEL

What's what?

SAVAGE

You've pocketed something.

JEWEL

I haven't.

SAVAGE

Let me make sure.

JEWEL

Sure of what?

SAVAGE

That you haven't taken something out from under the mattress.

JEWEL

Is there something under there? I'll look.

SAVAGE

No, no, I was only pulling your leg. Don't look.

JEWEL

We had a verbal agreement, no secrets; have you gone back on your word?

SAVAGE

Oh! these are terrible eggs; take them away.

JEWEL

Have you gone back on your word?

SAVAGE

I suppose I have. My word is portable, you know.

JEWEL

What do you mean?

SAVAGE

Don't be angry, *please!*

JEWEL

Explain.

SAVAGE

(*Slyly*)

My word is lightweight; I can take it back with no strain at all.

JEWEL

(*Starts to look under the mattress*)

Ah-ha, what's this?

SAVAGE

Common sense, that's what it is. Costs only cents to operate.

JEWEL

(*Pulls out a microphone and headset*)

Hot-dawg!

SAVAGE

Don't take it away, little honeypot, I need it.

JEWEL

Where's the rest of it?

SAVAGE

Under the bed.

JEWEL

You've dripped through. You've wet it. (*Pulls a tiny tape recorder out from under the bed*)

SAVAGE

It's precision engineered, renders the same functions as a, I've forgotten what. Faithfully records, perfect for recording interviews, and and—

JEWEL

Dance nocturne? (*Does a whirling turn*)

SAVAGE

Costing five times as much, captures the magic of speech—ingenious—records, plays back, erases.

JEWEL

Okay, play something, convince me.

SAVAGE

(*Takes the apparatus in his lap and fiddles with it. Finally gets it going. Tape hisses like steam, then a steady drip, drip of water.* SAVAGE *speaks, his voice under seven wagons of cotton*)

The secret is you demanded them. She made astonishing statements: Bubbles Darlene used a dirty towel and left a ring around the tub. I got wet too at my navel, who's to blame. *She* Pepper Powell, roach eggs coffee dregs and sister of Dick, took my Dick with the astonishing ability to relieve pain, to shrink without surgery. Cherry Knight strode in to say Jubilee of joy be with you. Flame Fury seared Gay Dawn who was trying to come up. You are Gray, Miss Gay I ventured. Dawn was to be shot at Dawn, I preempted my load. Shot your bolt she gaily cried. Fifty-foot adult, and let 'er roll! You don't need a projector. See sparkling lifelike, fast or slow motion.

JEWEL

Turn it off.

SAVAGE

Then I may keep it?

JEWEL

Innocent fun. Why be lonely?

SAVAGE

An extra bonus for you, daughter of Eve.

JEWEL

I don't care about your age, I hope you meet the kind of woman you hope to meet. There must be a woman somewhere screaming to meet you. If you meet that kind of woman, maybe you'll stop.

SAVAGE

You have a nicely curved smile. You're not only an employee, you're a real friend. Don't worry, I'll take care of you someday.

JEWEL

(*All broken up*)

I must finish making the bed. (*Resumes bed-making*)

SAVAGE

The extra bonus is. (*Weak singing fanfare*) A luxurious negligee to complete the most feminine set ever. Specifically designed to enticingly hide and yet show. Sheer black lace nylon, jet black, in extra large.

JEWEL

(*Turns on him savagely*)

Extra large is not sheer enchantment! Save your bedroom fashions for sizes 32 to 40.

SAVAGE

Would you prefer a trio of love-pledge panties? They come in stretchable nylon bespangled with rhinestones.

JEWEL

(*Crying, throws her arms around* SAVAGE'S *neck*)

You're so good, so very kind, but one man tells another.

SAVAGE

No one shall know. This time my word is permanent.

JEWEL

Dare I? (*Bravely*) Why not meet the sun halfway!

SAVAGE

Bravo, brutiful, now is the time to display that powerfully developed form. I'm tired.

JEWEL

Bed's made. Do you want that thing back under the mattress?

SAVAGE

I'll hide it myself. Gonna play a trick on Jan.

JEWEL

Come on, Corrupt dear, back to bed.

SAVAGE

Someday I'm gonna have me a custom made bed with lots of room for wet fun.

JEWEL

You can afford it. You can afford a whole field of beds; why don't you get what you want?

SAVAGE

(*Shakes head dreamily*)

I just don't know.

(JEWEL *carries him in her arms. She walks around the room a few times*)

JEWEL

At my risk, in your home, a walk around the room.

SAVAGE

Nice. So nice to be pressed against your genuine heavy equipment, it's really ringside isn't it.

JEWEL

Say the word and anything goes, Corrupt dear. Tangle with the best.

SAVAGE

Age forbids. A milder tonic for me.

JEWEL

Jan? (*She puts him on the bed*)

SAVAGE

What she lacks in skill, she makes up in merchandising.

JEWEL

Want anything else to eat?

SAVAGE

(*Winks lasciviously*)

Oo-la-la.

JEWEL

Here's your reading material. (*Spreads the mags on the bed as before.* SAVAGE *opens a wide one on the pillow and puts his nose in the center fold. He is lying on his belly*) Can't see much that way.

SAVAGE

(*Mumbles*)

Let me be the judge of that. It's a double delight no matter how you look at it.

JEWEL

Well then, please excuse this staggering hunk of earthiness.

SAVAGE

While you're out there, see if I've received my new Talent Portfolio. Scram!

JEWEL

(*Under her breath*)

Sucker. (*She exits and the lights dim and out*)

SCENE 2

Scene takes place in the kitchen of CORRUPT SAVAGE'S *apartment.* JAN, JEWEL, *and* JORDAN *are seated around a small white work table, smoking pot. There is a bowl of salad on the table (lettuce, carrots, tomatoes, green pepper).* JAN *is giggly,* JORDAN *horny, and* JEWEL *is withdrawn and a trifle paranoiac.*

JORDAN

Well? (*He takes a carrot and breaks it in half*)

JAN

(*Giggling*)

Well? Well, well, well, well, well.

JORDAN

(*He hands* JAN *a piece of carrot*)

Good for your eyes. I want you to see at night. I want you to open those big beautiful baby blues and find out where the old fart hides his loot.

JAN

(*Takes the carrot and munches on it*)

Prob'ly keeps it in the bank.

JEWEL

(*Eating a slice of tomato*)

Uh-uh! Not him. Wouldn't be surprised if he swallowed it in a plastic bag and shit it out every Sunday to pay my wages.

JORDAN

(*Lighting a reefer*)

Here, have a drag. (*Offers it to* JEWEL. *She takes it and drags a long deep one*) Up to now we haven't got a clue. Ladies, I think you stink. In fact, I believe you're not following instructions.

JAN

(*Takes a drag of* JEWEL'S *pot and speaks trying not to let the smoke out*)

I am following instructions. I kiss him, and touch him, and ask him to do dirty, nasty things, and I use his toothbrush and towel and warm his feet, and kiss his toes one by one, and, oh golly, he says I'm the best in the business, and he's gonna give me a diploma and a letter of recommendation.

JEWEL

(*Daintily holding a lettuce leaf aloft, shaking it so that drops of water fall off*)

Remember, you're just a figment of his imagination, and mine.

JORDAN

And mine. He's just using you. He's like us. Wants to get! Wants to get without paying. I'll make him pay.

JEWEL

Through the nose!

JORDAN

Through the eyes, ears, mouth and the South of him! Through

Jan dear. (*He caresses her*) And when he's through with her he'll be finished, done in, a panting, pitiful old man with just a bowl of soft, hot cream of farina to dip his finger into.

JEWEL

I'll take the spoons, they're gold-plated.

JAN

So are his teeth. They feel so heavy when they bite into me. He likes to bite me and I ask him to stop because the human bite is poisonous. I have poison all over in my skin and my clothes and my hair. It makes me so mad to be bitten at.

JEWEL

I'll take his teeth too. They make him look like a donkey anyway. Ever heard him bray?

(JORDAN *laughs*)

JAN

He only brays when he makes love. He taught me how to bray. (*Brays*) He says it's a sign of passion, real passion when partners in love make animal sounds. He pulls his lips up and makes a terrible racket. It reminds me of a story my mother used to read to me called "The Musicians of Bremen." All these animals got together and stood on each others' shoulders and brayed and meowed and barked and crowed and what not to scare the robbers in the house. The robbers in the house. (*She giggles*)

JORDAN

Sounds like he's on to us. Why should he have chosen that sound?

JEWEL

He's foxy, that wolf. But he can't frighten me. I've heard everything there is to hear. I've heard him gurgling like a sewer, laughing like a hyena, crying like a virgin in a cat-house, cooing like a pig's foot buried in sauerkraut, screaming like a man who can't find his lost limb but still feels pain in it. (*She smokes some more pot*)

JAN

(*Jealous*)

He never did that for me. He never made me hear his sound effects. (*She munches loudly on a carrot and anything else on the table*) He never tries to amuse me at all.

JORDAN

He despises you. What are you to him?

JAN

He calls me Jan.

JEWEL

He calls *me* his little honeypot.

JAN

No wonder—you're sticky and you look like a pot. You look like a pot that stayed in the fire too long. You've got a dirty bottom, you're bruised and bashed in, your handle is so hot you burn the flesh right off, and it smells and you smell and there's nothing in you, nothing at all, nothing at all, nothing . . . (*She weeps*) . . . nothing, nothing but a charred bone—the remains of a poor meal—a poor, cheap meal evaporated—floating in the clouds.

JEWEL

Speak for yourself, Jan. You're the one in the clouds. Food for the Gods, eh! The Gods who keep their mouths open waiting for you to enter them? The Gods who don't bite? The Gods who don't swallow? No substance to you or your Gods!

JAN

(*Goes over to* JORDAN *for comfort*)

I don't believe in Gods, I don't believe in men. I don't believe in people. You're right, Jordan, everybody wants to get!

JORDAN

Getting and spending we lay waste our powers. (*Pats her head as if She is the child She is*) But it's only human, Jan, dear. Only human to coax and pull the donkey to where we want to go. (*Takes the carrot and dangles it in front of her nose*) Only human . . . (*He gets up and makes her follow the carrot*) . . . to show it what it wants—to get it going, and then—jump on, to make the donkey carry us. You're the carrot, baby, and Corrupt Savage has enough back on him to carry us all. He may be old, but he makes an excellent beast of burden.

JAN

But he can't hardly get out of bed. I don't follow you.

JEWEL

You weren't hired for your brains, you were hired to enter his world and yank him out of it. (*She gets tough and yanks* JAN *around*) There are mountains in his room, dangerously high mountains, and lakes, great big round deep lakes with a whirlpool in each one. You're the lady in the lake.

JORDAN

The lady who rises out of the depths and lures tired, parched, hot old donkeys to their death.

JEWEL

Right down the drain with the rest of the hair!

JAN

I can't do it. I can't hurt him. I'm sort of his friend.

JORDAN

You don't have to stop being his friend. After we get away with the lettuce. (*He stuffs a huge handful of lettuce into his pocket*) You can stay with him if you want to and hustle for him, you can doll him up like a regular pimp and give him the take, and when he drops dead, you can stuff him and make a fancy pillow out of his shapeless shaggy showcase, and shove him under your ass when the customers want to go deeper. And you won't mind, because that old fat pillow will have you in its spell, softening each thrust, drinking in each protein spurt that leaks out of you. But you'll be friends, the human blotter and you—friends to the bitter, bitten end!

JAN

You, you're just a runt!

JORDAN

And you, Jan dear, are just a cunt! Just.

JEWEL

It's his fault we're fighting among ourselves. Come on, Jan, chin up, we've got a job to do and we might as well attend to it. Can't back out now. Corrupt is on to something. He's keeping a tape recorder under his mattress.

JAN

So?

JEWEL

He has evidence. We must destroy the evidence. At least I think it's evidence. It's spoken in code.

JORDAN

He's clever all right, but if A follows B, I believe that Mr. Corrupt Savage will relinquish his fortune, cheerfully, even if Jewel has to beat it out of him . . . (*ominously*) . . . drop by ruby red drop. How about it, Jewel, is the old boy kinky or isn't he?

JEWEL

I haven't prepared my report on that yet, Jordan, but if you think I should order a whip, I will.

JORDAN

See if you can't engage him in harmless kinky talk. Converse with him about matters of flagellation and Dalmation.

JEWEL

Don't you mean damnation?

JORDAN

I say what I mean and I mean what I say—Dalmation!

JEWEL

Okay. Then what?

JORDAN

Loosen his tongue, arouse his ardor. If things don't work out, I have an alternate plan. Something that will be strictly between Mr. Corrupt Savage and myself.

(*Blackout*)

SCENE 3

The bedroom of MR. CORRUPT SAVAGE. *Totally dark.*

SAVAGE

I'm all alone in the dark and yet I see magnificent unretouched pictures. I tingle at these pictures that can't be obtained anywhere else. My response is beyond my wildest expectations. Let's face it, Corrupt, you'll never take advantage of the money-back guarantee. You don't have to. (*Chuckle*) Now I have a treat in store for myself again. Push-button memory isn't everything. Door's locked. Miss Jewel Glass kept at bay. Ah, here they are in the automatic feeder. Come to me, Meg Myles, in your most daring, most revealing pose.

(*Familiar poses by Meg Myles projected onto opposite wall by slide projector from bed of* CORRUPT SAVAGE)

Christ, Meg, you're the megaton! Lethal rosebuds (*Sucking sounds*) taste so good. (*Suddenly total darkness again as projector plug pulls out*) Damn plug! In, in damn plug. (*Projector works again. Another slide of Meg appears on wall. Meg with whip*) Ah, there it is! Buxom bombshell, be mine. Destroy me.

Explode in my face, ooze milk, float those rosebuds, feed me, flood me, smother me. Where are you going to put it?

(*Loud knocking on door*)

JEWEL

Mr. Savage, are you napping?

SAVAGE

No, I'm nipping.

JEWEL

I thought I heard you talking in your sleep.

SAVAGE

You did, you did.

JEWEL

That's dangerous, I'm glad I stopped you.

SAVAGE

They all are. They stop me and they're glad of it.

JEWEL

Can I get you something?

SAVAGE

Go away.

JEWEL

I have something for you.

SAVAGE

(*With joy*)

The new talent portfolio?

JEWEL

No, Jan's here.

SAVAGE

(*Groans*)

She's too real right now. Tell her to wait.

JEWEL

Okay, Corrupt, you're the boss. Shout when you want me.

SAVAGE

(*Sings*)

I'll shout, sister, shout, I'll tell the whole world what it's all about.

JEWEL

Every nation in the whole world has a flag. I love the way flags hang and blow. When I was a little girl I knew every flag by heart.

SAVAGE

Well, keep your eyes peeled, baby, there's a flag in the field now that's head and shoulders above all others.

JEWEL

You!

SAVAGE

Red and purple above a split crest.

JEWEL

Silence! I suspect the deepest secret of your secret soul.

SAVAGE

Hit home! Hit home!

JEWEL

One day I shall bleed it out of you, torturous drop by torturous drop.

SAVAGE

Majesty! (*In awe*)

JEWEL

I am going to punish others . . . and you shall only watch!

SAVAGE

Refined torture at its best. Inflict it upon me, sweet tyrant.

JEWEL

Let me in.

SAVAGE

I'm too stiff to get to the door. Go speak to Jan while I limber up.

JEWEL

Mr. Savage, when I return I expect you to strip yourself before my royal eyes.

SAVAGE

Bring the little electric heater with you.

JEWEL

Certainly, Corrupt.

SAVAGE

I can't get too much of a good thing; relentless debasement, and abject suffering, now and forever as hard as you can!

JEWEL

I'll force you to respond by dealing with you.

SAVAGE

As it suits your fancy, oh mistress.

(*Footsteps going away*)

Now she thinks I'm a masochist and in her power. She has another think coming. She will expose her evil plans with my capable assistance. I know she wants my fortune and so does Jan; I'll go along with it and have some fun. Adult fun!

(*Projector off and regular lights go on. Reaches under his pillow and pulls out a wig. He tries to put it on but it keeps slipping off his head and out of his hands*)

Hmm, seems to have a life of its own. Wants to get back to the original owner; I'd let it go, but I can't believe my wig prefers a horse's ass to my head. (*Jams it back under the pillow. Calls loudly*) Jewel! Let's put the show on the road! Jewel!

(*Footsteps outside door and then crash!* JEWEL *smashes door in and steps through it. Immediately following her is* JAN *dressed in a rubber deep-sea diving outfit, fins and all, spear, etc. She makes feeble swimming movements with her hands as She walks forward*)

JEWEL

Howd'ya like them apples, Savage?

SAVAGE

Quick, the sex-o-meter! Have you forgotten it?

(JEWEL *takes a kind of grip-o-meter with attached thermometer and bell out of her apron pocket, hands it to* SAVAGE. *He starts squeezing*)

JAN

I'd love to go underwater spearfishing in Yucatan with you. I'd love to go underwater spearfishing with you in Yucatan. (*Stops at the foot of the bed, makes several inept thrusts with her spear and bumps and grinds*)

SAVAGE

(*Squeezes as hard as he can*)

Nope no go baby, it don't mean a thing to me, but don't give up.

(JEWEL *and* JAN *leave*)

If they only knew how easy it could be.

(JEWEL *comes through the broken door again. And announces*)

JEWEL

The Fire Dance!

(JAN *enters dancing, dressed in scarfs of orange and red*)

SAVAGE

I can put that fire out! I know how to. Jewel, you pump and I'll direct the hose.

JEWEL

Are you excited?

SAVAGE

False alarm.

(JEWEL *shrugs her shoulders and marches out with* JAN *following*)

It can't be the fault of the meter, it's worked before.

(JEWEL *re-enters and announces*)

JEWEL

How to use a sun lamp!

(JAN *enters, rolling a sun lamp in front of her: She is fully dressed in skirt and blouse, black hose, and five-inch heels. She is wearing a mask and long black leather gloves. She stops somewhere midstage and* JEWEL *brings a chair to her. She strips, starting with the gloves, but leaves on a black waist cincher, black bra, and her hose and shoes. She takes various poses using the chair as she would a man: supposedly getting a sun-ray treatment*)

The little lady is a sun worshiper. Notice the nice tan. If you wish she can administer a tanning too. Though your hide be thick as an elephant's she promises to get under your skin.

SAVAGE

(*Grips the sex-o-meter*)

Sorry, doesn't ring a bell.

JEWEL

Honey, are you tired of not getting what you want?

SAVAGE

I thought you were a hot promoter.

JEWEL

Breathe easy, daddy, your troubles are over.

SAVAGE

I wish I could believe that.

(JEWEL *motions to* JAN *and they leave together*)

Monkey business and stage props! That Jewel lady knows exactly what I want and yet she rings in a fringe area. Last week it was Pagan Fables of a Human Horse told with the aid of bit and bridle. She thinks me complicated, and yet I'm a simple fellow.

(JEWEL *enters alone*)

Has she gone?

JEWEL

She has.

SAVAGE

Did you pay her?

JEWEL

I did.

SAVAGE

What did she say?

JEWEL

She said: "If I'm not in, my answering service will take the message."

SAVAGE

You told her you'd call her again?

JEWEL

Yes.

SAVAGE

You're jealous of her that's why you give her the wrong get-ups.

JEWEL

Are you ready to be turned?

SAVAGE

Damn ready! And this time powder me with cornstarch, I perspire too much.

(*Blackout*)

SCENE 4

The bedroom again. MR. CORRUPT SAVAGE *is seated in a rocking chair.* JORDAN *comes in swiftly and glances back through the door to see if he is being followed.*

JORDAN

Mr. Savage, I have something for you.

SAVAGE

I do not know you.

JORDAN

Jordan's the name. You know me now.

SAVAGE

Who sent you?

JORDAN

No one. I am here on my own.

SAVAGE

What do you want with me?

JORDAN

Everyone, whether rich or poor, should have a will.

SAVAGE

I have a will.

JORDAN

Not a strong will.

SAVAGE

A will to win.

JORDAN

A willy-nilly.

SAVAGE

A willfull will.

JORDAN

A will or won't.

SAVAGE

A will.

JORDAN

A wilt!

SAVAGE

Why are you attacking me?

JORDAN

Want to know the ins and outs in simple language?

SAVAGE

Yes.

(JORDAN *takes a 64-page booklet out of his pocket*)

JORDAN

Take this. (*Hands booklet to* SAVAGE) *Wills: How to Make and How to Break Them.*

SAVAGE

I'm not about to die. (*Whispers*) Not about to die.

JORDAN

Will!

SAVAGE

Won't!

JORDAN

Prove it! I'll wait.

SAVAGE

I still consider myself a red-blooded adult who wants to love, live, and laugh.

JORDAN

Even those kind die.

SAVAGE

They die in the future.

JORDAN

Wipe out all debts now!

SAVAGE

I owe nothing, I am happy most of the time, I like pets, I like city life, I like country life, I've been in love. My name is Corrupt Savage. I've spoken to you confidentially although you're not the HELP COMPANY.

JORDAN

I can help you assemble artificial lures at home.

SAVAGE

What do you want?

JORDAN

Adopt me and make me the beneficiary of your will.

SAVAGE

I like you, you're outspoken. What kind of girls do you like?

JORDAN

Burly girls; and you, sir?

SAVAGE

Perhaps, perhaps.

JORDAN

I can help you publish your book. Join our successful authors.

SAVAGE

Perhaps, perhaps.

JORDAN

Play guitar in seven days!

SAVAGE

Perhaps, perhaps.

JORDAN

Be a fingerprint expert.

SAVAGE

I have some song ideas too, but no, no, you are right—

JORDAN

About what?

SAVAGE

I have a premonition that I don't even have time for the one-week course.

JORDAN

Desperate? You are surrounded by strangers. Let me be your son.

SAVAGE

You don't appeal to me.

JORDAN

But you are at the end.

SAVAGE

I am holding the end and I am turning the rope very slowly. It is your turn to jump.

JORDAN

A girl's name.

SAVAGE

We are interlopers, but nevertheless it is your turn to jump.

JORDAN

I'll try.

(SAVAGE *turns an imaginary rope.* JORDAN *gets ready to jump and then jumps up and down as if he is jumping rope. He trips and hurts his ankle*)

SAVAGE

Missed!

JORDAN

Interference. Someone got in the way.

SAVAGE

Not someone, me, I pulled the rope tight and made you miss. The ender is in control. (*Laughs*)

JORDAN

Have you ever heard of a steady ender?

SAVAGE

No.

JORDAN

A steady ender never gets a chance to jump, keeps turning till everyone goes home. Know how you got to be steady ender?

SAVAGE

What's your considered opinion?

JORDAN

That you are suffering from a bad heart, and cannot under any circumstances be allowed to jump.

SAVAGE

I can jump whenever I wish; I am active, active—
(SAVAGE *rises from his chair and jumps in a sickening way: out of breath, clumsily, and finally falls to the floor*)

JORDAN

See, I told you! Need some help?

SAVAGE

Call Jewel.

JORDAN

I want your signature and your name. Here are the papers. (*He hands a folio of papers to the sick* SAVAGE *on the floor*)

SAVAGE

(*Spits on the papers*)

I'd rather die.

JORDAN

The ink is waterproof, Mr. Savage; your spit won't blur the script. Oh, and here is a pen.

SAVAGE

(*Weakly calls* JEWEL)

Jewel!

(JEWEL *comes in as if she had been waiting right outside the door*)

JEWEL

You called, sir?

SAVAGE

Lift me onto the bed.

JEWEL

Okay. (*She does so without warmth*)

SAVAGE

Jewel, this man wants my life or my money.

JEWEL

I know.

SAVAGE

Are you the witness?

JEWEL

Yes, dear. I do and say what graduates say.

SAVAGE

What do you mean?

JEWEL

Graduates say: I am doing very well in my spare time.

SAVAGE

I was a fool to think you really liked me.

JEWEL

If you liked me you would have been generous.

JORDAN

We've all provided practical experience for each other.

SAVAGE

You can't force free gifts.

JORDAN

If you don't sign we'll raid the premises anyway.

(JAN *runs in, breathless*)

JAN

Mr. Savage, I have something for you. I picked it up accidently with my costumes.

JEWEL

Give it to me.

JAN

It isn't for you.

SAVAGE

They promised that no salesman would call. Give me my package, it's the long-awaited New Talent Portfolio. A last look.

JEWEL

Okay, give it to him. Let his lecherous eyes bug out.

JAN

Here you are, sweet old man. Do you want me to turn the pages?

SAVAGE

Do you mean it?

JAN

I can be false to no man.

SAVAGE

Sit here and hold it close; I don't see very well.

(JAN *tears the package open and looks at the magazine with* SAVAGE. JEWEL *motions to* JORDAN *and they go out*)

JAN

Is it nice?

SAVAGE

This is where loneliness ends. The milk of human kindness.

JAN

No more hilarious situations, just you and me.

SAVAGE

Personalized! I want to give you all I own. Not because you deserve it, but because I always make last-minute decisions, and also, the album we are perusing is an especially exciting one.

JAN

Thank you, dear. (*She kisses him*)

SAVAGE

You are forever artlessly gowned in my mind.

JAN

Thank you, dear. (*Kisses him again*)

SAVAGE

I believe that I am now ready to be privately released.

JAN

Really?

SAVAGE

On this bed of pain.

JAN

Now?

SAVAGE

For the last time. I know what I want, and you've got it.

JAN

But any minute now my business manager will burst in.

SAVAGE

Screw him, girlie. The price is high and the moon is high.

JAN

But Jewel and Jordan might—

SAVAGE

Terrific! Hot! Young! Luscious! (*He embraces her*)

JAN

Help! Oh, help.

(*He pins her beneath him*)

SAVAGE

Wow! Wow! Grrrr!

(CORRUPT SAVAGE *suddenly goes limp, but* JAN *is trapped*)

(*Voices of our friends are heard coming to the rescue*)

(JEWEL, JORDAN *and* JAKE.)

(*Blackout*)

(*Sounds of thunder on tape. General confusion of sound*)

(*Curtain*)

Epilogue

The bedroom. MR. CORRUPT SAVAGE *is laid out on the bed. The rest of the cast is turning the room upside down, looking for money, jewels, etc.* JEWEL GLASS *pulls the tape recorder out from under the mattress. She starts it going.*

TAPE RECORDER

You're all under arrest!

(*All arrest their activities sharply and gasp with surprise*)

Line up quickly! This is Corrupt Savage speaking, coming to you from the great beyond. Go on, line up, no pushing. Size places will do.

(*All line up with much measuring of height and pushing*)

You are about to hear my last will and testament, but first I must be properly mourned. Jewel, you are to intone the dirge.

(JEWEL *shakes her head*)

Reluctant? Then repeat after me, with expression: "Night and day he perused America's picture magazines for entertainment."

JEWEL

Night and day he perused America's picture magazines for entertainment.

TAPE RECORDER

"He ignored peepers choice for inside story, and found it naughty but nice. Skyscraper heels, approximately five inches high, gored his patent leather soul."

JEWEL

He, he—

TAPE RECORDER

"He would try anything once: The magic key to love and sex in eight volumes for only $4.98. Curious from the bottom of his heart he read complete instructions."

JEWEL

I read those out loud to him.

TAPE RECORDER

"But the mechanism was faulty. Even Donalda Jordan sporting a circumference of 41″ and adoring Sinatra, Presley, Monroe, and Siamese cats, which she raised for love or money, couldn't fill the bill. He wanted to shout: 'Own me,' or 'You'll never know what I have to offer'; cover to cover they couldn't wait, they flipped over backwards for more interesting shots. Female fighters knocked him out, after declaring in 'caps': We Like Men Friends. He specified and he received. The only means of access to his life was by subscription only."

JEWEL

Just like him to hog the whole dirge.

TAPE RECORDER

Jewel, turn me off, turn me off, turn me off. Wait! I meant to tell you and Jan who's been so kind to me, I meant to tell you where the money is.

JEWEL

He's going to tell.

TAPE RECORDER

In the basement where you store the magazines you'll find a batch from 1956–1958, there's money between each page, I have a habit of paying off the photos according to appreciation. You'll have to look carefully so as not to miss any of it, and, please, when you come to the more expensive pages, say good-by for me. Say: "He's tantalizing himself in the breathtaking sky blue, and is no longer yours alone!"

(JEWEL *turns off tape recorder, and shrugs her shoulders*)

JAKE

Maybe there's life in the old boy yet.

JEWEL

Dead or alive he'll fog your mirror for you. Come on.

(JORDAN *holds the door open and then all go out*)

(*Blue light on the bed and* SAVAGE—*who smiles—then:*)

(*Curtain*)

Gallows Humor

BY JACK RICHARDSON

The structure of *Gallows Humor* (a cycle of two loosely related plays the second of which is presented here) is that of an outright joke. Indeed, this portrait of a modern-day hangman who wants to wear a black hood because this essential of medieval penal costuming "would lend me a little more—well, personality out there," plagued by a warden who considers this too old-fashioned and "unsanitary" and a wife who regards such impulses as "morbid," is a bit reminiscent of that latter-day version of Surrealist blackness: the Sick Joke. The hangman who boasts of monstrous powers but is browbeaten by both boss and wife is a familiar type in the modern rogues' gallery, which is fully capable of accommodating its little men whose monstrous crimes are committed by "just following orders." What keeps Richardson's play a comedy is that the anti-hero, Phillip, is, in conventional terms, "unbelievable." Is it possible that this man whose finest statements are uttered while drying the dishes, who wants to surpass his situation but cannot even open the kitchen door when challenged to do so by his wife, and who is cowed by the dropping of a pepper mill, is really a monster? Under this comedy of contrasts lies the play's seriousness; the suggestion that even the most innocent and average reality may be the real monster, the real prison. Richardson brilliantly limits his "innocent" but ultimately triumphant reality to the most scrupulously innocuous naturalistic household surfaces and casually homey "realistic" dialogue. One might note that it is to this reality-subverting role that many recent European dramatists of imaginative protest have also firmly assigned the techniques of verism and illusionism.

Gallows Humor

CHARACTERS

THE WARDEN
PHILLIP
MARTHA

The curtain rises on the early-morning confusion of a suburban kitchen-dining room. PHILLIP, *the prison's executioner, and* MARTHA, *his wife, are standing at the kitchen table.* PHILLIP *is a small, erect man. He is dressed in the trousers, shirt, and tie of his official uniform. The hat and coat are placed on one of the kitchen chairs. His wife, her hair in curlers and dowdily attractive in a morning housecoat, begins busying herself at the stove. A large red pepper mill is the only conspicuous object on the table.*

As the lights come up fully, the WARDEN *is seen pacing back and forth across the table from* PHILLIP.

WARDEN
(*with rhetorical self-pity*)
When I think how I stayed up nights as a boy learning the penal code by heart so someday I would be a prison warden!

PHILLIP
What I asked for isn't going to prove you wasted your youth. It seems quite reasonable to me.

WARDEN
Reasonable? How can you, the last and most important link in society's chain of punishment, how can you think it reasonable to want to dress up like a headsman from the Middle Ages?

PHILLIP

I just want to wear a black hood over my head. I think it would lend me a little more—well, personality out there.

MARTHA

(*setting a pot of coffee on the kitchen table*)

Well, if you ask me, the idea of a hood, especially a black one, strikes me as a little morbid.

WARDEN

There you are; from your own wife. Can you imagine what others will have to say about it? Why, it smacks of thumbscrews, iron maidens, and unsanitary dungeons.

MARTHA

(*to* PHILLIP)

I wish you'd come sit down and finish your oatmeal. (*Looking into one of the bowls set on the table.*) It's getting crusty and beginning to stick to the edges of the bowl.

PHILLIP

(*a look of exasperation at* MARTHA)

I don't want any oatmeal now. I simply want, as an employee with some twenty years' service behind him, to have a request granted. (*With a little petulance.*) I want to wear a black hood at today's execution!

WARDEN

But think of what it will do to your reputation! Instead of being a finely edged instrument in a clinical, detached operation, you become a villain—a strangler—a black knight.

MARTHA

(*vigorously buttering a piece of toast*)

I can just imagine the treatment I'd get then from the girls in my bridge club.

PHILLIP

Let them jeer and hiss at me; it's better than not being noticed or thought of at all.

WARDEN

But behind a hood your face won't even be seen.

PHILLIP

(*slightly angry*)

My face? Don't you think I know what this collection of scribbles, bumps, and creases looks like? Any real expression I call on it to take looks ridiculous on me. But with this hood, this mask, it comes alive. My eyes, outlined by slanting black slits, crackle with perception; my mouth grows full and moist; and my chin, as if obeying a command from these other features, squares itself and, just a little arrogantly, juts forward.

MARTHA

(*now beginning to pour out three cups of coffee*)

It sounds as if you'd look like you were in a bad accident, Phillip.

WARDEN

I think you'd frighten the men to death before you had a chance to hang them.

PHILLIP

Then I would at least have some contact. (*A sigh.*) Oh, I didn't mind being your instrument when those condemned arrived like patients drowned in ether. But things have changed now. You yourself know that they come up those steps trembling, warm, talkative—exuding a scent so full of living that *my* head sometimes starts spinning because of it.

WARDEN

There are rules and regulations governing these things. An executioner's uniform can be blue, black, or gray; the buttons can be bone or brass; and the cap is optional. But by no stretch of interpretation is there any mention of a black hood.

PHILLIP

Hang the regulations! I'm trying to get a little color into things. (*Pleading.*) Don't you understand? I need a change.

WARDEN

You have your vacation coming up in a few months. Get in some fishing, and you'll feel better. I've always found that just dangling your line in a mountain stream relaxes the muscles, improves the digestion . . .

PHILLIP

I don't want to fish, Warden. For twenty years I've gone to little mountain streams on my vacation and caught nothing more interesting than a trout with one eye last summer.

WARDEN

A one-eyed trout? What kind of bait were you using?

PHILLIP

Don't change the subject. Now, do I or do I not wear my hood today?

WARDEN

I've already given you an answer on that.

PHILLIP

Just look at me in it, that's all. Just one glance.

WARDEN

I couldn't be less interested.

PHILLIP

All you have to say is yes or no. Just yes or no.

WARDEN

(*giving in with a long sigh*)

It's a waste of time; but, if you want to, go ahead.

PHILLIP

Fine; it's just upstairs. (*Starting to leave.*) Oh, I may be a little time adjusting it, though. It has to sit just right, otherwise it droops a bit and I find it difficult to breathe.

MARTHA

If you're just going to leave the oatmeal, should I have some scrambled eggs ready for you when you come down?

PHILLIP

Forget about breakfast, Martha. (*To the* WARDEN.) I hope, once I'm in my hood, that I won't have to take it off until the ceremony's over with. I wouldn't want any food stains to get on it. (PHILLIP *exits.*)

MARTHA

He used to eat such a big breakfast on special days like this. Why, I can remember when six eggs and a quarter-pound of ham were just enough for him.

WARDEN

Well, I must say I find his behavior this morning a little peculiar. The whole thing just isn't like Phillip. He's always been someone you could count on, someone who knew the importance of a good shine on his buttons and a sharp crease in his trousers.

MARTHA

(*sitting down dejectedly and absently stirring her coffee*)

Well, something's definitely been happening to him in the last months. If you'd been living with him every day, this business with the hood wouldn't surprise you in the least.

WARDEN

I haven't noticed anything until now.

MARTHA

Oh, he's kept these changes fairly well hidden, even from me. But you can't eat, sleep, and take out a joint bank account with a man without noticing the slightest change in him.

WARDEN

Now that you mention it, he hasn't come to any club meetings in the last months and his weekly reports have been dotted with erasure smudges—very unlike him.

MARTHA

(*putting the coffee down and nervously smoothing her hair*)

It's beginning to show on the outside too? Oh, I'd hoped to keep it confined to the rooms in this house.

WARDEN

(*reaching down and taking* MARTHA'S *hand*)

Is it something you can tell me, a very old friend? Is there another woman involved in all this?

MARTHA

(*hitting the kitchen table with her free hand so that the* WARDEN *turns the other loose*)

Oh, how I wish there was! How I'd love to be able to sink my nails into the flesh-and-blood reason for the way things are beginning to wobble on their legs around here! Just to see a larger bosom or a firmer behind leading Phillip down a street would let me spit at him with a clear conscience. If I just knew where the weakness was, I could make life miserable for him and then forget it!

WARDEN

But you don't?

MARTHA

(*rising from the kitchen table like a prosecutor at a trial*)

About four months ago, after Phillip had left for work, I got up from bed and, like I do every morning the first thing, reached down for his slippers to take them to the closet. For twenty years he's always left them on his side of the bed, neatly placed next to one another, toes pointed to the wall.

WARDEN

And that morning?

MARTHA

One was underneath the bed and the other, after being used for an ash tray, was tucked beneath his pillow.

WARDEN

(*shaking his head*)

A bad sign!

MARTHA

Only the first, though. In the next weeks I began making all sorts of discoveries: in his bureau drawer, tucked among his underwear, I found a book of Swedish lessons; in the hall closet, squeezed behind the Christmas decorations, I uncovered a banjo with two of its strings missing; and under one of the sofa cushions, I turned up a pair of red socks with "World's Fair—1939" stitched down their sides. Red socks! I can't decide what to do with them, and just knowing they're sitting in the house drives me half out of my mind.

WARDEN

(*approaching* MARTHA, *he puts his hands on her shoulders and speaks as the comforting male*)

Go on, Martha. My home's not a happy one, either.

MARTHA

Well, after that, Phillip himself began upsetting things. Since we were married, he's always slept on his stomach, one hand folded beneath his chin; but a month ago I woke up to find him snoring on his back. Then his favorite chair, that he always settled in after dinner, began being neglected; and, the dishes done, I'd come in and find him pouting in a corner or sitting cross-legged like an Arab on the floor.

WARDEN

(*oozing sympathy*)

And you've been suffering through all this, Martha, without a word to anyone?

MARTHA

I kept hoping it would all pass over; but I see now it won't. Last night, behind a stack of bathroom towels, I discovered a box of very expensive cigars with an unpronounceable name—and then this morning the hood. (*She utters a long sigh and turns to put her head on the* WARDEN'S *chest.*) Oh, Warden!

WARDEN

(*a smile hinting now a little more than sympathy*)

There, there. Please call me Harry.

MARTHA

(*a brief smile as she pronounces the name*)

Harry! (*Now the defenseless little girl.*) Oh, I just don't know what to do any longer.

WARDEN

I really can't stand thinking of you being unhappy.

MARTHA

Just last week Phillip refused to renew our country club membership or donate to the Red Cross.

WARDEN

You need help, Martha. Can Harry, an old, old, *old* friend do anything for you?

MARTHA

Don't let him wear that hood today. No matter how he coaxes, put your foot down.

WARDEN

(*a vigorous nod*)

You can depend on it. I'll simply tell him his pension won't be raised if he does.

MARTHA

Oh, Harry, you've always been so kind. Just having you here this morning makes everything seem much easier.

WARDEN

(*lifting up her chin*)

We're cut from the same timber, Martha. Perhaps we can help each other. (*He starts to kiss her.*)

MARTHA

(*pulling away*)

No, Harry! Even if Phillip has taken to collecting red socks and turning nasty remarks about my friends, I couldn't deceive him. It would be playing his game.

WARDEN

He does nothing but hurt you, Martha; and I've loved you ever since the day you came to my office to try to get a raise in salary out of me for Phillip.

MARTHA

(*now enjoying being pursued*)

Really? I remember coming out feeling you hadn't noticed me at all. And Phillip didn't get the raise.

WARDEN

You were wearing an orange-and-blue print dress, white gloves and, as it was right after lunch, there was a little drop of mayonnaise on the left side of your chin.

MARTHA

Harry! And you didn't tell me.

WARDEN

(*walking up to her and speaking in a hoarse voice*)

I found it terribly exciting. All the time you were going on about those extra five dollars a month, I was trying to imagine just what you could have eaten to put that tiny white mark there.

MARTHA

(*pretending embarrassment*)

You shouldn't talk that way. What a woman eats for lunch is an intimate matter.

WARDEN

And you? Did you notice me at all?

MARTHA

I'd only been married six months at the time. I wasn't noticing anyone but Phillip, such that he was.

WARDEN

(*somewhat hurt*)

You mean I made no impression at all?

MARTHA

Well, I do recall you had on a tie with a palm tree painted on it.

WARDEN

(*nostalgically*)

In the dark it lit up and formed a pair of woman's legs.

MARTHA

(*almost warmly*)

And I noticed how bloodshot your eyes were, and I thought how hard you must work to have popped so many of those little vessels.

WARDEN

Twenty years ago! Twenty years ago! If we could only have spoken frankly to each other then.

MARTHA

And why didn't you?

WARDEN

I thought of doing so, Martha. That very night I paced about in the dark of our five-room house, trying to decide just how bold I should be.

MARTHA

And then you saw your wife asleep, her head placed at just the right angle on the pillow, and you were ashamed of your thoughts. A good wife holds on even when she's unconscious.

WARDEN

Heavens no! It wasn't my wife. She'd already begun sampling the line of manual laborers that began with a teen-age elevator operator and just last week was kept going with a streetcar motorman. No, Martha, it was the twins, aged one, I think, at the time, who kept me from sending you a warm note about the stain on your chin. I wandered into their room, heard them breathing, in unison, and something made me switch on the light. I saw them: their eyes opened simultaneously, blinked once in disbelief at the questions written across my face, and gave me such a stare of clear-sighted respectability that I backed, shamefaced, from the crib. Oh, if you could have seen those accusing blue pupils daring me to jeopardize their owners' position. Martha, their plump faces were as solid as the walls of my prison, and they left me no choice but to forget your lunches and start saving for their college education.

MARTHA

(*with a sigh of genuine understanding*)

Well, I don't blame you for that.

WARDEN

Oh, it was the right thing then when I thought you were happy with our hangman. But now . . .

MARTHA

Now, now it's too late. I can't put mayonnaise on my sandwiches any longer and fit into last year's dress.

WARDEN

And I wouldn't dare wear a tie with a palm tree painted on it. (*Suddenly throwing off the gloom that has settled over him and tumbling out his words.*) But my sons are almost chemical engineers and my wife never stops riding streetcars and my house is empty and no matter what size dress you wear, I love you!

(*He kisses* MARTHA *enthusiastically, and, for a moment, she returns in kind. Then, however, she pushes him away.*)

MARTHA

Oh, no, Harry. No, no, no. (*She walks back to the kitchen table and steadies herself with it.*) Let me reheat your coffee or make you some toast.

WARDEN

(*again advancing*)

Please, don't drop back behind breakfast. We're both beyond that now.

MARTHA

(*again escaping*)

No, not here. Phillip may come down any minute.

WARDEN

Then we must have a meeting, a rendezvous as soon as possible. Twenty years, Martha. Twenty years!

MARTHA

(*after a brief pause*)

All right: tomorrow, three o'clock, in front of the supermarket steps.

WARDEN

Tomorrow? (*A pause and a frown, as he consults a small black engagement book.*) No, I'm afraid tomorrow's out for me. A government inspection team is coming down for the day. (*Brightening.*) But Saturday, in the afternoon, I know a little bar . . .

MARTHA

But I've promised myself as a fourth in three card games that afternoon.

WARDEN

Cards, Martha?

MARTHA

(*with just a little less enthusiasm*)

We could try Monday morning. No one suspects you of anything on a Monday.

WARDEN

(*a little impatient*)

That's because everyone's too busy to get into mischief. If I went away from my desk for five minutes after a weekend, it'd take me a month to catch up.

MARTHA

Well, I could slip away Tuesday night and say I'm seeing a movie.

WARDEN

(*dejectedly*)

That's the night the twins call from school to ask for money. (*With now but faint hope.*) But Wednesday?

MARTHA

(*flatly, as she checks a calendar on the kitchen wall*)

Cancer Fund meeting. Thursday?

WARDEN

(*in equally funereal tones*)

Parole Board all day, and I visit my mother at night.

(MARTHA *turns and goes to the kitchen table where she pours a fresh cup of coffee. The* WARDEN *continues as though trying to explain something to himself rather than to her.*)

I've visited Mother every Thursday night since leaving her to get married. Every Thursday night, and I don't think she really enjoys seeing me at all.

MARTHA

(*after a pause*)

Would you like cream in your coffee, Harry?

WARDEN

Black; make it as black as you can.

MARTHA

(*making conversation*)

Do you suppose it will rain? I always think hangings should take place in bad weather, even if it does make Phillip's back stiffen up a bit.

WARDEN

(*taking up the coffee cup and staring moodily into it*)

Are we back to hangings, your husband, and another official day?

MARTHA

Your twins' eyes are still following us.

WARDEN

(*putting down the cup*)

Ah, but for a moment, for a moment . . .

MARTHA

(*sharply*)

We were being fools. Now drink your coffee.

WARDEN

(*slinking around the table to her*)

At least one more kiss, Martha. The second and last one in twenty years.

MARTHA

(*dryly*)

It would just be a wet sound to me now, Harry.

WARDEN

But not to me.

MARTHA

Your kiss would mean nothing but that I had to breathe through my nose for its duration.

WARDEN

And if I don't, I'll never breathe properly again. I feel as if I'm being sealed away forever in a very small hall closet.

MARTHA

And no matter what you do, I'll always be on the other side of the door. You won't even be near me, Harry.

WARDEN

(*like a painful prayer*)

Oh, just this once let those damned chemical engineers look the other way!

(*He begins kissing* MARTHA'S *neck passionately while she remains immobile. After a second,* PHILLIP, *his black hood over his head, enters. His voice, because of the mask, is somewhat muffled.*)

PHILLIP

And just what is this going on?

(MARTHA *utters a cry and jumps back from the* WARDEN. *He turns around and is equally upset by what he sees.*)

WARDEN

Good God!

PHILLIP

(*moving toward them*)

I'll ask again: what were you two doing?

WARDEN

(*catching his breath and paying no attention to the question*)

Do you know how ridiculously ferocious you look? Your creeping in like that's sent a chill through me all the way down to my feet.

PHILLIP

Your feet? What do I care about your feet? You were kissing my wife.

WARDEN

What? That thing's covering your mouth and making it very hard to follow what you're excited about.

PHILLIP

(*taking off the hood*)

I *say* you were kissing my wife!

WARDEN

It's not very well-mannered to come right out and say it that way, but I suppose I was.

PHILLIP

While I was upstairs, trying to adjust this hood so you'd see it to its best advantage, you were making love to my wife. You, the Warden of the prison, who, in less than half an hour will be raising a solemn forefinger and signaling me to hang a man—you were making love to my wife in my own kitchen.

WARDEN

(*really confused by all the fuss*)

Man to man, Phillip, I apologize. These things happen all the time—a little slip that sets one in the bushes alongside somebody you've no business being in the bushes with. Yes, it's an unfortunate, uh, occurrence, and, as I said, I *do* apologize for it.

PHILLIP

(*somewhat stunned*)

Apologize? Oh, no, please don't do that. I—I couldn't accept. I don't *want* to accept.

WARDEN

Now, Phillip, I understand how you feel. I've found my wife in much more than an embrace with a plumber. He was covered with grease, too, and had . . .

PHILLIP

Oh, no, it's not that at all. I was a little shocked just now and perhaps I did sound like a predictable husband. It just seemed that, under the circumstances, bellowing was expected of me.

WARDEN

I'm not following.

PHILLIP

It's simply that, while I was in my room, I was thinking what a failure I'd be in the hood. I was thinking, Harry, that the only thing that would save me would be to turn tail on this house, this uniform, this prison—everything that keeps me jogging along in step with the rest of you. So, Harry, friend and lover of my wife, I almost opened the window, slithered down the drainpipe and slipped out of your sight forever. I was going to run away—are you listening too, Martha?—run away and find out just where those men I've been dropping through gallows' doors come from.

WARDEN

Phillip, call me names, knock me down if you want to, but don't psychoanalyze yourself in public this way. At least not while you're in uniform.

PHILLIP

Let me just say that it was my old, well-trained conscience that kept me off the drainpipe. I thought of you two, standing firm on this dreary morning, washing your misery down with coffee, keeping to the rules of the game, and I bowed my head, covered it with the hood, and came downstairs ready to go on as Phillip, the old executioner. But now, now that you two have kicked up your heels a little bit, I see no reason why I shouldn't follow suit. You don't know how long I've waited to find a crack in the wall that being Martha's husband has built around me. But now that I see it's there, I'm going through it and down the drainpipe without a regret.

WARDEN

Phillip, this is all impossible, you know that, don't you?

PHILLIP

No more so than my finding you wrapped around my wife is impossible. If you two, at breakfast time, can stomach each other to the point of embracing, then I don't see how the line of impossibility can be drawn anywhere.

WARDEN

And just who, in all honesty, is responsible for this embrace?

PHILLIP

(*looking at* MARTHA, *who, during the foregoing, has folded her arms and kept her back to both of her champions*) Who, indeed?

WARDEN

You, yourself. You with your black hood, your Swedish lessons, your scattered slippers, and your brooding in the corner. You sent her into my arms, Phillip.

PHILLIP

(*smiling at* MARTHA *who doesn't respond*)

So you did notice these things.

WARDEN

Of course she has; and that's why what happened happened. It explains . . .

PHILLIP

At five-thirty in the morning it doesn't explain . . .

WARDEN

(*raising his arm for silence*)

No! No! I am now speaking in my official capacity and I don't want to be interrupted by subordinates. (*The* WARDEN *takes the deep breath of one preparing for platitudes.*) Life, Phillip, is like a long sea voyage—the comparison's an old but apt one. We begin by deciding whether we favor temperate, tropic, or arctic waters. We decide what ports to put into with proper ceremony and what savage islands to sell trinkets and contract diseases on. We select the style of ship and the type of crew that suits us; and if one turns out to have a few leaks hidden in its bottom and the other to be bad-breathed and mutinous, we don't let that force us to drift off course. For, Phillip, staying within the latitudes and longitudes we've marked out for ourselves is all that matters. There can be no floating about to take closer looks at a curvaceous coast line or a sensual horizon. There can be no seeking out restful doldrums when your nerves get a bit frayed or poking about for a good typhoon when calm seas prove somewhat tedious. No, we keep to the prescribed path, and when other ships plow past us, flaunting well-laundered sails—well, we scrub ours up too, send every one with scurvy out of sight, keep a good mile of sea water between us and our short-lived neighbors, and leave them with the impression of nothing but that we're occupying the exact bit of ocean marked out for us. But you, Phillip, you just weren't sticking to the chart. You were sailing into harbors that weren't even marked on the maps of your second-in-command; you were tossing sensible and costly cargo overboard to make room for unmarketable baubles; you were tilting the compass to suit yourself. Now, is there any wonder, as you were approaching the dangerous waters of middle age, that Martha should lower a dinghy over the side and paddle her way to a vessel that looked, at least from a distance, to be completely shipshape? And, of course, having a good set of sea manners and seeing your wife bobbing next to me, I took her aboard, gave her, so to speak, a change of dry clothes and am now ready to return her to your schooner which, I'm sure, will be polished up and made ready for inspection. And if you don't want her to think she has to abandon ship again, tighten the hatches, throw out your World's Fair socks; secure the rigging, don't use slippers for ash trays; scrub the decks, go to club dances; check your compass hourly, burn that revolting black hood; and, finally, appear at today's execution as if you knew what your coordinates as the state's official hangman were. For remember, Phillip, no matter how attractive you find the mermaids or the rocks they wrap their appealing green tails around, the important thing is to keep sailing on course. Take that as an old captain's advice—just keep sailing on course.

(*The* WARDEN, *who during the speech has edged his way to the door, exits through it.*)

PHILLIP

(*running to the door after him*)

That's the same speech you gave at the club's Christmas dinner last year and the summer picnic the year before! Well, you old pirate, you'd better get your ship's lifeboats ready because there isn't going to be a hanging today. Do you hear? The person you thought you temporarily rescued is now your permanent passenger. I resign! From everything! I resign! (*Phillip pauses for a moment, comes back into the center of the kitchen, looks at his hood, then at* MARTHA, *and laughs softly.*) I'll have to admit you surprised me, Martha. It was pleasant, but a surprise nevertheless. (*Silence.*) Well, don't you have anything to say? After all, I just said I was leaving you.

MARTHA

(*disinterested*)

If you're not going to touch breakfast, I'll put the dishes away.

PHILLIP

(*relieved*)

Oh, I thought after twenty years of marriage that a little piece of flesh had begun to sprout, connecting us together like Siamese twins. You don't know how upset I was by the idea. And now, Martha, you've shown me that it's nothing but a flimsy band-aid —nothing more.

MARTHA

(*beginning to remove the dishes and wash them*)

A band-aid?

PHILLIP

(*with real admiration in his eyes*)

One that you had the courage to tear off. Oh, if I'd only known how simple it would be. There I was, trying to sneak into a black hood and leave little hints about the house.

MARTHA

Hints at what?

PHILLIP

Hints that I was unhappy; that I thought I'd become little more than the brass and flannel of my uniform; that I wanted to run away from everything that I was and had been. It never occurred to me that you might feel the same way. But then, seeing you pressed up against the Warden—well, Martha, I confess I underestimated you.

MARTHA

And are you planning now to go out and make love to the Warden's wife?

PHILLIP

Oh, no. I'm going to leave you and this little piece of the world forever. I'm going to become—to become . . .

MARTHA
(*sharply*)

What?

PHILLIP
(*a visionary smile*)

To become—to become something like those fellows I've been hanging in the last few months. Do you know, Martha, there's a light in their eyes, a pulse behind their ear that beats faster than mine, and an interest in the weather that makes me envy them. Oh, they're frightened all right, but it's a healthy fear—something I don't think I would ever have had.

MARTHA

As the Warden said, they've just left those official ladies. Maybe if you didn't read all night in bed we could . . .

PHILLIP

Oh, no, Martha. I need a complete and total break.

MARTHA

And when do you plan to start breaking?

PHILLIP

In the past a step like this would have meant travel folders, reservations, exact calculations down to the dollar. But now, Martha, I'm not even going to bother to pack. I'm walking straight out the door without a glance over my shoulder.

MARTHA

(*holding out a plate to him*)

Will you help dry first?

PHILLIP

(*abstracted but pleasant*)

What? Oh, certainly. (*Towel and plate in hand, he goes back to his vision.*) First, I'm going to a tailor. I'm going to have him make me something for every mood I'm going to try—silk vests, lace collars, green tweeds for reflective moments . . .

MARTHA

(*handing him another dish*)

Tweeds always make you break out in a rash.

PHILLIP

(*thinking for a moment, he takes the new plate and stacks the old one*)

That's true. Well, perhaps, I'll give up reflection—there won't be much time for it, I hope, anyway.

MARTHA

And after the tailor, then what?

PHILLIP

Ah, I want to go where the climate's very hot; where it steams, as a matter of fact; where oversized plants seem to couple with one another before your eyes and produce offspring so colorful that they look indecent.

MARTHA

(*now a cup in her hand*)

You never liked me to wear loud clothes: always gray, black, and brown.

PHILLIP

(*taking the cup*)

No offense, but you're just not a tropical plant, Martha.

MARTHA

It wasn't me who had to have an air-conditioner last summer. Put the cup face down, Phillip.

PHILLIP

(*he does so and receives a bowl in its place*)

Now I want the heat to prevent anything from taking on too solid and sensible a shape. I want everything about me to shimmer, sway, and change in a second's time as if it were all one big sleight-of-hand trick. People, too, should melt and harden in front of you. (*He starts to put the bowl away.*)

MARTHA

That still looks wet to me.

PHILLIP

(*retrieving the bowl*)

And, Martha, there might be mirages. Can you imagine, scenes floating about purely for your own amusement. Do you know, I think I've wanted to see a mirage for the last ten years.

MARTHA

You're getting water on your trousers, Phillip. (*She opens a cupboard and takes out an apron.*) Here, put this on.

PHILLIP

(*getting into the apron*)

I used to try to force a mirage on myself. On days like today, when I'd see the man I was to hang being escorted toward me, I used to widen my eyes, clench my fists, and try to make my brain turn the entire scene into something else. It never worked, though: my eyes would begin to water and soon I was receiving reprimands from my superiors for what they took to be my emotional attitude while on duty.

MARTHA

(*handing Phillip the last dish*)

All you want, then, is to see mirages?

PHILLIP

I want my pores to open and let out of me all the bubbling perspiration that's been stopped up by the civil service code. Think of it, Martha! Me, in the middle of a jungle, where everything's raw and fresh, where only the hungry and alive do the executing, where . . .

MARTHA

I think some grounds are still in the coffee pot.

PHILLIP

(*giving the pot another rinse*)

And then, Martha, once I've filled my lungs with that wild air—well, then I'll be ready to—to . . .

MARTHA

To what, Phillip?

PHILLIP

(*modestly, with some embarrassment*)

Oh, grow a beard perhaps.

MARTHA

All this trouble just to avoid shaving?

PHILLIP

No, what I mean is, once I've finally shed this old skin, I'll be ready to—to take up my old profession again with a fresh hand.

MARTHA

You mean after all that sweating in the tropics you'd still want to be an executioner?

PHILLIP

(*soberly*)

That is my profession, my trade, the only thing I can do passably well. (*Brightening.*) But, Martha, I won't be an official piece of cloth and brass, tying the knot around living necks because someone, somewhere, has underlined their names in red ink.

MARTHA

(*as if humoring someone not too sound of mind*)

You're going to do free-lance work?

PHILLIP

(*slowly winding the dishtowel into a strangling cord*)

I'm going to have an eye peeled for all the dead branches that need pruning—for all those who want to measure away the few wild patches of weeds left to us and turn the ground, teeming with savage centipedes, into a middle-income housing development.

MARTHA

(*still indulging him*)

And just how do you go about determining when a branch is dead?

PHILLIP

(*moving about the kitchen table, towel in hand and eyes agleam*)

Oh, that won't be hard, Martha. (*He begins circling the table, his eyes on the pepper mill as if stalking it.*) Just suppose I'm standing on a busy corner at lunchtime. Oh, there'll be a lot of dead wood about, but I'll find the one beyond the help of insecticides. I'll know him: perhaps I'll notice that his tie, socks, and handkerchief match; or perhaps I'll see he doesn't cross the street until the exact moment the light blinks in his favor. Oh, I'll know him as one of those who'll spend what energy he has trying to make tomorrow a line-for-line copy of yesterday; one of those who has a favorite chair, who sees no difference but age between the woman he married and the woman he keeps. (*Phillip pauses, narrows his eyes, and moves in on the pepper mill.*) He won't notice me, but I'll be behind him all the time. I'll watch him stuff himself with just the right calorie count; I'll smile as he leaves the proper tip and takes the long way back to his office to get in a little exercise; I'll peek around a corner as he tells an off-color joke to his secretary and pats her knee. And then, when he's alone in his office, about to balance another day's equation, I'll just tiptoe up behind him, hold the loop for a moment over his head, and then—snap! (*He catches the pepper mill in the towel's knot and lifts it up level with his eyes.*) There won't be any struggle or sound. He might have just enough curiosity to turn and see just who's doing him in, but the only thing I'd find in his eyes would be the gleam of one whose funeral arrangements were planned down to the last flower, tear, and comma in his epitaph. Already dead, Martha, he'd be only too happy to lie down. (*Phillip lets the pepper mill drop to the floor.*)

MARTHA

(*getting down to retrieve it*)

That pepper mill was your birthday gift from my mother!

PHILLIP

(*as if suddenly startled awake*)

What?

MARTHA

(*putting the object back on the kitchen table*)

It must have cost twenty-five dollars. (*Sharply.*) Find something less expensive to play games with, Phillip.

PHILLIP

(*hurt*)

Games? Martha, I was trying to share a secret with you. For the first time in our marriage, I was telling you something I really felt.

MARTHA

Don't be open-hearted and frank with me, Phillip.

PHILLIP

But aren't you at least interested in what I'm really like?

MARTHA

If I was interested in what you were really like, I don't think I'd have stayed married to you for twenty years.

PHILLIP

But you might find me—well, exciting.

MARTHA

(*coldly*)

I've grown used to the lies, Phillip. They make up the comfortable husband I know.

PHILLIP

(*realizing he's made a mistake in confiding in her*)

Oh, I see. All right, then, you keep the comfortable husband! The new one, Martha, won't bother you any longer. No, he's simply going to close his eyes, turn around, and head straight through the door.

(*As he speaks,* PHILLIP *performs the above gestures. As he is halfway to the door, however,* MARTHA *speaks up.*)

MARTHA

You'd better take off my apron first.

PHILLIP

(*angry with himself for not having noticed it*)

Oh, yes. How did I get into it in the first place?

MARTHA

(*as if she were discussing a shopping list*)

And another thing: I don't see how you can pick up and leave today, Phillip.

PHILLIP

(*repeating the above gestures*)

And why not, Martha? Why shouldn't I just close my eyes, turn around, and . . .

MARTHA

Because you have a dentist appointment first thing tomorrow morning.

PHILLIP

(*turning about in confusion*)

Dentist? Dentist?

MARTHA

(*innocently*)

You remember. The molar in the back has to come out? It's infecting the gum? Because of it you can't eat sweets?

PHILLIP

I don't want to eat sweets. I just . . .

MARTHA

We've been invited to my sister's for dinner Friday, and you know how partial you are to her chocolate mousse.

PHILLIP

(*at last rather angry*)

Damn the chocolate mousse! I'm not going to your sister's for dinner anyway.

MARTHA

I've already accepted. And with the weekend whirl coming up, I don't see how you can plan to leave before next Wednesday.

PHILLIP

Plan? Something like this can't be planned and put on schedule. I'm giving up knowing where and what I'll be a week, a day, or even an hour ahead. I'm going to be . . .

MARTHA

(*again sharp and bitter*)

A man-eating, jungle plant—I know. Well, you'll have to wait until *after* my sister's dinner to start blooming. And by that time, there'll be other things popping up to detain you.

PHILLIP

(*a little unnerved*)

Martha, maybe you didn't understand or listen to what I was saying. I'm sweeping all the old laws, manners, and invitations under the rug. There's nothing here that can hold me now.

MARTHA

Oh, yes, there is—me.

PHILLIP

You? Martha, I don't want to be brutal, but if nothing else were pushing me through that door, you, in your breakfast face, would be all the reason I'd need.

MARTHA

(*now in full attack*)

Maybe my face won't charm you into bed, but you're going to look at it, speak to it, and—yes, even kiss it in a businesslike way every day of your life. Because, Phillip, covered with cold-cream or skin oil, it's the face of your wife. And "wife," Phillip, means a thousand obstacles for you to get over before you're free to start chopping down dead branches.

PHILLIP

(*in the tones of family argument*)

Wife? Hah! And were you my wife with the Warden pawing over you?

MARTHA

More than ever, Phillip. That little moment with him only reminded me how snug I was with you—even with your red socks under the sofa seat. My life depends on all the little functions you perform. You're like the telephone, electricity, or underground plumbing. My life takes you for granted, but would be lost without you. Maybe we're not held together by a little piece of flesh, but there is something there even harder to snip apart. It's the word "and" in "man *and* wife." It's official and keeps us together through mistresses, dreams, bills, and burned toast. "Man *and* wife"—that's our world, Phillip; and everything in it has long ago been discovered, named, and placed in its proper corner.

PHILLIP

No three-letter word's going to drag me after it. Not when I finally have the chance . . .

MARTHA

You *had* the chance, Phillip. For the briefest second, when you caught the Warden and me, you had the chance. But no; you stayed and helped me with the dishes.

PHILLIP

That was just habit.

MARTHA

No, dear, that was the law of gravity yanking you right back to earth.

PHILLIP

Well, I'm breaking the law of gravity, Martha. From now on you'll have to find someone else to eat off and dry your dishes. The first day of creation is waiting for me on the other side of the kitchen door, and all the rules of marriage or physics aren't going to keep me from it. (*He starts for the door.*)

MARTHA

Touch that door and you'll find out how unpleasant the truth about yourself can be.

PHILLIP

I have all the truth I need, Martha. Goodby. And if we ever meet again be careful I don't mistake you for a dead branch. (*Phillip makes to open the door, but finds it refuses to budge. He begins tugging at the knob.*) It must be the dampness has made the wood swell.

MARTHA

(*taunting*)

You'll never get it open, Phillip. You know too well what's on the other side.

PHILLIP

(*increasing his efforts*)

It's not locked. There's no reason for it to be this stubborn.

MARTHA

You don't want to strain yourself, Phillip. Remember that awful rubber girdle you had to wear after cleaning out the attic last year.

PHILLIP

(*more and more effort*)

Shut up, Martha!

MARTHA

Ha! Don't yell at *me!* You, I, and the door know on which side of it you belong.

PHILLIP

(*losing all control*)

I'll tear the damned thing off its hinges.

MARTHA

That door's the speed of light—a permanent boundary fence. It can't be broken.

PHILLIP

(*now pounding on the door*)

Open, damn you! Open!

MARTHA

It won't because you don't want it to. You know that all your jungle will give you is athlete's foot, diarrhea, and swollen joints.

PHILLIP

(*turning from the door to* MARTHA, *he pleads with desperation in his voice*)

I'm going to tear down every kitchen door in the world. I'm going to strangle, murder . . .

MARTHA

You, murder? Hah! Come on, Phillip, the game's over. You're an official executioner, a little paunchy through the middle, with thinning hair and an obedient attitude. That's as close as you'll ever be to a murderer.

PHILLIP

(*menacingly*)

If that door doesn't open you'll be the first to know how wrong you are.

MARTHA

(*with an incredulous smile*)

Are you threatening me?

PHILLIP

If you're keeping me in this kitchen—yes!

MARTHA

Oh, poor, poor Phillip. Look at you; out of breath already and not even one step away from the house yet.

PHILLIP

I won't stand you laughing at me!

MARTHA

Then don't make jokes about doing me in. You're not on your gallows now; no twenty-five forms have been filled out in triplicate authorizing you to snap my neck. (*Shouting.*) You're my husband! And that makes you the most harmless person in the world as far as *I'm* concerned!

PHILLIP

(*picking up the black hood from the kitchen table and beginning to knot it ominously*)

For the last time: make the door open!

MARTHA

How can I, Phillip? You're the one who's keeping it shut. If you really wanted to leave, it would spring open like a hungry mouth.

PHILLIP

(*stepping toward her*)

Then I'll have to prove I'm in earnest, Martha.

MARTHA

Don't be an ass. One of the things that will make the rest of our life together tolerable is that you can keep your mind buzzing with plans to murder me. Don't try it now and find out you can't. It'll make you sour, bitter, and even more difficult to get new hats and dresses out of than you are now.

(PHILLIP *begins testing the hood's strength and continues his advance.*)

MARTHA

(*quite earnestly*)

I'm warning you. With as much love as I can squeeze out of me after twenty years, I'm warning you not to do this to yourself.

PHILLIP

As the books say: there's no good reasoning with a murderer.

MARTHA

(*throwing back the challenge*)

All right, murderer, if you won't listen—(*She picks up one of the kitchen table chairs, places it downstage, facing the audience, and sits in it with her neck thrust out as if for a sacrifice.*)

All right then, go ahead. Try and squeeze the air out of my windpipe. Just try it! Well, what are you waiting for, Bluebeard? Come on, let me feel some of your jungle sweat dripping down the back of my neck.

PHILLIP

(*a little startled by* MARTHA'S *action*)

Are you just going to sit there as if you were having your hair done?

MARTHA

You'll have to supply the noise and screams, Phillip. I'm just going to sit here and talk.

PHILLIP

Talk? Then that's just the last bit of incentive I need. (*He knots the hood around* MARTHA'S *neck and begins tightening.*)

MARTHA

(*not affected at all by* PHILLIP'S *attack*)

Oh, you'll have to pull harder than that. I'm still getting in more than enough air to tell you that the ivy plants over our bed are all the jungle you'll ever know.

(PHILLIP *gives an extra hard tug, and* MARTHA *starts, as if tickled.*)

And it's your turn to water them next week. You'll take care of them every other week for as long as you're on this planet.

PHILLIP

(*hopefully*)

Is the blood beginning to pound in your head? Do you find it difficult to focus your eyes?

MARTHA

Hah! I've never felt better. This is the closest we've come to sex in years.

PHILLIP

(*increasing his efforts*)

And now, Martha, is your past popping up in front of you?

MARTHA

Only my future. And you, Phillip, growing stooped, absent-minded, and a little sloppy at the table, are in every minute of it.

PHILLIP

(*becoming frustrated*)

You should at least be gagging now, damn it!

MARTHA

(*sweetly*)

I don't know how to gag. But I could cough a little if it would make things easier for you.

PHILLIP

(*pleading*)

Please stop breathing, Martha. Please, my arms are getting tired—please stop breathing.

MARTHA

At this rate, you'll stop before I will. Oh, what a story this will make at cards Saturday!

PHILLIP

(*makes one last supreme effort, and then, with a groan, drops his hands*)

I just can't do it. My wrists and fingers just aren't strong enough. (*He sits in one of the kitchen chairs.*) I can't even get out of the kitchen.

MARTHA

(*rubbing her neck and rising from the chair*)

I told you, Phillip, but you wouldn't listen, would you? Now look at you—panting and overheated. (*She takes the hood and begins mopping his brow.*) And you have to go out right away. I'm sure this will mean a cold by tomorrow.

PHILLIP
(*docilely*)

Go out?

MARTHA

There's not fifteen minutes till the execution begins. There now, that's the best I can do. (*She takes* PHILLIP'S *coat and holds it out for him.*) All right, come on, get into this. If you keep all the buttons closed there's still a chance I won't have to spend a fortune on nose drops and cough syrup.

PHILLIP

So the execution's going to take place after all?

MARTHA
(*buttoning up the coat*)

Of course it is; and you're going to be on those gallows, stiff and tall, the way I, the Warden, and the man you're going to hang expect you to be. The whole thing will go very smoothly now, won't it?

PHILLIP

I suppose it will.

MARTHA

(*finishing the buttoning,* MARTHA *steps back to admire her work*)

There! Now you look like my husband and the state's official executioner. You can tell at a glance that you're a fish in the right waters now.

PHILLIP

I guess you can.

MARTHA

(*picking up* PHILLIP'S *cap*)

Now, don't be so gloomy. Look on the bright side of everything to come. Think of the certificate of merit and pension bonus you'll receive when you successfully hang your thousandth man. Think of the speeches you'll be asked to give to college students on the fine prose in the penal code. Think of the jokes you'll tell at your retirement dinner and the little cottage our insurance policy's going to give us. Think how peaceful things will be when you're certain that there's only one world and one way to live in it.

PHILLIP

Will that come with the retirement policy too?

MARTHA

(*putting the cap on his head*)

It just might, Phillip. It just might. And now, you're complete; not a wrinkle in you. (*She takes his arm and starts to lead him toward the door.*)

PHILLIP

My hood? Can I at least have that?

MARTHA

I'll put it under the sofa with your socks. And, on holidays, you can take them, your banjo, and the other things out to look at for a while. And on New Year's Eve, you can even sit on the floor and flip ashes into your slippers if you want to.

PHILLIP

I think I'll go back to my chair. The floor's very hard.

MARTHA

That *is* more sensible, I suppose.

(*They reach the door*)

Well, come on now. Out you go.

PHILLIP

But it won't open.

MARTHA

(*she touches the door knob ever so lightly with the tips of her fingers and it springs open*)

There's nothing holding it shut now.

PHILLIP

(*taking a step toward the opening*)

It is very cold this morning.

MARTHA

Do you have a handkerchief with you?

PHILLIP

(*feeling his pocket*)

Yes.

MARTHA

Well, then, you'd better be off.

PHILLIP

(*turning toward* MARTHA)

Martha, I just wanted to be . . .

MARTHA

But you couldn't, Phillip. Some things just can't be broken. So you'd better just try to keep warm out there and forget all about it. Now, kiss me goodby.

PHILLIP

But isn't there any chance for me at all?

MARTHA

(*in a command voice and pointing to her cheek*)

Kiss!

(PHILLIP *does so, and then slowly turns and leaves.* MARTHA *waits for a moment and then calls out to him.*)

Keep bundled up, dear. Don't work too hard. And tonight—tonight we'll have something very special for dinner. Something you really like, dear, something you really, really like.

CURTAIN

The Falling Sickness
BY RUSSELL EDSON

The most immediately striking characteristic of Russell Edson's *The Falling Sickness* is its fierce, slam-bang kinetic energy. The characters who populate this sealed-off microcosm of conventional reality, this inescapable domestic hell, engage in perpetual protest against it and one another by dancing about, jumping up and down, screeching at, insulting, or attacking one another, donning wigs, and changing clothes. There is none of the acquiescence evident even in, say, Richardson's unhappy household. Scenes end as characters collapse on the floor in fits of frustration and exhaustion; subsequent events resume full tilt. The speech of the characters echoes the mimetic vigor. They converse extravagantly, wildly, sometimes in their frenzies forgetting or exchanging identities, sometimes considering one another as objects or obstacles. Conversely, objects tend to become people, and in their furious dissatisfaction people address the furniture, walls, corners, and other details of their surroundings. Author of *The Very Thing That Happens,* a book of tales and prose poems, Edson has a haunted imagination that is close to Surrealism. In the theatre, his wealth of effects and the comic violence of his attack suggest the added influence of circus or vaudeville slapstick.

The Falling Sickness
A PLAY IN THREE PARTS

CHARACTERS

FATHER
MOTHER
SON (TWIN SISTER)
TOILET

PART I

A man, the SON, *walks out and collapses. He gets up, walks a few steps and collapses again. Gets up, goes to window and screams. Walks to front, screams again; collapses and doesn't move.*

MOTHER *and* FATHER *enter.* MOTHER *is fat and wears a big white apron.* FATHER *is slight and bald.*

FATHER

Shall we dance?

MOTHER

No, no, let's just walk in.

FATHER

Should we curtsy?

MOTHER

No, no, we don't have to be afraid to walk into our own kitchen; even if the walls are covered with those that watch.

FATHER

That watch? Why do they watch us? Whose kitchen is this, the kitchen's or ours?

MOTHER

Why do you keep asking me questions? Didn't I take my clothes off in front of you once?

FATHER

But, Mother, I'm so afraid of your head . . .

MOTHER

My head is my place to make up things to do.

FATHER

Please do not make up anything against me.

MOTHER

Now listen to me before I let my mouth punish you . . . (*Works her jaw at him*)

FATHER

Oh, please do not let that terrible thing get at me . . .

MOTHER

Our son . . .

FATHER

Something else . . .

MOTHER

Thirty or forty years old, named exhibit A . . .

FATHER

Who criminally assaulted my view . . .

MOTHER

For that he could easily be loved.

FATHER

Why is it that the husband does not inspire worship?

MOTHER

Because the husband is a stupid fedora who is really an old lady's dress.

FATHER

That is not true. I was once an old lady's stocking hanging at her ankle as she trooped around a grocery store trying to impress the grocer with her varicosity. But she kicked me off with a sudden desire to put the calloused one in the grocer's face so that he could look down her leg to better things.

MOTHER

I never did such a thing. That's a dirty rotten lie. Perhaps I stooped to pull up my stocking to relieve his curiosity about my sitting organ, which he hid by talking to another customer . . .

FATHER

That is a dirty rotten filthy lie; he didn't say a word to me.

MOTHER

Don't you remember, he asked to see your knee.

FATHER

That isn't so, my attention was deviated to a handsome young woman wearing a mustache leading a dog on a chain.

(*Their* SON, *still on the floor, screams*)

FATHER

Something is hurt, Mother.

MOTHER

Something is always complaining, Father.

(*Their* SON *screams again*)

FATHER

I think we better call the plumber, the toilet's complaining again, Mother.

MOTHER

Well, call the plumber . . . As if I didn't know why you want the plumber.

FATHER

(*Goes to window and screams*)

Plumber, plumber, greengrocer, anyone, help!

MOTHER

Please do not tell the neighbors about our toilet.

FATHER

Neighbors, neighbors, please do not listen to our toilet!

(*Their* SON *screams again*)

MOTHER

The door just screamed, I heard it scream, Father.

FATHER

Why does it scream, Mother?

MOTHER

It is hungry, it wishes to eat a stranger.

FATHER

The door is a mouth and I am a digestive organ.

MOTHER

You're a silly old man who looks like an old lady's dress.

FATHER

No no, Mother, I wear a fedora which shows people that I have love with a trunk in the attic, which gives birth to an old lady's dress. Now that makes sense. And maybe they say to the old lady's dress, *my, you look just like your father.* See, that's why you think I look like an old lady's dress. You see, it is really an old lady's dress that looks like me . . .

MOTHER

I don't care to hear what you do in the attic.

FATHER

But, Mother, please listen . . . Just the other day a newspaper got quite fresh with me. I had been crossing and uncrossing my legs . . .

MOTHER

Oh, Father . . .

FATHER

Yes, and I noticed my shoe was pinching my foot quite deliberately; not to mention that the easy chair was holding me in its arms . . .

(*Their* SON *screams*)

MOTHER

Something is very wrong; and you go on like a coquette.

FATHER

What is wrong? Just because the walls want to have love with me, and the house falls down because the walls get into bed with me . . .

MOTHER

Father Father Father, I hate you . . .

(*Their* SON *screams again*)

FATHER

Why do things scream!

MOTHER

Because it is possible . . .

(MOTHER *and* FATHER *collapse on floor*)

PART I, SECOND SCENE

(MOTHER *and* FATHER *still where they collapsed, still collapsed*)
(SON *on floor convulses like a dog that dreams of running. He whines and yips moving his arms and legs*)

SON

Coming awake, coming awake . . . Awake . . . When I snap my fingers you will be awake; you will remember nothing. (*He snaps his fingers. He points a finger at his face*): Who are you? Wait . . . (*He goes over to his* MOTHER *and lifts her apron, looks under it, shakes his head and pulls the apron up over his* MOTHER'S *face*) Where I came from isn't there anymore. (MOTHER *convulses*) (*He points to the seat of his pants*): Who are you? (*Looking over his shoulder at the seat of his pants*): I'm up here. (*He goes over to his* FATHER *and looks up one of the pants legs*): Oh, my God, Father's knee! (*Sits at table, picks up a cup*): Cup because a cup is shaped like a cup; as is a spoon after the shape of spoons. Identity is more shape than essence—that a thing comes because of its absence, which is an emptiness for it to enter . . . (*Stands looking at his shadow*): If one is nothing, still, one is an object, one has a shadow . . . (*He collapses*)

PART I, THIRD SCENE

(SON *still where he collapsed.* MOTHER *and* FATHER *wake up where they had collapsed*)

MOTHER
(*pointing to* SON)

There's something wrong with the floor.

FATHER

A small mountain begins, the earth is changing.

MOTHER

No, no, what is that thing?

FATHER

It is something not too near us, yet not that far away at to be said to be *that* far away . . .

MOTHER

Stop it, stop it, Father, you drive me crazy.

FATHER

But, Mother, perhaps we can carry on our lives without noticing it.

MOTHER

Go to it, Father, and ask it what it is.

FATHER

Oh no, Mother . . .

MOTHER

Ask it!

FATHER

(*To his collapsed* SON)

Who are you, sir? . . . No, don't answer, I'll take it for granted that you are either God or a person of awesome power. Our kitchen is completely at your disposal . . .

(*no answer*)

MOTHER

Kick it, Father.

FATHER

It might bite me.

MOTHER

Light a light.

(FATHER *lights a lamp*)

[25] *Gas*. The Parade at Southampton. "'Liquid Hips' (riding) the hovercraft dressed in a spangled bathing suit." At left, Charles Frazier. Photo by Peter Moore.

[26] *Gas*. The Parade at Southampton. "Men and women joined in turning kerosene barrels over and over, rolling them down the main Southampton street." Photo by Peter Moore.

[27] *Gas*. Events at the Beach at Amagansett. The fifty-foot-high "soft sky-scraper." "...The children scrambled around, positioning themselves to giving the building a push back up whenever it lurched dangerously. It stood upright for about ten feet and then the rest of it kept weaving and bending." Photo by Peter Moore.

[28] *Gas*. Events at the Beach at Amagansett. "...the skyscraper was allowed to topple and the kids were let loose to pull it apart, which they did with great savagery." Photo by Peter Moore.

[29] *Gas*. On and Around the Shelter Island Ferry. "The word FIRE (sprayed) inside the window...policemen...leaped from their squad car and sprayed the entire truck." Photo by Peter Moore.

[30] *Gas.* On and Around the Shelter Island Ferry. "The nurses could be seen waving and laughing as the ferry pulled into the dock (before) someone drew a black curtain in front of them." Photo by Peter Moore.

[31] *Gas.* On and Around the Shelter Island Ferry. "About half a mile from the dock, the nurses turned up—piled five in a cot in the middle of the highway, kicking their legs, waving their arms." Photo by Peter Moore.

[32] *Gas*. Pilgrimage Through the Fire-fighting Foam at Montauk. "When everyone was in place…the foam machines began to churn out sudsy stuff which at first blew into the air like tiny clouds." Photo by Mordi Gerstein.

[33] *Gas*. Pilgrimage Through the Fire-fighting Foam at Montauk. "Below, on the beach, other participants stretched . . . black plastic over several wooden frames. These pyramids were designed to echo the crevices and peaks of the dunes, while standing out starkly against the foam." Photo by Peter Moore.

[34] *Gas*. Pilgrimage Through the Fire-fighting Foam at Montauk. "The foam poured down the bluffs—a sudsy waterfall which mounted to the knees, thighs, necks of those crossing the beach at the base of the bluffs." Photo by Mordi Gerstein.

[35] *Gas*. Picnic in the Auto Graveyard. "For about three quarters of an hour the children painted the cars." Photo by Mordi Gerstein.

MOTHER

What is it?

FATHER

It might be one of us . . .

MOTHER

WE are in our own selves.

FATHER

(*His back to* MOTHER)

Where are you, Mother?

MOTHER

In this old woman.

FATHER

What old woman?

MOTHER

Your wife, that pretty young thing.

FATHER

(*Looks upward*)

Help me to know the right thing.

MOTHER

What is it, Father?

FATHER

It is someone, far away, asleep; but by a certain proximity in our kitchen.

MOTHER

If it's mobile tell it to go.

FATHER

Oh, Mother, I don't know anything about it. Although it seems to have legs, but they may be phony ones. It seems to throw a shadow. But I can't tell whether it's a drawing with the shadow drawn in, or a hole in the floor.

MOTHER

Well, walk on it!

FATHER

But it might be a hole in the floor.

MOTHER

Experiment freely.

FATHER

You mean if it's a hole, fall into it. If it's a mountain, rise with it.

MOTHER

A God, author of goodness, author of cruelty . . .

FATHER

Let's not fool with this thing anymore.

MOTHER

Let's not do anything anymore.

FATHER

Let's just wait.

MOTHER

For what?

FATHER

For the external to make itself known.

MOTHER

No, no, I've been hidden all my life; let the external hide itself for a while.

FATHER

Oh, but, dear wife and mother of my child, you are the external. *I* am internal all my life; the supressed explosion inside of an old man.

MOTHER

You are nothing!

FATHER

I have a shadow which allows I am something mounted on legs.

MOTHER

I don't care for your legs.

FATHER

The world is perfectly willing to mind its own business while someone is dying inside his greatcoat.

MOTHER

Your greatcoat can be used as a rug.

FATHER

Wife, wife, love my hairy belly!

MOTHER

In the springtime . . .

FATHER

Yes . . . ?

MOTHER

In the time of pubescence, in the green wood, birds fluting the air . . .

FATHER

From the high hill the sea as blue as Hokusai said it was . . .

MOTHER

The maiden, half girl, half woman . . . I loved myself then . . .

FATHER

I adore you!

MOTHER

No, no, you are not there to adore.

FATHER

But pretend that I am.

MOTHER

No, no, you're spoiling it.

FATHER

No, no, Mother, let me be in it too.

MOTHER

No, no, you're home masturbating over pictures of your father.

FATHER

I ruined my mind, visualizing Father wearing his fedora in strange landscapes . . .

MOTHER

Oh, please, is there no end to the end?

FATHER

It goes on and on. The beginning is always with us. Let us go to the green wood.

MOTHER

No. It is over, thank God.

FATHER

Never to be again?

MOTHER

Over, over, over!

FATHER

As is this time?

MOTHER

As is any time seen far from itself.

FATHER

Ah, Mother, the romance of it . . .

MOTHER

But it is always *now*. (*She sobs*)

FATHER

Soon to be *then*.

MOTHER

To get past this time, to be safe in the future.

FATHER

But, Mother, this is the future.

MOTHER

No, no, this is right now.

FATHER

But it is also the future of some other unhappiness.

MOTHER

And see how it turned out.

FATHER

It is still turning out.

MOTHER

Oh, Father, will it ever stop?

FATHER

Not as long as it doesn't.

MOTHER

What *doesn't?*

FATHER

I forget . . . That's how it sneaks up on you.

MOTHER

What is sneaking up on us?

FATHER

I forget . . . And again, that's how it sneaks up on you.

MOTHER

Oh, Father, what are we doing here?

FATHER

We've come to kill something.

MOTHER

Then why do we wait?

FATHER

Because to *be* is most of the battle . . .

MOTHER

And now that we *are* . . . ?

FATHER

If we *are,* then we are ready to branch out.

MOTHER

Oh, Father . . .

FATHER

. . . As to what this is . . . (*Points to* SON)

MOTHER

Unavoidably . . .

FATHER

Exactly what?

MOTHER

That which was become of us in our coitus.

FATHER

Which was . . . besides the huffing and puffing . . . ?

MOTHER

So to speak . . .

FATHER

So to speak what?

MOTHER

It is something that has been with us.

FATHER

Why is it with us?

MOTHER

Oh, because it is there on the floor in our kitchen, where it has lain for thirty or forty years . . . because I'm so sick of it and you and this kitchen.

FATHER

Was it the son we had not loved?

MOTHER

It was something.

FATHER

Was it the son?

MOTHER

Do I know? It was someone who often came as a baby.

FATHER

A baby?

MOTHER

You know, something that cries through the noise of the birds at sunset.

FATHER

At sunset?

MOTHER

Yes, yes, the closing of the day.

FATHER

And it cries . . . ?

MOTHER

The baby!

FATHER

Why?

MOTHER

Out of pity for itself, that it should stir again . . .

FATHER

What stirs . . . ?

MOTHER

Life out of the safety of un-being.

FATHER

And so it cries . . .

MOTHER

Because its comfort is lost forever.

FATHER

Who is this baby?

MOTHER

It's the one I was talking about; our son!

FATHER

And all this talk is about him?

MOTHER

Do you not remember how he came out of my body?

FATHER

You mean this man who hangs around here came out of your body?

MOTHER

Of course, don't you remember?

FATHER

I only remember you going into a big building and then coming out of it with a miniature person who kept yelling.

MOTHER

That person is your son.

FATHER

I don't like it. Something is very wrong with this whole business. You'd better go back to the big building.

MOTHER

There is nothing to be done for it now.

FATHER

Then we are in trouble.

MOTHER

Why?

FATHER

Because it is the son we do not love.

MOTHER

There is also you.

FATHER

And you. (*He sticks his tongue out at her*)

(*They collapse to the floor*)

Part I, Scene Four

(MOTHER *and* FATHER *wake up moaning.* SON *also awakens with his mouth formed to scream an unscreamed scream*)

MOTHER

(*to her husband*)

Who are you?

FATHER

I am whoever I was. By the way, Miss, who are you?

MOTHER

That's hardly your affair.

FATHER

Wait a minute, you're the greengrocer's wife, and you've been having an affair with me.

MOTHER

I've never seen you before in my life . . . unless you're my husband . . . ?

FATHER

I'm not married to an old lady; I would have married my mother if it came to that.

MOTHER

You old fool, you are my husband; and that thing over there is our son.

FATHER

I am not.

MOTHER

No, no, that thing with its mouth open is the son.

FATHER

Then you must be the daddy . . .

MOTHER

No, you are the daddy . . . I mean the *father*. It's your fault.

FATHER

I had been reclining on the floor so as to look up the legs of a chair, when you came in; and thinking I was a rug stood on me. Yes, you thought, what a luxurious rug, as you dug your shoes into me. As you perched on my face one of my eyes only partly covered by your instep happened to see how the woman is different from the chair . . . the rose in scent, the glands most liquid . . .

MOTHER

Enough! You are like some old woman's dress that blew off a clothes line through my window. You kept insisting: "Let me show you how I am a man." I said, damn you, whatever you are, let me sleep. Although you kept reminding me of an old woman's dress. You were like something belonging to Mother . . .

FATHER

Who am I? Am I you talking to myself? Why am I on the floor? Did I fall from someplace? What situation is this? . . . I'm getting out of here!

MOTHER

Sure, go down to the grocer's . . . But your son . . .

FATHER

My son?

MOTHER

Your son . . .

FATHER

But I'm a child myself, I cannot father another child.

MOTHER

Down to the grocer and up his ass!

FATHER

But I'm a child myself.

MOTHER

You're a terrible old rag that needs a woman to give it shape.

FATHER

How dare you say that I require female company!

MOTHER

Come and do love with me. (*Holds out arms*)

FATHER

My mother would blush.

MOTHER

Your mother's cheeks are worms' shit.

FATHER

Besides which, once is enough.

MOTHER

Once what?

FATHER

You do not expect me to father this thing again? (*pointing to* SON)

MOTHER

No, no, this time for love . . .

FATHER
(*to himself*)
It's just that I'm having dirty thoughts . . . At the greengrocer's one can think . . . Ah, there's a place . . .

MOTHER

For what?

FATHER

It is more the journey . . .

MOTHER

The anticipation?

FATHER

It is something or other; but mainly leaving here.

MOTHER

The woman with the mustache?

FATHER

Yes, yes, damn you, the woman with the mustache.

MOTHER

Who is really a man.

FATHER

If it turns out that way . . .

MOTHER

Which it always does.

FATHER

Is it my fault if in the dark I discover it?

MOTHER

Why do you stay after discovering it?

FATHER

Because then I know it is nature that made the mistake. And when I am quite sure that it is not my error, I am free to pretend that I am the victim of mistaken identity.

MOTHER

But it never happens, does it, Father?

FATHER

No, I see to it that it doesn't happen; it would be too shameful . . .

MOTHER

(*points to* SON)

Him.

FATHER

Don't start with that now. I'm on my way to the greengrocer's, and I don't want anything to do with that; that's a decision I'm not ready to make.

MOTHER

But supposing it doesn't love us anymore?

FATHER

Supposing it never did . . .

MOTHER

Get out of here, you have made me unhappy.

FATHER

(*Sticks tongue out at her. Steps out of door and collapses*)

SON

(*Moans*)

MOTHER

The voice of God . . . ?

SON

Mother . . . ?

MOTHER

To become incarnate again?

SON
(*screams*)

Mother!

MOTHER

Yes, yes, I can't say no.

SON

I'm hungry.

MOTHER

Anything, my God.

SON
(*screams*)

I'm hungry!

MOTHER

Come to me; or show Yourself that I might come to You.

SON

Where are you?

MOTHER

Has God become blind in His old age?

SON
(*screams*)

Mother, Mother, Mother!

MOTHER

Please, You frighten me; show me how I might serve You.

SON

Do you still love me?

MOTHER

You . . . (*to her* SON)

SON

Do you love me?

MOTHER

I do not love.

SON

Please love me.

MOTHER

How can I love you?

SON

Feed me.

MOTHER

I do not like to feed you.

SON

Feed me!

MOTHER

Lick the dirt from the floor.

SON

Feed me!

MOTHER

I'll kill you!

SON

Why?

MOTHER

Because you interrupt me.

SON

From what?

MOTHER

Myself.

SON

What are you doing that you cannot feed me?

MOTHER

I'm trying not to think of anything.

SON

But I'm hungry.

MOTHER

Go to the cupboard. Die. Stop interrupting me.

SON

I need you.

MOTHER

For what?

SON

To feed me.

MOTHER

Why?

SON

Because I need you to love me.

MOTHER

I do not love you. I will not feed you.

(SON *collapses*)

PART II

(FATHER *and* MOTHER *and the* SON *all collapsed on floor*)

SON

Coming awake . . . coming awake . . . awake . . . When I snap my fingers you will be awake. You will remember nothing. (*He snaps fingers*) (*He turns a finger to his face*) Who are you? (*Goes over to* MOTHER, *lifts apron, looks under*): Nope. (*Pulls apron over* MOTHER'S *face.* MOTHER *convulses*) (*He goes to table and raps on it with knuckles*): I hear my twin sister at the door. (*Goes to door, steps out, then enters back again wearing an obviously phony blond wig*): Hello Mom and Dad; I've been in the world. I've just come off the street. (*Looks at collapsed parents on floor*) I was passing by like anyone passing by. I could have been anyone passing by. But suddenly I was your daughter. In the world I was a woman who ran a school to teach airplanes to be tender. (*He runs to the door and puts his head out and shouts*): I'm hungry, feed me. (*Returns*) A school to teach airplanes to be tender after having lost my mind while dressing one day. Thinking it was a cuff button that had rolled under the dresser. But no, it was my mind, because I had become quite insane. An airplane flying by winked at me; that's nice, I said. But I couldn't think anymore; I would have to remember how I used to do things . . . (*Takes wig off and says*): I'm hungry! (*Puts wig back on*): . . . How I used to do things. I used to fall down stairs because it saved me the effort of walking down. (*Takes wig off*) Please! (*Puts wig on*) Once fallen I used to stay there unconscious for several hours, which saved me the effort of having to climb back up to my bedroom to sleep. (*Takes wig off*) Hungry! (*Puts wig on*) I would stand in the yard and teach airplanes to be tender. As they would fly over I would scream to them: BE TENDER! And they would fly away and be tender wherever they went. (*Takes wig off*) But I must eat! (*Puts wig on*) When dinner-time came I would go into the kitchen to see if the kitchen had cooked anything. But the kitchen is always too busy entertaining flies. I was able to solve all my problems by setting fire to the house. I was able to find cooked things; such as a feather pillow, which I decided could be a chicken, if *you* shut your eyes . . . (*Takes wig off*) No more, dear sister, I'm hungry . . . (*Puts wig on*) Through my enterprise I was able to save myself the effort of cleaning house, which was a dirty house, a dirty rotten filthy house; which made no effort to keep its hair combed. I asked it once, will you please serve me my breakfast in bed? Will you please run my bath . . . ? No! You see the walls just stood around like hoodlums in their corners. (*Takes wig off*) This story's too long, it never stops . . . (*Puts wig on*) From disorder into greater confusion . . . that I was forced finally to scream from a window. Which, I admit was not unpleasant; and which grew into somewhat of a side occupation, perhaps a hobby; and became, I must admit, after a time more important than airplanes . . . Surely I would spread tenderness, but screaming was perhaps the better way . . . I needed only a window and a mouth. I had a window, and so I felt around my face for a mouth. Yes yes, I have a mouth, I screamed—yes, my mouth is screaming! But then I saw a vase, and its mouth was open too. Could it be screaming? If it is, I thought, I shall be very envious, which is very negative. I said to the vase, If you are screaming please do not scream. But the vase continued to scream and I became very envious; until I smashed it. (*Takes wig off*) (*Sobs*): It's too long . . . (*Puts wig on*) But the screaming continued, and I noticed that the door was open: Please door, do not scream because I am becoming very envious. But the door continued to scream. I thought, must I clear the whole world of screaming things before I can scream? And now the toilet bowl began to scream. It was a time of much screaming. (*Takes wig off*) (*Screams*) (*Puts wig on*) I will be forced to fall out of the window because I have not learned to fly. I said to myself, You must fall out of the window because you don't know how to fly. And so I said, Very well then (*throws wig into air, and falls to floor*) and fell out of the window. (*Puts wig on again*) As I was falling an airplane passed, and in my fall I screamed, BE TENDER! (*Takes wig off*) Be tender! (*Puts wig on*) When I came awake after that interesting experience I was stone deaf; I could hear no more screaming. I saw a stone and said hello to it . . . (*Takes wig off*) No no, it has no ears. (*Puts wig on*) And I noticed that it didn't have any eyes. So now I asked the stairs to carry me to my room in their banister arms. But they refused. So I dragged myself up by the hair of somebody's head. (*Takes wig off*) Mother, I'm hungry! (*Sobs*) (*Puts wig on*) Then, while dressing, my mind rolled under the dresser. At first I thought it was a cuff button; but no, because I noticed I had become quite insane . . . that it was my mind that I had lost . . . And now an airplane winks at me, which is a good start toward the way I have not yet determined . . . something . . . yet, toward what thing? . . . My cuff button begins to think . . . (*Takes wig off*) Go away, you keep talking while I hunger. (*Puts wig on*) I'm Father's favorite. (*Sticks tongue out*) (*Takes wig off*) (*Makes a face*) (*Puts wig on*) (*Makes a face*) (*Takes wig off*) (*Makes a face*) (*Puts wig on*) (*Makes a face*) (*Takes wig off*) (*Makes a face*) (*Puts wig on*) (*Makes a hideous face*) (*Starts to punch self on shoulders and chest*) You get out of here, get out, get out! (*Pushes and beats self out of the door*) (*Enters again, minus wig. Looks at audience with great sadness*): Mother, I'm hungry . . .

(*Collapses*)

PART III

(*All are lying on the floor in collapsed state. The* FATHER *is wearing the blond wig. The* MOTHER *is wearing a mustache. The* SON *is wearing his mother's apron*)

(MOTHER *convulses,* FATHER *moans*)

FATHER

Oh, God . . . Because comfort is lost forever . . .

MOTHER

What stirs . . . ?

FATHER

It is lost forever . . .

MOTHER

AM I loved . . . ?

FATHER

Was anything ever loved?

MOTHER

(*Sits up suddenly. To her husband*)

Who are you?

FATHER

I am whoever I was, whoever that is. By the way, Miss, who are you?

MOTHER

That's hardly your affair.

FATHER

You could be the greengrocer.

MOTHER

You could be somebody's daughter.

FATHER

Perhaps I'm the father of a daughter.

MOTHER

You look more like the daughter.

FATHER

Wait a minute (*points to* SON *on floor*), there's my wife.

MOTHER

You look more like her daughter.

FATHER

Oh yeah, you look like a hermaphrodite.

MOTHER

Are you the greengrocer's wife who's been having an affair with me?

FATHER

I've never seen you before in my life . . . unless you're my husband?

MOTHER

I'm not married to an old lady; I would have married Mother if it came to that.

FATHER

Somebody better be somebody!

(*The* SON *sits up with mouth formed to scream. Pulls up apron, looks under it, and screams. Falls back pulling apron over face*)

MOTHER

I think my wife is going to have a baby!

FATHER

Help, help, not that again!

MOTHER

A son?

FATHER

Something else . . .

MOTHER

Thirty or forty years old, exhibit A . . . ?

FATHER

Who criminally assaults my view . . . ?

MOTHER

For that he is easily is loved . . .

FATHER

The journey!

MOTHER

The anticipation?

FATHER

It is something or other, but it's mainly leaving here.

MOTHER

(*Holds arms out to him*)

The woman with the mustache . . . ?

FATHER

(*Falls into her arms*)

Yes, yes, damn you, the woman with a mustache . . . (*He sobs*) Did we ever love anything?

MOTHER

We did love something once in a while, didn't we, Father?

FATHER

Earlier there was the lovely feeling that we would soon love something.

MOTHER

But something had to love us first, didn't it, Father?

FATHER

A dog licked my hand once . . .

MOTHER

That is a lovely dog, and I love that dog.

FATHER

Why do you love a dog and not your husband?

MOTHER

That is a lovely dog, and its tail wags . . .

FATHER

I was forced to beat the dog because I knew it was just a matter of time before he fastened his jaws to my throat.

MOTHER

Did you hurt the nice dog, Father?

FATHER

The dog had secret plans to open my throat; either out of curiosity or hunger—or perhaps just out of parental cruelty.

MOTHER

Did you hurt the nice dog, Father?

FATHER

And I do not like people who like animals instead of people.

MOTHER

But that was a nice dog, Father; that was a good friend.

FATHER

It was an enemy disguised as a friendly dog. But soon he was yelping and running from me. And I was able that very night to tell Mother and Father that I hated them. Uncle George said, that is not nice. I said, Uncle George, keep out of this.

MOTHER

Did you ever see that nice dog again?

FATHER

Yes. The next time I saw it it growled and chased me home.

MOTHER

You didn't hurt it again?

FATHER

No, no; it chased me home. And when I got home I said to Mother and Father, I love you. Uncle George said, That's the way I like to hear my nephew talk. And I said, Uncle George, will you please keep out of this.

MOTHER

So what did the dog do?

FATHER

Will you stop annoying me about that dog? It lifted its leg and pissed.

MOTHER

And then what happened?

FATHER

It met another dog and mated with it; but, discovering that its partner was male, blushed.

MOTHER

Oh, Father, you mean he was queer?

FATHER

No; I said he blushed. He made a mistake. He was really queer for my throat.

MOTHER

Did we ever love anything?

FATHER

It is this, Mother, everyone wishes they were loved, but no one will love anything.

MOTHER

But, Father, can't they pretend?

FATHER

It is too much bother.

MOTHER

What else is there to do?

FATHER

Well, why doesn't our son love us?

MOTHER

He's trying to get even with us for not loving him.

FATHER

He's spiteful that way.

MOTHER

I try to ignore him.

FATHER

He's trying to break our hearts, so he can say, Ha ha, fooled you, you love me, but I don't love you . . .

MOTHER

Why does he want to hurt us, Father?

FATHER

Why . . . ? Because he's no different than those that hurt him.

MOTHER

He's a copy-cat . . . and who hurt him anyway?

FATHER

He thinks we did.

MOTHER

What did we do to him?

FATHER

I think he wanted us to worship him, to cuddle him . . .

MOTHER

I wouldn't do that for my own child . . .

FATHER

But, Mother, he is your child.

MOTHER

So what? I just said I wouldn't do it for my own child.

FATHER

So he's out to ruin us by denying us the love he owes us.

MOTHER

What can we do to protect ourselves against this cruel denial?

FATHER

We must carry on as if we didn't care. I for one just pretend he's my mother; and I say to him, Mother, I don't love you either. He just looks at me. Did we ever teach him to talk?

MOTHER

I never taught him anything. I thought, If you can get yourself born you can teach yourself to talk. He may have picked it up from the radio.

FATHER

I just wonder sometimes if we shouldn't just kill him?

MOTHER

I would love to knock his head in. Did you ever notice how much he looks like my father?

FATHER

I would love to knock your father's head in.

MOTHER

I would love to knock everybody's head in. Oh, if I could only murder the world!

FATHER

Mother Mother, do not murder the world because I'm still in it.

MOTHER

Oh, Father, I wouldn't hurt the world; I'd just like to squeeze it a little.

FATHER

Your mind wanders . . .

MOTHER

My mind can go anywhere it wants.

FATHER

I do not like your mind, nor do I like your body.

MOTHER

Have I ever liked you?

FATHER

I'm not asking you to like me.

MOTHER

That's good, because I don't.

FATHER

That's what I mean about you . . .

MOTHER

Ho ho, you can't make me like you . . .

FATHER

See how you're way off the subject?

MOTHER

Well, damn you, what is the subject?

FATHER

Don't you remember?

MOTHER

Remember? Remember what? What have I known worth remembering?

FATHER

Mother, sometimes I would love to put the vital tubes of your neck between my fingers . . . and squeeze all the rottenness out of the world.

MOTHER

Ooh, I wish you'd try it . . .

FATHER

Damn you, damn you.

MOTHER

Oh, damn yourself! (*She sticks her tongue out*)

FATHER

(*Starts to cry*)

Don't you (*Sob*) remember . . . ?

MOTHER

Remember what? Father's day.

FATHER

No, no, no, no! (*On the floor kicking and sobbing*)

MOTHER

What, you fool?

FATHER

Our son!

MOTHER

Well, what about it?

FATHER

You just want me to say it.

MOTHER

Say what?

FATHER

That we're going to knock your father's head in. (*more tears*)

MOTHER

Well . . . ?

FATHER

No, no, no, that's not it! (*rage and tears*)

MOTHER

Well, what is it?

FATHER

That we're going to knock . . . your father's head in!

MOTHER

Well, knock his head in.

FATHER

No, no, I don't mean him!

MOTHER

Then who?

FATHER
(*Screams*)

Your father!

MOTHER

I'm growing out of patience with you!

FATHER

I'll kill God!

MOTHER

Then do it.

FATHER

I'll kill a homosexual dog!

MOTHER

Kill anything you damn well please!

FATHER

(*On floor screaming and kicking*)

I'll kill you, I'll kill you, and your son; I'll kill him, I'll kill him . . .

MOTHER

Kill him then.

FATHER

I'll kill him. (*looks at* SON)

MOTHER

Let me help.

FATHER

Help me.

MOTHER

I said I'd help.

FATHER

Then do it.

MOTHER

Do it? I said I'd help you . . .

FATHER

(*Approaches* SON *in old-fashioned, comic boxer's attitude*)

Stand up and fight like a man. (*Dances around collapsed* SON)

SON

(*Looks up, screams*)

Don't, don't, don't!

FATHER

Come on, I ain't afraid of you!

SON

(*Gets up shrinking, hands protecting face; screams*)

Don't, don't . . .

FATHER

(*Still dancing in comic boxer's attitude*)

Oh, think you're tough, huh? (*Dances around without landing a blow*) Come on, Mother, help me, he's tougher than I thought.

(SON *still shrinking, hiding face*)

(MOTHER, *in same comic stance as husband, dances around* SON)

(SON *cries with real sadness, begins to wet on himself*)

FATHER

He's pretty good.

MOTHER

S'got a nice left.

(SON *is sobbing very loudly*)

(*The* MOTHER *and* FATHER *begin to land blows on him. They start to beat him to the ground. The scene is no longer comic*)

SON

(*High scream*)

Don't, don't, don't . . .

(*Parents breathing with sexual intensity. When they finish the* SON *lies crumpled and bloodied, and doesn't move*)

MOTHER

Sonofabitch didn't want to die!

FATHER

Bastard!

MOTHER

I suppose we better call the police.

FATHER

(*Going to telephone*)

They're rather nice to talk to when you're lonely.

MOTHER

Oh, do hurry, I'm feeling real lonely since my baby died.

PART III, SECOND SCENE

(SON *wearing mustache walks from center and sits on edge of stage, seemingly talks to audience*)

SON

(*Holding hand mirror*)

Hello, pretty self. Eyes for myself alone. Makes traveling circular . . . stationary. I realize I need not have left. And not having left, I am neither surprised nor disappointed. Or, if I have left, it is still the same. What was I talking about? I have been buzzing, be assured of that. The human voice is only a series of buzzes. Soliloquy is no more than an idle fly buzzing in a kitchen. What he said . . . and then he died; his age passes over. What they said; but their age passes . . . And so I will talk some . . . Perhaps I will make a small scream that passers-by will take for a mosquito at song . . .

(*The door bursts open, and two policemen enter. They are the mother and father fully uniformed in blue. The* mother *policeman is wearing her apron over her uniform. The* father *policeman is wearing the blond female wig*)

MOTHER

Where's the parricide?

FATHER

What a terrible weapon.

MOTHER

All that blood.

FATHER

I say he's a brat.

MOTHER

A brat? Did you see what he did to his folks?

FATHER

What a cruel weapon.

(MOTHER *and* FATHER *lift* SON *from stage edge by his shoulders to unsteady standing position*)

MOTHER

(*To* SON)

Have you seen the parricide?

SON

The who-cide?

MOTHER

Do I know? It was someone who often came as a baby.

SON

A baby?

MOTHER

You know, something that cries through the noise of the birds at sunset.

SON

At sunset?

MOTHER

Yes yes, the closing of the day.

SON

It cries . . . ?

MOTHER

The parricide!

SON

Why?

MOTHER

Out of pity for itself; that it should stir again.

SON

What stirs?

MOTHER

The parricide!

SON

And who is the baby?

MOTHER

The parricide! the one I've been talking about.

SON

(*Begins to sob*)

I'm hungry.

FATHER

(*To* MOTHER)

The witness is hungry.

MOTHER

So is the parricide, let's be careful. (*To the* SON): You mean you're hungry . . . ?

SON

(*Sobbing, fist in eye*)

I'm hungry.

MOTHER

(*Takes out note book, writes*)

. . . First requirement of love . . .

FATHER

We're not here to have love.

MOTHER

(*She writes*)

. . . Not here for love . . . (*To her husband*) We were never here for love!

FATHER

But can't we pretend?

MOTHER

It is too much bother.

FATHER

But what else is there to do?

MOTHER

Come and do love with me then.

FATHER

Do I dare?

MOTHER

Of course, old boy; my old boy.

FATHER

You love me?

MOTHER

Please don't ask that. But do come to me, I do care for you some.

FATHER

May I kiss you?

MOTHER

You may kiss my badge.

FATHER

Oh, my darling! (*Kisses badge with passion*)

MOTHER

There there, old boy, love-starved old sweety . . .

FATHER

I've been so alone, so alone . . .

MOTHER

Poor old boy; my poor old boy . . .

(*Their embrace is loose, and he wanders out of it like a blind man, his arms out, until he comes to a chair, which he embraces*)

FATHER

(*To chair*) Oh, please let us be foul! (*begins to feel under seat of chair as he kisses the chair's back*) . . . Oh, you are more lovely . . . I adore you, you are my potency . . . (*He goes down on the floor with the chair*) . . . You are the most beautiful of women . . . (*He loses contact with the chair; rolls over like a blind man, his hands feeling out*) Oh God, I'm too unhappy to live; I'm alone! (*Wife begins to strike him with night stick. He screams*): Kisses!

MOTHER

The world is filled with pain . . .

FATHER

And cruel kisses . . .

MOTHER

It is too sad.

(*The* FATHER *on the floor finally finds wife's feet, he clings to them. The* SON, *who had all this while been whimpering, goes to and kneels before his* MOTHER)

MOTHER

Oh, ganging up, huh?

SON

(*He lifts his mother's apron and looks under it*) Where I came from is policeman pants; all comfort is lost; nor is there any food to console . . . (*He buries his face in the apron, weeping*)

(*The* FATHER *on the floor is crying into* MOTHER'S *feet*)

MOTHER

Compassion . . . ? Of course. Toward something else . . . ritual . . .

(FATHER *and* SON *loudly crying*)

MOTHER

Uplifting . . . ?

(FATHER *and* SON *loudly crying*)

MOTHER

(*To audience*)

Shall we dance?

(FATHER *and* SON *crying*)

(*Toilet flushes*)

CURTAIN

Poem-Plays

BY RUTH KRAUSS

Ruth Krauss, the author of *A Hole Is to Dig* and dozens of other very popular children's books, has written texts for the stage that possess on the one hand the clarity and simplicity of children's literature and, on the other, as great a sophistication as the theatre can perhaps aspire to. They strongly suggest that the essential aspect of theatre may not be dialogue, however fresh and unconventional; but rather a play's projection through extra-textual proliferations. The characteristic Krauss play usually consists of a few lines of dialogue and some slight suggestions as to accompanying action. She has invented the term "poem-play" to characterize her work; the pieces are in fact satisfying both when read as outright poetry (the form in which they have been widely published), and when presented in interpreted form on stage. Considering the gaiety pervading the plays, it may seem arch to mention the ideals of the much-misinterpreted "Theatre of Cruelty" here, yet Ruth Krauss' suggestion that text is only the beginning of theatre comes close to the ideal of only incidentally verbal drama espoused by Antonin Artaud. For Artaud, too—whose texts are brief as well as rare, and who considered himself a full-fledged theatrical author although his contributions were mainly in what would ordinarily be considered the area of the directorial—the essence of any play lay outside of its spoken elements. For their mounting as stage pieces, Ruth Krauss' plays require exceptionally close and insightful collaboration on the part of their directors. In Lawrence Sacharow and Remy Charlip, Ruth Krauss found exceptional, virtuosic, directorial collaborators. In their versions, the poem-plays are not only subject to considerable interpretation, but are also presented according to different organizational schemes. Most often they have been presented as individual playlets or as a linked series of events (in the latter form, most notably in Charlip's setting entitled *The Cantilever*

Rainbow, which is also the title of a recent Krauss book for children incorporating several of the poem-plays included here). On more than one occasion a single play has been presented several times in one evening, in successive yet varying versions. To give a better sense of directorial elaboration than the texts alone might provide, Charlip's notes on the multiple presentation of Ruth Krauss' first poem-play, *A Beautiful Day,* are also included here.

A Beautiful Day

GIRL

What a beautiful day!

(THE SUN *falls down onto the stage.*)

END

In a Bull's Eye

(1500 HORSES *rush by going east in profile.*)

(1500 HORSES *rush by going west in profile.*)

(1500 HORSES *rush by going east again in profile.*)

(GIRL *begins undressing.*)

(FIRE *breaks out.*)

(CROWD *rolls over a cliff.*)

MAN

It's very hot I'll leave my hat and jacket here*

(BATTLESHIP *sinks.*)

(BULL'S EYE *closes.*)

END

* Line from *An American Tragedy.*

Pineapple Play

NARRATOR

In a poem you make your point with pineapples.

(PINEAPPLES *fly onto stage from all directions.*)

SPY

And it would be nice to have a spy going in and out.

END

There's a Little Ambiguity Over There Among the Bluebells

ONE

What a poet wants is a lake in the middle
of his sentence

(A LAKE *appears*)

TWO

Yes and a valid pumpkin

(A PUMPKIN *appears*)

THREE

and you should slice up language like a
meatcutter abba dabba dabba dabba yack

(SLICED-UP-LANGUAGE *appears*)

FOUR

It's fine we have inhibitions
otherwise we'd all be dead

(*all drop dead*)

FIVE

or flat on our backs

SIX

yes and everyone on roller skates in bed
would be nice

(EVERYONE-ON-ROLLER-SKATES-IN-BED *appears*)

SEVEN

and a delayed verb

EIGHT

and an old upright piano

(AN OLD UPRIGHT PIANO *appears*)

(*all bow together to the audience and to each other*)

NINE

goes to the piano and begins to play

(*everyone dances*)

END

The 50,000 Dogwood Trees at Valley Forge

HEADLINE

The 50,000 dogwood trees at Valley Forge
are at the peak of their—

TREES

Bow! Wow! Wow!

HEADLINE

according to the Pennsylvania Department
of Forests and Waters.
Special details of State Police have been
assigned to—

POLICE

Bow! Wow! Wow!

HEADLINE

and to direct the—

AUTOMOBILES

Bow! Wow! Wow!

HEADLINE

automobiles—

TREES

Bow! Wow! Wow!
Bow! Wow! Wow!

POLICE

Bow! Wow! Wow!
Bow! Wow! Wow!

HEADLINE

Bow! Wow! Wow!
Bow! Wow! Wow!

ALL

Bow! Wow! Wow!
Wow! Wow! Wow!
Wow! Wow! Wow!
Wow! Wow! Wow!

END

Directorial Notes for "A Beautiful Day"

Four versions of *A Beautiful Day* were interspersed in *The Pocket Follies* on June 10, 1963 at the Pocket Theatre, New York City. It was produced and directed by Remy Charlip and performed by Viola Farber (GIRL) and Burton Supree (SUN). The following are Charlip's directorial notes of these four versions.

1

Stage black.

Lights dim up slowly as golden sun appears from hole in ceiling.

GIRL *asleep on stage, awakens, stretches, sits up, rubs eyes, looks at* SUN, *smiles and says, "What a beautiful day!"*

SUN (*tied to ashcan cover*) *crashes to the floor.*

Black-out.

2

Stage black.

Lights up, as fully inflated orange balloon is lowered from hole in ceiling.

GIRL *enters watching.*

When balloon is fully visible, GIRL *smiles and says, "What a beautiful day!"*

BOY *explodes balloon with pin.*

Black-out.

3

Stage black.

Lights up.

GIRL *seated on chair reading.*

Looks up to see and hear an empty orange balloon being blown up by BOY *through a hole in ceiling.*

GIRL *closes book to watch.*

When balloon is full, GIRL *smiles and says, "What a beautiful day!"*

BOY *releases balloon.*

GIRL*'s eyes follow in amazement as air empties out propelling balloon, zig-zag, all over stage to final sputter on floor.*

Black-out.

4

Stage black.

Lights dim up, as GIRL *grimly and cautiously pushes head through trap door.*

Lights suddenly up full and warm.

GIRL *smiles and says, "What a beautiful day!"*

Big orange ball thrown from hole in ceiling, hits GIRL *on head, knocking her back down as trap door closes.*

Black-out.

A fifth version of *A Beautiful Day* with Florence Tarlow (GIRL) and Charles Adams (SUN) was directed by Remy Charlip and presented at Judson Memorial Church in December 1965. This was added to the other four.

5

Stage brightly lit.

GIRL *enters covered in a dark blanket.*

Huge orange balloon floats down from above.

GIRL *throws off blanket and catches balloon as* BOY *climbs down and jumps onstage.*

GIRL *walks out with* BOY *and balloon staring in disbelief from one to the other.*

Before exit GIRL *shouts, "What a beautiful day!"*

Black-out.

What Happened
BY GERTRUDE STEIN

Plays are "the things anybody can see by looking," Gertrude Stein once wrote. She has also been quoted as having remarked about literature in general and the theatre in particular, "If it can be done, why do it?" When Gertrude Stein wrote this, her first play, she could hardly have expected—at least according to any theatrical ideal then current, even internationally—that it would ever be performed. Though blithely described by its imperturbable author as a "Five Act Play," *What Happened* bore very little resemblance to any previously seen theatrical text. Each act consists of a block of words printed prose-poem style—somewhat in the manner of Stein's first collection of poetry, *Tender Buttons,* which appeared shortly after the composition of *What Happened.* No indications as to the characters in the play appear anywhere. Each "act" seems unrelated to any other, except in terms of the barely definable, verbally energetic style common to all. "The idea in *What Happened* . . . was, without telling what happened, to make a play the essence of what happened," Gertrude Stein is said to have once remarked. Perhaps the aptest comment on what happens in this text, as well as in most of Stein's works, was made by reviewer E. E. Cummings, who wrote that "Gertrude Stein subordinates the meaning of words to the beauty of words themselves." The logic of this play is verbal: that is to say, imagistic, and even aural.

When the work was finally performed, a full half-century after its composition, it was produced according to the canons of a theatrical style that was still unusual in the context of the English-speaking stage. It was performed as a theatrical "pretext" or "theatre piece," but not necessarily as a play. Although when Stein wrote this work Antonin Artaud was still a young poet who had not yet turned to the theatre, it was of course Artaud who eventually eloquently argued the distinction between the textual side of theatre and what he called "total" theatre. In *The Theatre and its Double* he noted:

> To change the role of speech in theatre is to . . . combine it with everything in the theatre that is spatial and significant in the domain of the concrete;—to manipulate *it* like a solid object . . . It is in the light of magic and sorcery that the *mise en scène* must be regarded, not as the reflection of a written text, the mere projection of physical doubles to be derived from the written work, but as the burning projection of all the objective consequences of gesture, word, sound, music, and their combinations. This active projection can be made only upon the stage and its consequences found in the presence of and upon the stage; . . .

What Happened was premiered in 1963 at Judson Memorial Church in New York City with Lawrence Kornfeld as director, under the general aegis of Al Carmines, the assistant minister of the Church and also a theatrical man of remarkable talent and insight. Kornfeld and Carmines wove from the original a texture of "gesture, word, sound and music and their combinations," a *mise en scène* that included text but which presented it as of no greater value than any other quality of the total production. Carmines himself provided it with a musical setting; he himself played the piano on stage during a performance which involved three male singers and five female dancers—the latter drawn from the members of the dance group informally associated with the Judson Poets' Playhouse, the Judson Dance Theatre. Not only was there a conversation between music, singing, and dancing throughout the piece, but these roles were constantly interchanged. Dancers called out the text; the chorus began to dance, the pianist sang and spoke and sometimes danced as the other members of the company combined forces to move his piano around the stage, or attempted to perform while sitting on or even in this instrument. Thus even the piano was converted from one medium (musical instrument) to another (portable sculpture). The whole was converted into a theatrical conversation in which, appropriately enough, not individuals but whole arts took part.

The connections with the original that remained during these activities were as general and fresh as Artaud himself could have hoped. A certain maxim-like, sing-song quality in the original might be suggested by the child's-play-like actions of the dancers. The ceremonial and processional quality of the realized *mise en scène* seemed to correspond to hints in the original about slicings, archbishops, and birthdays. In so general an interpretation, such a setting becomes not *a* version but, especially if it works as this one did (Richard Gilman reviewed it as "a triumph of total theatre . . . the most hopeful event this increasingly desperate pilgrim of the theatrical apocalypse has witnessed in many a week, month, and even year"), *the* version—indeed, *the* play.

In such a radical a treatment of text, written or printed representation is rendered even more inadequate than such representation usually is. Included in this book, as well as the original Stein text, is a series of photos of the Judson production. Although highly selective, they are intended to be suggestive with respect to the wide variety of interpretations of the basic text possible in this style of setting.

What Happened
A FIVE ACT PLAY

ACT I

(*One.*)

Loud and no cataract. Not any nuisance is depressing.

(*Five.*)

A single sum four and five together and one, not any sun a clear signal and an exchange.

Silence is in blessing and chasing and coincidences being ripe. A simple melancholy clearly precious and on the surface and surrounded and mixed strangely. A vegetable window and clearly most clearly an exchange in parts and complete.

A tiger a rapt and surrounded overcoat securely arranged with spots old enough to be thought useful and witty quite witty in a secret and in a blinding flurry.

Length what is length when silence is so windowful. What is the use of a sore if there is no joint and no toady and no tag and not even an eraser. What is the commonest exchange between more laughing and most. Carelessness is carelessness and a cake well a cake is a powder, it is very likely to be powder, it is very likely to be much worse.

A shutter and only shutter and Christmas, quite Christmas, an only shutter and a target a whole color in every centre and shooting real shooting and what can hear, that can hear that which makes such an establishment provided with what is provisionary.

(*Two.*)

Urgent action is not in graciousness it is not in clocks it is not in water wheels. It is the same so essentially, it is a worry a real worry.

A silence a whole waste of a desert spoon, a whole waste of any little shaving, a whole waste altogether open.

(*Two.*)

Paralysis why is paralysis a syllable why is it not more lively.

A special sense a very special sense is ludicrous.

(*Three.*)

Suggesting a sage brush with a turkey and also something abominable is not the only pain there is in so much provoking. There is even more. To begin a lecture is a strange way of taking dirty apple blossoms and is there more use in water, certainly there is if there is going to be fishing, enough water would make desert and even prunes, it would make nothing throw any shade because after all is there not more practical humor in a series of photographs and also in a treacherous sculpture.

Any hurry any little hurry has so much subsistence, it has and choosing, it has.

ACT II

(*Three.*)

Four and nobody wounded, five and nobody flourishing, six and nobody talkative, eight and nobody sensible.

One and a left hand lift that is so heavy that there is no way of pronouncing perfectly.

A point of accuracy, a point of a strange stove, a point that is so sober that the reason left is all the chance of swelling.

(*The same three.*)

A wide oak a wide enough oak, a very wide cake, a lightning cooky, a single wide open and exchanged box filled with the same little sac that shines.

The best the only better and more left-footed stranger.

The very kindness there is in all lemons oranges apples pears and potatoes.

(*The same three.*)

A same frame a sadder portal, a singular gate and a bracketed mischance.

A rich market where there is no memory of more moon than there is everywhere and yet where strangely there is apparel and a whole set.

A connection, a clam cup connection, a survey, a ticket and a return to laying over.

ACT III

(*Two.*)

A cut, a cut is not a slice, what is the occasion for representing a cut and a slice. What is the occasion for all that.

A cut is a slice, a cut is the same slice. The reason that a cut is a slice is that if there is no hurry any time is just as useful.

(*Four.*)

A cut and a slice is there any question when a cut and a slice are just the same.

A cut and a slice has no particular exchange it has such a strange exception to all that which is different.

A cut and only slice, only a cut and only a slice, the remains of a taste may remain and tasting is accurate.

A cut and an occasion, a slice and a substitute a single hurry and a circumstance that shows that, all this is so reasonable when every thing is clear.

(*One.*)

All alone with the best reception, all alone with more than the best reception, all alone with a paragraph and something that is worth something, worth almost anything, worth the best example there is of a little occasional archbishop. This which is so clean is precious little when there is no bath water. A long time a very long time there is no use in an obstacle that is original and has a source.

ACT IV

(*Four and four more.*)

A birthday, what is a birthday, a birthday is a speech, it is a second time when there is tobacco, it is only one time when there is poison. It is more than one time when the occasion which shows an occasional sharp separation is unanimous.

A blanket, what is a blanket, a blanket is so speedy that heat much heat is hotter and cooler, very much cooler almost more nearly cooler than at any other time often.

A blame what is a blame, a blame is what arises and cautions each one to be calm and an ocean and a masterpiece.

A clever saucer, what is a clever saucer, a clever saucer is very likely practiced and even has toes, it has tiny things to shake and really if it were not for a delicate blue color would there be any reason for every one to differ.

The objection and the perfect central table, the sorrow in borrowing and the hurry in a nervous feeling, the question is it really a plague, is it really an oleander, is it really saffron in color, the surmountable appetite which shows inclination to be warmer, the safety in a match and the safety in a little piece of splinter, the real reason why cocoa is cheaper, the same use for bread as for any breathing that is softer, the lecture and the surrounding large white soft unequal and spread out sale of more and still less is no better, all this makes one regard in a season, one hat in a curtain that in rising higher, one landing and many many more, and many more many more many many more.

ACT V

(*Two.*)

A regret a single regret makes a door way. What is a door way, a door way is a photograph.

What is a photograph a photograph is a sight and a sight is always a sight of something. Very likely there is a photograph that gives color if there is then there is that color that does not change any more than it did when there was much more use for photography.

Flower

BY ROBERT WHITMAN

The Happening has been described in a variety of more or less relevant ways. It seems appropriate to present it here as an extreme development of theatre. The Happening could be defined as a genre of anti-realistic drama in which non-textual elaborations entirely occupy the key place ordinarily given to words.

Like all the more explorative plays and theatre pieces presented in this collection, the Happening's deepest roots are in the visual media. Allan Kaprow, the former painter, sculptor and Rutgers Art History instructor who in 1959 appears to have both named and invented the form with his *18 Happenings in Six Parts,* has traced the Happening to ". . . Futurist manifestoes and noise concerns, Dada's chance experiments and occasional cabaret performances, Surrealism's interest in automatic drawing and poetry, and the extension of these into Action Painting . . ." While emphasizing the contributions of such disparate contemporary artistic phenomena as modern dance (particularly the Merce Cunningham troupe), costume design and lighting (particularly that of the assemblagist Robert Rauschenberg, who once worked with the Cunningham company), and music (particularly that of John Cage, with whom Kaprow briefly studied), Kaprow notes that for both himself and his fellow Happening authors, "our prime sources were visual, whatever non-visual outcome these led to." Indeed, as Kaprow also points out, most of the initial explorers of the Happening form were painters or sculptors.

Thus, though the Happening has much in common with such plays as those already presented in this volume, it has a distinctness: whereas we have been observing a genre of theatre become, in part, more visual, the Happening is a visual form become theatrical, converging with developments from within the theatre itself.

Although the Happening begins with Kaprow (notwithstanding the fact that Kaprow himself has documented both a European ancestry and analogies in his study ***Assemblages, Environments and Happenings***), it seems appropriate that the first example here should be by another leading Happening producer, Robert Whitman, a former student of Kaprow's. Whitman's Happenings are closer than many such events to recent concepts of experimental theatre, rather than those of experimental sculpture or painting. His events involve several basic and specifically theatrical departures from the standard Happening style as its originator has defined it. Whitman even likes to avoid the term Happening, characterizing his events as "Theatre Pieces" (a term which, of course, we have usurped to describe the presentation on stage of material, such as Stein's, that seems unplayable in conventional theatrical terms). Kaprow has listed a series of useful rules of thumb for the Happening genre, at least as he practices it; these rules begin:

(A) The line between art and life should be kept fluid, and perhaps indistinct as possible;
(B) Therefore, the source of themes, materials, actions and the relationships between them are to be derived from any place or period *except* from the arts, their derivatives, and their milieu.
(C) The performance of a happening should take place over several widely spaced, sometimes moving and changing locales;
(D) Time, which follows closely on space considerations, should be variable, and discontinuous.
(E) Happenings should be performed once only.
(F) It follows that audiences should be eliminated entirely.

Most of these rules of thumb relate to a particular guiding principle: that the line between actors and audience, art and life, be kept indistinct. In Whitman's Happenings actors and audience remain distinct to the end. Moreover, Whitman often evokes quite directly the trappings of an artistic milieu. His audiences are usually settled in a standard theatre setting. The pieces often include hints of an area-environment, footlights, sometimes even a stage or multiplicity of stages. He tends to use the same actors from work to work, suggesting the lineaments of a theatrical troupe. Kaprow's final rule (G) provides that "The composition of a Happening proceeds exactly as in Assemblage and Environments, that is, it is evolved as a collage of events in certain spans of time and in certain spaces." The kind of plotless, non-sequential structure which Kaprow recommends and practices, and which some critics have aptly characterized as "non-informational," seldom appears in Whitman's works, which conduce to a relatively specific end. Finally, Whitman seems to design his Happenings to encourage the possibility of repetition, of the re-evocation of his pieces as distinct works of art. *Flower,* for example, had the longest run of any Happening up to its time—a record later broken by Whitman himself, who has tended increasingly to elaborate his works through the introduction of film, light, and other mixed-media phenomena—qualities which, as the reader will see, underlie *Flower* as well.

Since it is part of Whitman's intention that his Happenings be repeated, he has created a script in retrospect for this collection. Included with it, in addition to photographs of the original production, is a description of *Flower*'s original performance, emphasizing some of its theatrical and "informational," plot qualities. The review, by this editor, appeared in the *Village Voice* during the piece's original and successful run.

Flower

Part One

The audience is in rows outside a space about twenty feet square. There is space around the outside of the audience and some holes for coming and going.

The lights go out. A man walks around the outside of the people. A noise is heard and a flash from a camera flashgun illuminates a cascade of aluminum foil in mid-fall. The foil stays hanging from ten or twelve feet down to the floor. The cameraman lights a flashlight which he aims at the foil and leaves that way for the rest of the part. He sets off a flashbulb during each of the following occurrences:

A balloon about two feet in diameter floats up about fifteen feet, where it stays.

A short, anonymous noise, not loud.

A thin stream of water starts to fall from ten feet high. It goes on through the part.

A person is brought into view by the cameraman.

Nothing.

A loaded burlap sack, appears in full view of the audience.

Also a large filmy plastic cloud.

A chair shoots up and bounces up and down from a big piece of elastic tubing.

These things are loosely arranged around the outside of the space outside the audience.

A light shines on the sack. A thin green vine is upraised from it. The top stops fifteen feet up; and the part of the vine at the mouth of the sack begins to rise separately, pulling more vine up until it too is at fifteen feet; then the end of the vine now at the mouth of the sack is brought up to the same height. The three points of the vine at the top are close together. This is all done very slowly.

Five slides of woods and landscapes are projected on a screen for about ten seconds each. After these there are pictures of a face, mouth, eye, ear, nose, which are run off a few times, mixed, and interchanged with one another. Each is on for from ten to thirty seconds at a time. When the face slides start a movie also begins. This is on a different screen within the same field of vision. It's of the same subjects, only with a bluish cast, a ghost movie of the slides. The slides are in no particular order and any imagistic or durational relationship between the images on the slides and the movie is coincidental. A minute after the bluish ghost movie starts a second movie in black and white begins on a third screen. This is separated from the others so they can't all be seen at the same time. This second movie continues through part one. It begins with a woman in bed. She is moving around under the covers. This movement becomes more and more restless as the piece goes on. She has a lot of clothes on. As the movement becomes more nervous the covers are thrown off, there is jumping on the bed, throwing clothes off into a pile, and so on. There are always many clothes on the woman. After a few minutes the ghost movie ends. It and the slides are shut off at the same time.

Two people run out, a man and a woman. They are pulling and tearing off each other's clothes. They both have on ten or so layers of coat, jacket, sweater, and shirts. This action is done in the most direct way. It is very physical and the people are all over the place. When one of them is down to the last layers, the movement is carried off, out of sight.

The man who was brought out in the beginning by the flashlight man leaves. He returns rolling a young woman in a ball costume. Only her head and the bottom part of her legs are visible sticking out from the ball. She is set upright, and the man goes to another place and rolls in another Ball Girl. One girl is in blue and the other in white. Once the two girls are upright in the center of the space, the man begins to drape them with bits of cloth which he finds around the place. Some pieces of cloth have parts of the body drawn loosely on them: arms, hands, etc. They fall over the girls so that they are roughly in place. When the man is finished, he leaves the girls and goes off. When he is gone, each girl begins to hop gently, each hop a few seconds apart. They head irregularly off stage. The man returns and leads them back to the center of the place. Slowly he removes the cloth and stuff that he had draped them with. As he does this he becomes more active and nervous. Finally he's taken off all the cloth. He continues and tears open the balls. They are stuffed with soft white paper, like newspaper. The paper is torn out and the action becomes more frenzied. When he is about one-third through the job of emptying out the costume, six or eight other people come running in and take the paper that is flying around and attach it to anything in sight as quickly as possible. The place is covered with white paper. In the movie the person in bed has thrown all the stuff out of the bed into a pile beside the bed. She throws herself out. Then she throws everything back onto the bed. The last part of the movie is in color. When the movie ends, the camera-flashlight man comes back and turns off the flashlight.

Part Two

A giant sugar cube slowly absorbs coffee. When the coffee reaches the top, three flowers pop out of the top of the sugar cube.

Light comes on in the center of the area and four girls enter, one at a time. They all walk slowly, deliberately, formally. They are dressed in white satin dresses. They spread out in the area, each girl walking in her own pattern. Each girl should try to cover all areas evenly. The only sound is the clicking of the heels of the high-heeled shoes as the girls move about. There are pauses and changes of direction. After about one minute the girls begin to change the colors of their costumes. The top of each dress unhooks to fall down and form a new skirt of a different color, and a different colored blouse is revealed. Each girl makes this change roughly at her own pace, that is, not necessarily together with or apart from any other girl. After white, every dress becomes a brilliant red. The red is kept for about forty-five seconds, then the dresses turn to blue. After another forty-five seconds, they turn to gold. These changes have been made in the same way as the first one. After these changes have been made, the girls go on to try still different ways that the dresses can be organized.

The girls find spray cans of paint and shake the cans, making a rattling noise. Then they paint stripes vertically on the walls behind the audience. The stripes are red, green, blue, and yellow. They are made at random along the walls. The smell of the paint fills the air. This goes on for one minute. At this point the girls stop, and four suspended walls descend to enclose the space around the outside of the audience. The walls on the sides are hinged in the middle and have been half unfolded, making a sort of canopy over the audience. They open to be flat then drop to the floor, four or five feet straight down. These walls release a bunch of vines that hang into the center of the space, and the girls untangle these fallen vines. The walls on the ends may be dropped, or pivoted from the ceiling and then dropped. They are soft white. Inside the new room the girls keep on walking. The lights change color: white to red to blue to yellow to violet. Each change is for about twenty seconds. Then darkness and silence for one minute. The girls have stopped. This silence is broken by a loud noise, the lights go on and the walls go up. The noise goes on until the walls are all up. The noise is like a loud, distant roaring.

As soon as it is possible to go under the rising walls, a man joins the girls. When he enters he brings in a large sack identical to two others that have been hanging up. He takes down the two that are hanging, and the girls begin to empty them with his help. They are full of different pieces of cloth. The man goes on to empty the sack that he dragged in after him. In among the rags of this sack is another girl, dressed ordinarily. At this point the sound of a dressing room of a large department store comes on. The girl is helped to her feet, and the others begin to cover her with the pieces of cloth. The sound comes up a little: squeaks of hangers being scraped along the steel racks, snatches of voices, muzak, etc. They cover the girl until she is a large cloth statue. Then they leave. A light goes on a big red flower. After about ten seconds it begins to open. It opens wide, slowly. It stretches to about nine feet in diameter. When it's all open there's a circular bunch of cloth that's the center of the flower. This begins to ooze and push out and drop on the floor. When the whole pile is on the floor two small flowers begin to rise up from it. They are different from each other and go about four and seven feet off the floor in short, jerky movements with many pauses.

There's another flower, this one a giant white one. A large, massive something descends to cover this flower. When it is still, a cloth of flowers falls down over it. All the lights come on and the girls return in the gold layer of the costumes. They are smiling, running, and throwing flowers to the audience. They run off when they are finished.

(From *The Village Voiçe,* April 4, 1963)

HAPPENING: FLOWER

In a loft at 9 Great Jones Street, the occupants of which have resolutely refused it an identifying name during the period of the theatrical activity there (and during the exhibitions of painting and sculpture shows there previously), Robert Whitman's happening "Flower" was played twenty times during the month of March. "Flower," a two-act piece by a man whose work in the plastic arts has appeared fairly regularly around town in past years, is, happily for its anchored audience, far more related to theatre than to painting or sculpture. To this reviewer, "Flower" is a remarkably successful work.

The material of which "Flower" is constructed is as disparate as its structure is superficially wayward. Any member of the audience searching for the usual relationships of character and plot in this structure will go away from Mr. Whitman's piece in a well-merited state of nervous exhaustion. The playgoer approaching this piece from the relatively enlightened point of view of one who knows his Theatre of the Absurd will be equally disappointed. For the plot of Mr. Whitman's play is expressed, and advances, entirely through the relations between forms and colors. As in a well-balanced painting every color and line is justified by the presence of other, corresponding colors and lines (a system in which the nature of the colors and lines actually balanced somewhat loses significance), so in Mr. Whitman's happening *bien faite,* all the parts, whatever they are, circulate in a system which is as perfect as it is hermetic.

ALLEGORY OF ART

"Flower" has a theme: as is appropriate for an author who is also a painter, is the difficult and generally ugly struggle of the flower to reach maturity and decorativeness. The structure, which starts with dark, ominous events and ends with intense displays of color, reflects this subject; in a sense, Mr. Whitman's play is an allegory of the construction of any work of art, in which beauty is extracted from the material of chaos. In Mr. Whitman's treatment, this stolid subject—far from seeming less significant than the "problems" of the conventionally "Serious" "drama"—comes to intense and curiously appealing life.

Toward the beginning of the play a series of green rags knotted together rises out of a brown burlap sack directly beneath a sun-like lightbulb in the ceiling. Immediately afterward we move into a series of flashbacks reflecting, with the boldest of obliqueness, the growing of the flower. These flashbacks are accompanied throughout by a device indicating the diverted time-stream: movies, in which nothing much happens, projected at either end of the theatre. Like a radio constantly playing background music in a house full of unpredictable children, these films can only occasionally be enjoyed; a tape, apparently made during a bargain day at a department store, briefly provides additional diversion during pauses in the action.

PITCHED BATTLE

In the first of the flashbacks, the underground, primitive struggle of the awakening seed is indicated by a pitched battle between a woman and a man in which, far from observing beauty's augmentation, we see several layers of decoration violently stripped away. Shortly after, two young ladies encased except for heads and legs in vast, stuffed sacks are rolled into view, only to rise and hop about like two huge, about-to-bloom flower bulbs. They are then officiously draped with old rags by an actor who soon, apparently recognizing the futility of his premature course, rips apart the costumes of both, out of which sprout masses of old newspaper (certainly a brave decision as to substance during the newspaper strike; however, the depth of planning which went into "Flower" was roughly defined by an ad for a Columbus Day Sale on one crumpled page). The four performers who then run out, pounce eagerly on the disappointingly colorless bulb-released newspapers, and begin attaching them with stapling machines to the walls are in Mr. Whitman's scheme of things probably expressing nothing more unreasonable than the all-too-human eagerness for attractive things, especially the all-too-human desire which Mr. Whitman as a painter must especially understand, the desire for attractive things on walls.

Even the intermission announcement is presented in this happening's inimitable style, in which traditionally inert material is abstracted in theatrically interesting ways: a chair, hooked up in a pulley-like arrangement, is jerked ten feet in the air by its suddenly dropped counterweight; a voice cordially suggests: "And now we'll have a little intermission while we get ready for the second part."

FOUR COLORS

The second act—or rather second panel of Mr. Whitman's diptych—continues the expression of the genial and ingeniously presented theme. Act II is as full of fulfillments as Act I was compounded of frustration, struggling, and coloristic restraint. Three flower-like discs pop out from in back of a kind of abstracted embankment to begin the act. Four girls dressed in white begin to walk about the theatre, and then (in perfect deadpan) slowly effect the rearrangement of their costumes, which by a design more than worthy of a sculptor (although Balmain might flinch) unfold so that they are dressed first entirely in white, then red, then blue, then yellow. After walking as if in trances for several minutes, shifting their colors, these four actresses begin spraying the walls from spray-on paint-cans. The colors are white, red, and blue (was yellow unavailable in this brand?). The walls now decorated, a battery of lights in the ceiling turns the entire theatre red, then blue, then white, then yellow. With a grinding noise, new, white walls are lowered into place; some dangling brown bags are ripped open and are discovered to be full of various colored rags. The girls begin picking at these rags, as if at remnants in a department store sale; the tape of the department store sale day is played once more, this time with obvious justification. A girl in plain clothes who emerges from the heap of rags is gradually covered with the rags by the four costumed lady decorators, finally suggesting an enormous, intensely colored beanstalk. It is clearly the play's climax. An enormous mechanical flower at one end of the theatre comes to clumsy life; its yard-long petals open wide, and from the corolla another mass of colored rags is unceremoniously dumped. Thus the theatre has been decorated, the girls have been costumed, and the flower has come to light. The lights go out, and when they come on again, the four girls, smiling delightedly as befits flower-girls recently reclaimed for reality from a state of pure abstraction, walk through the theatre, throwing real daffodils into the laps of the audience.

TOTAL AUTHOR

Earlier happenings by Mr. Whitman, among them "Mouth," "Small Cannon," and "An Interior," have been presented, as have his painting and sculpture, at several galleries, among them the Green, the Reuben, and the Martha Jackson. The costumes and settings for "Flower" are, of course, entirely by Mr. Whitman—in this variety of drama the designer and the costumer are necessarily one with the author. It should be added that the entire cast of "Flower" is as devotedly at one with the author's intention as any playwright of any school could wish.

It is very seldom in any of the arts that an entirely new genre appears, but here the happening takes on a dimension which it seems must eventually prove as formidable to classifiers as it is, in Mr. Whitman's hands, delightful, lyrical, and thoroughly entertaining.

Meat Joy

BY CAROLEE SCHNEEMANN

Some of the impetus of the Happening, as Kaprow has noted, is derived from the style of avant-garde painting that was dominant in America during the 1950s; Abstract Expressionism or, as it is sometimes called, Action Painting. "I was concerned with the implication that Action Painting—Pollock's in particular—leads not to more painting, but to more action," Kaprow once wrote.

Meat Joy is a striking example of the way one author of Happenings—a painter and sculptor who once worked very much in the Abstract Expressionist vein—improvised the form almost entirely within the framework of Action Painting. It deserves to be termed a classic example of the Happening—if only because, when the average interested individual considers the Happening, he is apt to characterize it in the sensual terms of this particular piece, which was performed in New York and Paris, and which has ample "underground" fame. Its basic idea is also one of Abstract Expressionism's: that, in the context of a sufficiently active and gestural painting style, virtually any subject can serve to fill an essential abstract gesture or painting stroke with the necessary element of content. Schneemann's contribution to both a later phase of Abstract Expressionism and the Happening was to fulfill these gestures with an element that has seldom been treated as anything *but* abstract in both painting and theatre: the human form.

Like *Flower, Meat Joy* operates in a fundamentally plotted, "informational" way. It is structured around a progressive reduction or stripping-down of the flesh; but it is a stripping-down in largely conceptual terms—although elements of the actual and visual are obviously involved. The painting of the bodies that follows the actual undressing represents a step beyond mere stripping-down through removal of clothing; it is an ultimate reduction of the flesh to the status of any ordinary object. Thus, its climactic section, in which butchershop debris is flung amid the dancers, is simply a logical continuation of this reduction, to the point where animal flesh and human flesh are equated.

The serving-maid who effects this flesh mixture, in her formal black-and-white garb, might be considered a kind of priestess. Indeed, as its title suggests, *Meat Joy* is intended as a celebration of the flesh or, as its creator notes, as a kind of exorcism against the evil of "non-sensuousness—both in the theatre and out." Although the source of Schneemann's theatrical inspiration is Action Painting, its result is close to rite.

Meat Joy

Notes

Meat Joy began to evolve from dream sensation images in journals stretching as far back as early 1960; by February of 1964 they constituted a more elaborated series of drawings and notes. I was becoming increasingly aware of the possibility of capturing certain interactions between physical, metabolic changes and their effect on dream content, as well as on my sensory orientation upon and after waking; in capturing their releasing of random memory fragments (as well-defined sound, light, weather, and environment kernels from the past) in the immediate present.

At this time I made a photographic study called *Eye Body.* It involved the use of my body as source of collage transformations—its juxtaposition/extension to constructions, kinetic light boxes and the constructed environment I had been making in my studio generally; ambiguities both spatial and tactile; change of flesh forms by paint, grease, water, oil, powder, crayon, transparent plastic, combined with forms of the glass, wood, motors which I had been using in my work. The intention of *Meat Joy,* like all these images, was the visual transformation of the naked body-as-environment.

Then I received an invitation from Jean-Jacques Lebel to make a Happening for his first "Festival of Free Expression" in Paris, to occur in May. There was no financial possibility then of managing the trip, but the images which were to become *Meat Joy* increased with the provocation of the unknown, highly charged city—Paris:

In February of 1964 I wrote to Lebel:

> There are now several works moving in minds-eye towards the possibility of an extreme time/space change (that is, being in Europe), tentatively identified as *Meat Joy,* and

> *Divisions and Rubble;* . . . *Meat Joy* shifting now; relating to Artaud, McClure, and French Butcher Shops—carcass as paint (it dripped right through Soutine's floor) . . . flesh jubilation . . . extremes of this sense . . . it may involve quantities of dark fabric and paint drawn from performance area outward into audience to become inundation of all available space—action and viewing space interchanged, broken through. Smell, feel of meat . . . chickens, fish, sausages? I see several girls whose gestures develop from tactile, bodily relationship to individual men and a mass of meat slices. Specific sequence of collision and embrace . . . rising, falling counterpoints to bodies . . . very dark (very bright). Hand held lights spotting color cover movements.
>
> My Visual Dramas (Kinetic Theater . . . Concretions) can take substance from the materials I *find* to work with: this means that any particular space, any debris unique to Paris and any "found" performers (picked off the street!) would be potential structural elements for the piece. I've been working a great deal with the Judson dancers for love of their non-dance movement and their aggressive, expansive interest in changing the very physical traditions which have given their bodies extraordinary scope and strength, and my pieces for them impose space relations, provoke personal responses which will work inclusively with any chosen or found environment; so that I do not require or want any specially predetermined "set-up." What I find will be what I need.

At this point I should make it clear that my traditions are non-literary, non-verbal—"Kinetic Theatre" is my particular development of the "Happening." It is probably precisely my lack of connections with traditional theatre which left me free to evolve a new theatrical form. I am a painter, which means that even though I may not be working with paint on canvas, my sensibility is shaped in visual worlds and these are strongly tactile, plastic, concretely dimensional. I can trace three basic formal conditions which led me from painting to theatre:

1. The unlimited range of materials (in Kinetic Theatre)—objects, people, lights, sounds, etc.—all acting as an extension of the more gradually broadened range of materials which I

had used in my collages, painting-constructions, light-boxes, kinetic constructions, etc.;
2. The moving body in space (formal unit of Kinetic Theatre) as an extension of the eye-to-hand gesture that generates the paint-stroke;
3. The fluid, actually present environment (of Kinetic Theatre) as a metaphorical extension of an environment relatively fixed in painting by visual selection or inner-eye imagery.

Meat Joy was the first Kinetic Theatre piece I did in which I used performers almost entirely without previous experience in theatre. First in Paris, then in London and New York, I did actually pick (as I had suggested to Lebel) potential performers from crowds in bars, restaurants, concert halls, and streets. In Paris it was difficult and amusing, since I spoke only a few words of French. (The subsequent rehearsals were exceedingly strange; communication usually depending on hand and body gestures, facial expression and a raft of freshly memorized French words strung together to—hopefully—indicate my essential ideas.) I looked for people whose presence I responded to: simplicity, intensity, a self-contained yet open quality. In common they had a natural sexual presence—unself-conscious and vital and "untrained" bodies which moved integrally, rhythmically in commonplace actions. They might be shy or exuberant, plump or skinny —I found contrasting types, a spectrum of qualities.

The performers had to develop a rich and freely expressive responsiveness to one another. In choosing them I had always to sense that those who would provoke my conception of the piece would in turn be complimentary to each other and that the affinity they might feel for one another would develop through the nature of our work together just as the relationship between any of the performers within the context of their instructions would freely transform and intensify the quality of those instructions. My sense of the total quality of the piece was clear from the beginning—in some very internalized way—but was never explicitly imposed, because the performers had to slowly discover and reveal all those detailed experiences which would realize my images. It was like a journey we embarked on together. Only I knew the destination, but they would discover it for themselves.

The performers approached the work, not by assuming characterization or predetermined attitudes, but with what was spontaneously available and expressive in their own personalities. To maintain this the actions had to feel good to them, yet carry them beyond their own expectations of what was likely or possible, remaining clearly unique in the context of our associations. The performers transformed as well as realized the imagery of the piece. At every stage it was a collage process.

Since all the movements of *Meat Joy* take shape by sequences of bodily contact between the performers, we had to establish trusting and pleasurable feelings among ourselves. It involved what Lee Baxandall (describing his performing experience in Water Light/Water Needle) called "putting ourselves in one another's hands." (Literally and figuratively this was true.) A certain amount of surfacing intellectual and psychological trash had to be cleared for performers to feel free. This would necessitate leading them into actions, physical movements which would in themselves answer questions of feeling and response and relationship—the experiences of the body would re-form/inform their mental stance. Early rehearsals began with wrestling sessions: all eight of us on a small mat going through "exercises" of pinching, poking, rolling, tumbling, and crawling. We did other exercises of catches and carries, jumps and falls in which one person assumed responsibility for the weight, direction, and reactions of another: men to men, women to women, as well as men to women. We disposed of conventions of reserve exploring these modes of contact while concentrating a responsive attentiveness on one another. We conscientiously recognized the relation of muscular response and emotional engagement—handling, feeling, carrying, learning each other's weight, muscular strength, type of gestures, and rhythms in action. While these exercises centered on the entire body, I also made exercises for the hands, working with objects in preparation for the materials of the work to come: we made fish and chicken shapes, stuffing plastic with paper; we juggled, threw, kneaded, tossed, and drew on each other. The primary focus for all actions was the immediate animate environment, our relation to the immediate present.

It was important to avoid literal explanations of motive or circumstance to the performers. All "motives" grew directly out of their *physical* engagement with each other and our materials. The performers were free to explore a metaphoric scope of vesture as their own embodiment of tactile-kinetic sensation. The areas of actions moved between dream and banality, rooted in our particular present. Presence rather than interpretation. I told the performers: "The focus is never on the self, but on the materials, gestures, and actions which we generate and which involve us. Sense that we become what we see, what we touch. A certain tenderness (or empathy) is pervasive—even to the most violent actions: cutting, chopping, throwing chickens, for instance. Our senses—tactile, visual, aural—should be completely identified with our immediate environment; either in action, or simply sitting and not moving."

Finally, after intensive work on action/reaction spans, use of material, placement, time duration, co-ordination of movements, cue systems, the performers understood the work as a process combining my need to "see" it and their ability to realize it—that the piece belonged to them to enjoy, rummage in, recast. If their actions were unpolished, crude, sometimes amused or bewildered, then that was what they experienced and projected and would be aware of, rather than some imposed attitude outside of what they actually felt and experienced. All mechanical, intellectual, predicable notions of movement and relationship were behind us, and at this point I would vary materials and instructions to sustain a certain tension; to create an off-balance quality to ensure responses which were totally engaged—that is, both spontaneous and accurate. Just *before* the performers were comfortable and secure about procedure I would change sequences and instructions to keep them diverse, complex, and surprising so as to provoke not only the kind but the quality of involvement I wanted.

In *Meat Joy* I needed a natural, uncontrolled flow between physical action and facial expression, and this had to be learned —to work with a natural, unset fact; that they could laugh, grimace, screech, stare blankly, say ouch and even fart or belch.

My original intention was that we perform naked; I visualized the natural bodies in action—clear and present. The bikinis we wore were a reluctant compromise.

Certain parameters of the piece function unchangeably; others vary with each performance. Sequences, light, sound, materials are developed in rehearsal and co-ordinated with one another during each performance. Attitude, gesture, relationships between performers and performers and objects are structured in rehearsal and left to freely evolve in each performance. The fish, chickens, and hot dogs were never used before actual performance. The Paint Attack which occurs at the conclusion of the piece we rehearsed as a projective exercise with brushes, dry sponges, working with ideas of contour, mass, color distribution, and energy impulse being directed by the action of arm and body movements, as in painting.

The idea of using particular popular songs throughout the main sections of the piece was clear to me in the very early stages of co-ordinating fleeting or insistent images and motions. *Meat Joy,* in its over-all rhythmic structure and physical layout is circular in form—cut through by shafts of diagonal, vertical, horizontal movement and action; circular clusters of figures are a recurring element. And the rock-and-roll songs are not only circular in their very disk-spun nature but in their own thematic and rhythmic form. I planned on their regular three-minute durations and to break into the songs and between them with overlapped, faded, and dominating sequences of street sounds (which I intended to tape in Paris): a transposition of the current, permeating sound environment of the two cities—the sound ambiance that would persistently surround and move into my senses as I was making *Meat Joy.*

The popular songs I chose to use were mainly current American ones (with some English, Italian heard in Europe) and whether rock 'n' roll, Mersey sound, or Detroit sound, they formed a motley and rather "funky" selection. Most are full of speed, propulsive rhythms, sexual energy—no wilting, nostalgic, slow vibrato for lost, glimpsed, idealized, future-promised "romance"; songs about "making It"—without sentimental hypocrisy or artificial misery. What the gray ones found shocking and objectionable in The

Sound when it first appeared (and I remember the outrage and moral offensiveness older people felt) was its fervent, emotional intensity (often couched in "secret," metaphorical language or "nonsense" innuendo), explicit sexual vigor, and the movement this released in the new dances—crude, raw, energetic, "ungraceful"—which could involve the entire body—not just fancy footwork or a pattern of stylized leading and following—and which, further, might involve the entire culture.

The Rue de Seine sounds which intercut between each song are composed mostly of the cries and shouts of street vendors who were selling fish, chickens, sausages, vegetables, and flowers under my window—these cries dominate noises of street traffic—cars starting, stopping, honking, screeching—and often resemble bellowing cows, crying birds, humming animals. These noises are rich and strange; they induce a displacement of the sound continuity I have set up—enlarging, confounding the associative range of the songs.

I made a separate score for each aspect of the piece—one, for instance—in which the rock-and-roll Rue de Seine sounds and actions are related to lighting. Within certain areas of agreement the lighting technician and the sound technician were free to improvise, to vary and adapt their "scores" throughout the piece. They followed formal aspects of the piece, but were also responsive to subtle energy changes of both the performers and the audience. As with everyone else involved in the performance, they had to be very carefully attuned to the nature of the choices they were free to make; delicate balances in the over-all relations of the elements could be destroyed by wrong choices.

Each performer also had a "score" for make-up; there were certain colors, tones, and structural effects which I saw for each face. I worked out a make-up for each performer—almost painting the face, but without letting it become precisely like-a-painted-face; finally the performers were encouraged to adapt this further for themselves.

My lighting ideas are always difficult to realize, and I've had to have patient and imaginative lighting technicians to work with. I will know that I want "a muddy light in a pool over here which then turns to diffuse gold . . . in another area something blue and wet looking and a blast of green turning up over there." I make an elaborate painted light score, with diagrams of possible movement and duration, and then I find out what is actually possible. I've never wanted dramatic or "theatrical" lighting; the color focus must be integral to the work and must be on the performers themselves—that is, not so as to turn them green, but rather to have greenness come from them; not to dramatize a fixed space, but to provide a pacing of color in this particular environment. The lighting in *Meat Joy* was keyed to the larger rhythms of the piece in subtle washes, with concentrations of strong illumination for certain energy clusters, and so as to focus intensities.

There are four black-outs in *Meat Joy,* which I use to compact or shatter a sequence—to concentrate in the eye the sensory effect of actions and gestures usually aiming for a total sensory receptivity on the part of the audience; actions and gestures setting up an intensive demand on visual, aural, and kinetic response. The audience is assaulted with moving lights, colors, textures; shifting directions, lines of actions in space; units of small, contained gestures—any and all of which carry the essential character of the work, which contains them in this compressed time and space. To break this, then, is suddenly to insert a "blank" in which perception is halted, the imagery settling into the mind, fusing, spreading.

The figure described as Serving Maid functions in a way related to the function of the rock-and-roll sounds. She becomes an image of continuity—repeatedly moving in and out of the action to fulfill her banal tasks; her reappearance becomes as predictable or likely as the occurrence of another rock-and-roll song. It is as if this figure and the songs are some skin or envelope which enfold the action. The sound is conceived as almost a drone, with particular songs and particular sections of songs used for an intrusive, disruptive quality (in-gathering aural sense, provoking connections of popular culture and breaking these connections in the context of the pieces action—often ironically, humorously. *i.e.:* "My Boy Lollipop," as the fish, chickens, and hot dogs are thrown onto the fallen performers; "Anyone Who Had A Heart," during the "undressing walk."). The Serving Maid moves flatfootedly, efficiently, endlessly from task to task—dealing with fantastic refuse, rubbish, props, and then introducing materials matter-of-factly which will unleash the most extraordinary excesses and indulgences on the part of the performers.

I wanted *Meat Joy* to follow the direction which its formative drawings and notes had indicated: to be excessive, indulgent, a flesh celebration with all sorts of materials as extensions of flesh (the fish, chickens, hot dogs, paper-strewn floor, wet paint, transparent plastic, brushes, ropes); a propulsion toward the ecstatic; an emotional range shifting precariously between tenderness, banality, wildness, precision, and abandon—with these qualities so juxtaposed as to be ambiguously mixed—simultaneously comic, disturbing, exhilarating.

These interior processes which have become visions—which have become enacted imagery—assume a receptivity, a viewing response which is also fluid, engaged, open, enlarging; an unlimited possibility for perceptual continuities and juxtapositions in the viewer. I wanted my audience to be an energy complement enclosing and corresponding to the energy stream of performance. I placed the audience as close as possible to the performance area, surrounding it like a skin. My over-all conception is that of a sensory arena. Performance allows me involvement with changing metaphors, including every possibility of sensory ambiguity: the transference of aural to tactile, taste to feel, gesture to taste, shape to gesture to action: an inundation and intensification of sensory information.

Audience reaction to all this can be violently antipathetic: the pleasures of the body in free, energetic motion, erotic physical contact, may be considered "disgusting" or "boring" or an "imposition" or confused with an outright sexual act. On the other hand, and as I hope, the audience may take the action into themselves because it is present, immanent, and "real." Or, they may even become involved with dream/wish material: they may wish that would happen to them some time (they always wanted to be slathered with paint, to roll in piles of papers), they wanted to do that too, they could have imagined all this themselves. (And some, I have even learned, actually find emotional levels set off in them which lead them to change or enlarge some aspect of their own lives.)

The creation of *Meat Joy* was one way my own energies could be cast against fragmentation, depersonalization, and, in general, inertness, non-sensuousness—both in the theatre and out. I'm pleased when audience response to *Meat Joy* is: "Yes! —life is really like that . . ." For me it is. I'm not interested in "fantasy."

Meat Joy is dedicated to James Tenney.

Meat Joy Scenario

CAST

CENTRAL MAN
CENTRAL WOMAN
TWO LATERAL MEN
TWO LATERAL WOMEN
INDEPENDENT WOMAN
INDEPENDENT MAN
SERVING MAID

THE SERVING MAID *in black, with a huge starched white apron. She functions throughout as a stage-manager-in-the-open, wandering in and out of the performance area to care for practical details: gathering discarded clothing, spreading plastic sheeting, dumping the fish and chickens, distributing props. Performers call out to her when necessary. Her matter-of-fact actions are deceptive, since cues and co-ordinations of materials and sequences often depend on her.*

THE CENTRAL MAN *and* CENTRAL WOMAN *hold the major intensity and are the main energy source.*

THE LATERAL MEN *and* LATERAL WOMEN *perform as complements/doubles.*

THE INDEPENDENT WOMAN *sets up a private world on her mattress, at the perimeter of action; she joins the others during "men lighting women under plastic."*

THE INDEPENDENT MAN *joins the* INDEPENDENT WOMAN *from the audience. He arrives dressed in street clothes over bikini pants. All other men wear bikini pants under work clothes. The women wear bikini pants and bras covered with stringy, colored feathers. The* CENTRAL WOMAN *enters in blouse and skirt.* INDEPENDENT WOMAN *wears a kimono over a bikini covered with scrappy tiger fur.*

SETTING

The audience is seated in a long, narrow horseshoe curve, bisected by two narrow aisles. The curve moves right around the performing area. There are fewer seats than people to occupy them, and so part of the audience is seated on the floor as close to the performance area as possible. A separation of more than two feet between audience and performers creates a spatial energy lapse which I will wish to avoid in this work. The movements, colors, bodies, odors of the piece should overflow into the audience. The horseshoe curve faces a balcony or open tier; beneath the balcony the performers make most of their entrances and exits.

PROLOGUE

As the audience enters and is seated the tape of "Meat Joy Notes as Prologue" is begun. The tape combines an overlapping collage of my voice reading the written material formative to Meat Joy *(the entire piece is described, as well as discarded, unrealizable imagery); my beginning French exercises (from a French dictionary and a picture book entitled* Look and Learn); *a ticking clock and noises of the street recorded from the window in my room in Paris, Rue de Seine.*

At this time the performers carry in a long table, chairs, trays with make-up, cups, brandy, water, etc. The table is set facing the audience, close to the entrance-exit area. The performers wear old shirts and robes over their costumes; as they face the make-up table mirror, their backs are to the audience. The tape is twenty minutes long, and for its duration I move among the performers, who sit casually at the table, completing their make-up. We talk, sew last feathers on, smoke, and drink from cups. Before the conclusion of the tape the audience is restive, annoyed by the barrage of words from the amplified tape. The tape ends. We carry away the table. Lights out with exception of a small illumination above the balcony.

Lights and Sound	*Action*
Meat Joy Notes, French Lesson tape. Lights dim in hall; spot on table. 20 min.	SERVING MAID and stage hands cover entire floor with heavy plastic sheets. Performers assembled at long table. Make up, free movement, talk. Audience enters.
Small work light; work noises; black-out.	Make-up table cleared away. LATERAL MEN to balcony. LATERAL WOMEN lie down in audience area.
Rock-and-roll–Rue de Seine tape at full blast. "One for the Money," "Blue Suede Shoes." Narrow spot from balcony to floor below.	From the balcony LATERAL MEN drop huge plastic sheets to position. Five large paper scraps flutter down. Slow fall of paper to *inundation* making the central pyre below five feet high—momentum/cascade. (Huge hunks of paper, mostly shiny white, some gold, blue.)
Low-level light fans into center. "Tutti Frutti," Rue de Seine.	LATERAL MEN slide down rope from balcony; across floor to find their partners lying in audience area. They pull them out by their feet, lift and carry them to positions in front and to sides of center paper pile.
Soft spot follows.	CENTRAL MAN and WOMAN enter from under balcony, beginning of Undressing Walk—slow motion. She walks backward, always no more than a few paces separate them; they keep eyes on one another. The undressing is done as a slow series of exchange motions, one after the other but with a pause in between; only one hand is used at a time in a clear, sustained, slow reaching to the clothing of the other. If the action of undoing a button or pulling a shirt free takes more than a few moments that action is left uncompleted; the other takes his turn; the

uncompleted action is returned to. (Example: it takes about six slow, pulling gestures to pull out the man's shirt. Four separate moves to get it over his head/or down his arms since only one motion at a time is allowed.) Each article of clothing taken off is dropped slowly, clearly. The woman simply steps out of her skirt, which the man loosens, and keeps walking. The man's pants require a sequence similar to that of blouse-over-the-woman's-head; the exchanges are halted; he raises blouse, pauses, keeps walking, raises it further; her arms follow, pause, raise, lift it away. Their facial expressions are concentrated on one another.

Lights up on sides (over "Body Packages").

Rue de Seine.

Rue de Seine.

Rue de Seine, "From Me to You."

Simultaneously the LATERAL MEN begin Body Package. The girls rest on their backs where they have been carried, their arms remain free as the men slowly, deliberately walk into the paper pyre, select a few large papers and bring them back, placing them on the torsos of the girls; they pile up a nice fat mound of paper and tuck it around their hips, some of it vertically up over their shoulders, where it also functions as padding for the "Body Rolls." When the Body Package is sufficient they call to the Serving Maid: "Rope!" She brings a length to each one, and they tie in the papers at the girls' waists.

In related rhythms, each man gets up and begins walking away, looking back; they break into long, circling runs as approaches/feints to their Body Package.

Dull amber-gold light.	The INDEPENDENT WOMAN walks in and out carrying her mattress, tea set, pillows, books, cakes, and oranges, and sets up her space to right of pyre, beyond Body Package, at the edge of the audience—their feet nearly in her bed.
"Baby Love." Rue de Seine.	LATERAL MEN after several feints at top speed skid in by Body Packages (like skidding into First base), gather girls in their arms and in unbroken motion begin Body Roll. Their actions are not precisely coordinated; each has a particular speed and direction to his rolls (one cutting space laterally, fast; the other short, slower rolls in eddying circles). If they roll into each other or the Undressing Walk which occurs simultaneously, or part of the audience, they stop, rest, shift directions of rolling.
"Where Did Our Love Go." Rue de Seine.	When they wish, each man stops, raises his partner on her feet—papers flutter and spread; he adjusts the papers attentively; goes down and takes her on top of him and begins rolls again. Or he may rise onto his knees and lift her onto her knees: they stretch arms out slowly, and exchange slow pushes, bending back as far as the push propels them. They join and roll. CENTRAL MAN and WOMAN, now undressed, have completed their series of circling walks. They exit.
Brief black-out. Rue de Seine.	CENTRAL WOMAN hides in center paper pile completely covered by papers. SERVING MAID with flashlight walks about gathering up discarded clothing. INDEPENDENT WOMAN

"That's the Way Boys Are."

continues to eat, pour tea, shift things about in her space. CENTRAL MAN into audience opposite pyre; he sits on the floor between chairs. LATERAL COUPLES lie where they were as lights went out, resting.

Diffuse gold light.

Brightening light.

LATERAL MEN carry women forward, close to pyre, the women acquiescent, relaxed. They place the women on their backs, tuck their legs up against their chests. The men then run to and from the central paper pyre, carrying armfuls of papers, which they drop and spread over the women. (They are careful not to expose the CENTRAL WOMAN.) They are brisk and conscientious—watchful of what they do.

Rue de Seine.

"Baby Love."

INDEPENDENT MAN comes from the audience; he walks slowly to the INDEPENDENT WOMAN and speaks with her, asking if he may join her on the mattress. They speak together. He carefully removes his jacket, tie, shoes, and pants, and settles onto the mattress. She offers him tea and cake. They read something, talk, and play a game of bouncing oranges on their stomachs and then exchanging them by bounces.

"From Me to You."

When the LATERAL WOMEN are completely covered with papers, the LATERAL MEN rush to the central pyre, rummaging; they find the CENTRAL WOMAN's feet, which they seize and pull straight up into the air. She is raised on her hips beneath the paper, and immediately begins Leg Choreography—the legs moving as if dancing upright, walk-

Rue de Seine.

ing, pedaling a bicycle, etc. The men quickly pack the loose papers down around her hips to expose the legs; they run around the pile punching and hitting loose papers into the center. They return to their own partners, repeating these actions around them individually. They crouch down to watch the motions of the legs they have thus set off.

Flickering amber beam follows CENTRAL MAN.

CENTRAL MAN comes slowly, deliberately from audience, across floor to central pyre. He seizes moving legs of CENTRAL WOMAN and drags her out of the pyre, papers streaming behind her. He lifts her into an awkward hold, moving across the floor.

LATERAL MEN have slipped off their outer pants and jumped into the pile of papers; they lie flat on their backs, hips raised, buttocks touching women's buttocks. They scoop up and scatter papers over their heads and torsos until only their legs show: Leg Mixture.

"Anyone Who Had a Heart," Rue de Seine.

CENTRAL MAN, comes parallel to the paint table, suddenly drops CENTRAL WOMAN. Motionless. They look at each other, she raises her arms slightly and he grasps her hands and jerks her up in the air as high as he can, taking her weight against his chest. He shakes her as long and violently as possible until they fall over onto the paint table. He has fallen on his back, she on top of him.

Soft spot on paint table.

Motionless. Very slowly she slips off him, reaching under the table with one hand to pull out brushes, paint bowls (puts bowls on table at his side, keeping one in her hand, with brush); rising, moving toward his head.

Begins Love-Paint-Exchange, as she moves around in back of the table slowly painting his face, chest, arms, sex, thighs, feet, legs.

"Wishin' and Hopin'." Rue de Seine.	LATERAL MEN stand up out of leg and paper pile. They begin running jumps across floor and back into pile; then they leap over the women in the pile, alternating this with short bursts of running. The women, still with their legs in the air and on their backs, slowly swiveling, complicating the hurdle they present.
"My Guy." Rue de Seine. "That's the Way Boys Are."	As the CENTRAL WOMAN comes around the table, painting his legs, the CENTRAL MAN sits up, reaches for paint brush in her hand and takes it. He drops his legs over the side of the table and begins gently painting her face; slowly standing, painting her body. She takes up another brush and bowl and they start to exchange body-paintings, gathering speed across the floor where the LATERAL MEN still run. They drop brushes and bowls, mix wet paint on their bodies directly, surface against surface, twisting, turning, faster and faster. Exit.
Black-out.	LATERAL COUPLES exit in dark. SERVING MAID hands women plastic sheets; flashlights with cords attached are given to the men. She brings plastic sheet to INDEPENDENT COUPLE and gathers up brushes, bowls, clothing as LATERAL WOMEN and CENTRAL WOMAN go into performance area where they cover themselves with a plastic sheet; they sit apart in a roughly triangular formation. The INDEPENDENT COUPLE cover themselves with a plastic sheet but remain sitting up.

Black-out.

The men release lights on ropes in wide arcs . . . very slow, large patterns of movement. The lights are colored red and green. They mutually watch the lights, co-ordinating directions and rhythms as they walk in slow wide arcs: faster light arcs: variations of vertical, horizontal, diagonal patterns; over heads of the audience, as high as possible, as low as possible, with sudden shifts of light shafts back toward center; the men come closer together—staccato light sequence as they pull ropes in closer. They fall quickly to the floor and fan out in Alarm Positions (starfish). Women begin slow, *angular* movements under plastic: angling elbows, knees, feet (all pointed parts) to shape plastic. INDEPENDENT COUPLE do variations of this together. Rustling in the dark; men scuttle across floor to spot fragments, details of moving forms of women and INDEPENDENT COUPLE. Back and forth; abrupt. Movement subsiding as women turning under sheets slowly move into center of floor; men crawl on their stomachs . . . closing in, they flicker the lights off into the plastic . . . on . . . off . . . not moving. All these figures are now grouped closely together in a kind of heap. The INDEPENDENT COUPLE has rolled over into this heap. They lie still.

"Non Ho L'Eta." Slow central lights.

Rue de Seine, "Non Ho L'Eta."

Rue de Seine.

"Maybe I Know."

From their pile the performers call for "Rosette"—the Intractable Rosette (how to get four flesh bodies moving as one combined unit—as a water-lily, a carousel, a floating stone sculpture?). Men gather women into circular formation, back to back. This sequence of attempts to turn the women into sculptural shapes which can

Rue de Seine.

"My Guy."

Rue de Seine.

move as a unit is not pre-set. They all improvise. The women link arms or legs; the men may take ropes to tie their legs or arms together; they arrange them lying down, sitting up, spread-eagled, rolled in a ball, and they try to move them (star, wheel, flower, crystal) as if they were one solid structure. Each time the "unit" falls apart; they all shout instructions, suggestions, ideas, advice, complaints. And each time the women are set and the men begin to move them (synchronized) they roll apart, lose balance, fall over, get squashed, etc. The men may choose The Tree as the final arrangement; here the men stand the women up, raise their hands and fingers high over their heads, touching their hands together in the center. Each man stands close against the grouped women, encircling with his arms as many as he can. They all try to move as a free-wheeling circle, which is impossible. They all fall over, yelping. They lie motionless.

Full light.
"Non Ho L'Eta."
Rue de Seine.

"My Boy Lollipop."
Rue de Seine.

"Where Did Our Love Go."
Rue de Seine.
"Baby Love."
Rue de Seine.

SERVING MAID enters with dignity, carrying a huge tray of raw chickens, mackerel, strings of hot dogs. Slowly, extravagantly she strews fish, chickens and hot dogs over all the bodies. Wet fish, heavy chickens, bouncing hot dogs—bodies respond sporadically—twitching, pulling back, hands reaching, touching out of the pile, grunts and groans, giggles. Grasping one of the new objects they sit up to examine their situation. Individual instructions for fish and chickens are evolved: slips, flops, flips, jumps, throwing and catching, drawing, falling, running, standing still, patting, sucking, eating, stuffing, rubbing, slapping, exchanging, stroking. (Example: LATERAL WOMAN attacked by others; INDEPENDENT WOMAN concentrates her activities on the periphery of the group until someone pulls her in; INDEPENDENT MAN with fish follows contours of woman's body with it, while at the same time this same woman may be engaged with some one else or several others.) Tenderly, then wildly. All are to be inundated finally with fish, chickens, hot dogs. The smell of raw fish permeates the entire room.

"Bread and Butter."
Rue de Seine.

"Anyone Who Had a Heart."
Rue de Seine.
"That's the Way Boys Are."

Rue de Seine.

Call goes out for "hats." Women again propped in a circle, back to back. SERVING MAID brings plastic scarves and hairpins. Each man makes a secure but wild hat for a woman. Call goes out for "paint." SERVING MAID scurries back in with large green and orange buckets full of colored paints, brushes, sponges, which she distributes among the men. Deliberately each man paints a brilliant linear face on a woman; then each man thoughtfully paints a woman's body; they continue, faster and faster, to cover them with paint—stroked, streaked, thrown, hurled (three hundred years of painting techniques combined).

"I Only Want to Be with You."

The women may smile contentedly, amusedly at first. They watch the movement of the paint until finally they are yelling, howling, twisting, turning; trying to rise slipping and falling on the splattered plastic. Each man grabs up a woman and carries/drags her out over the littered floor as CENTRAL WOMAN hollers, "Enough, enough!"

Black-out

Time: 60–80 minutes

The Paris Cast		*The New York Cast*
Carolee Schneemann	CENTRAL WOMAN	Carolee Schneemann
Daniel Pommereulle	CENTRAL MAN	James Tenney
Danielle Auffrey	LATERAL WOMAN	Dorothea Rockburne
Romain Denis	LATERAL MAN	Tom O'Donnell
Annina Nosei	LATERAL WOMAN	Irina Posner
Claude Richard	LATERAL MAN	Robert D. Cohen
Rita Renoir	INDEPENDENT WOMAN	Sandra Chew
Jacques Seiler	INDEPENDENT MAN	Stanley Gochenouer
Claudia Hutchins	SERVING MAID	Ann Wilson

May 1964 Centre Americain
Blvd. Raspail
Festival de la Libre Expression I

November 1964
Judson Church

The Songs (Collaged with Paris Street Noises)

Blue Suede Shoes	Elvis Presley
Tutti Frutti	Elvis Presley
Anyone Who Had a Heart	Dionne Warwick
From Me to You	The Beatles
That's the Way Boys Are	Lesley Gore
Non Ho L'Eta	Gigliola Cinquetti
Rigazzi	Gigliola Cinquetti
My Boy Lollipop	Millie Small
Where Did Our Love Go	The Supremes
Baby Love	The Supremes
Bread and Butter	The Newbeats
I Only Want to Be with You	Dusty Springfield
Wishin' and Hopin'	Dusty Springfield
My Guy	Mary Wells

Gas

BY ALLAN KAPROW AND CHARLES FRAZIER

We have already noted qualities which the Happening, for all its visual-arts origins, has in common with the most recent developments of Anti-Naturalist theatre. In certain respects, the Happening also has increasingly evident connections with an earlier, more basic, even primitive dramatic style. *Gas* not only has the distinction of being the work by Kaprow in which this relationship is plainest, but from the point of view of Kaprow's basic rules, has the added distinction of being as ideal a Happening as has been performed. Moreover, it received about as widespread a public attention as has ever been accorded any Happening.

Gas was performed over a three-day period, on a series of six occasions in six locales toward the eastern tip of Long Island, New York. It fulfilled Kaprow's recommendations as follows: (B) its source of imagery was not artistic or cultural in origin in any ordinary way: it was structured around images of expansion and contraction mainly—parachutists, falling objects, fire-fighting foam, flying sculpture, ubiquitously appearing and disappearing individuals, weather and other balloons—and its materials were mostly scientific; (C) it fully involves "changing locales"; (D) "discontinuous time"; (F) and it "eliminated audiences entirely" by omnivorously consuming most bystanders with whom it came into contact, digesting them as actors. Thus Kaprow's key recommendation, that (A) "the line between art and life should be kept fluid" is more than satisfied.

One might almost place *Gas* as easily at a pre-naturalistic phase in theatrical history as one presents it here, as a recent experimental development. It bears close resemblance to a form of theatre which has been described as a theatre of:

> . . . mass movements, community expressions . . . Either a whole tribe worked itself up into a frenzy, or a group, which with or without initiation ceremonies stood open

> for everyone to join . . . a wild and frenzied dance is born of this ecstasy, a dance . . . with an extremely pronounced portraying character, on the one hand reflecting emotional tension, on the other indicating by mimesis the forces so stirring to the emotions.

This is a description of archaic ritual or rite, from Benjamin Hunningher's *The Origin of the Theatre*. Such events, generally taken to be the first sign of the human theatrical impulse, eventually through early Greek drama became an influence on the mainstream of theatre. Were it not for the intervening centuries, and the fact that the concerns of the producers of Happenings are clearly contemporary, such events might seem to have been the most direct influence on the Happening. Archaic ritual has in common with the Happening (reference once again is to Kaprow's own suggestions) that (A) the art-life line was kept indistinct, lost in the fact that as Hunningher notes, "all rites have a purpose"; (B) the image-source was not aesthetic but religious; (C) locale was unspecific, as revelers often wandered; (D) time might become "discontinuous" as a result of the convulsiveness of the celebrations; (E) repetition was made unthinkable because of the element of ecstasy; (F) audiences were all but abolished, since the rite was a matter of participants, not of spectators. Indeed, this issue of non-differentiation, which Kaprow places in an important position in his aesthetic, appears historically to be the distinction which rite had to raise before it could turn into a theatre "proper."

Although the aesthetic of *Gas* returns us to a time before (Thornton Wilder says in an essay) the stage was adopted as "a convenience in view of the weather in northern countries," Kaprow links it to an "increasing concern . . . with departing from the many quasi, unconscious rituals of our society and focussing on the possibility of conscious rituals." Kaprow's ritual differs from archaic ritual mainly in that—if it is ecstatic at all—it is not religious-ecstatic, but aesthetic-ecstatic. *Gas* relates to the idea (also expressed in Kaprow's simplest Happenings, which sometimes simply consist of people convening to watch other people) that when viewed from an art-perspective, a most absorbing form of theatre may be life itself.

We have been able to represent *Gas* not only through text, but by reference to the various public media for whose coverage the work was partially designed. Originally commissioned by the Dwan gallery (offices in Los Angeles and New York), it was also sponsored by CBS-TV. It was not only at every point qualified by photographic considerations, but Kaprow came to consider the numerous photographers who attended the piece as legitimately consumed/subsumed performers, just as he regards the CBS director, and a private film maker who made a remarkable short-subject version of *Gas* as partial collaborators. We augment Kaprow's original and quite incidental text (it was originally issued as part of a broadside distributed to those participants who wished to consider participation in advance) with some notes on *Gas*'s collaborative genesis; eyewitness notes by the *Time* reporter who covered the event; and photographs of high points of the piece, some enlarged from frames of the motion-picture edition.

A HAPPENING

by

Charles Frazier
Mordi Gerstein
Gordon Hyatt
Allan Kaprow

GAS

SATURDAY, AUGUST 6 - AM

slow parade of big weather balloons, crowds pushing - hover crafts manned by the Neutron Kid and Liquid Hips - seeing eyes - flares - barrel pounders booming

---

SATURDAY, AUGUST 6 - PM

weather balloons rise, burst, wash ashore, messages to area - plastic skyscraper on beach, destroyed, shrill whistles - laundry uncovered, day at washerette - bulging letters go up, ride waves - sky divers descend, yells, noise - blimp hoves in - skywriter's secret word - seeing eyes

SUNDAY, AUGUST 7 - PM

bluffs above sea - fire trucks, squad cars, red flashers on, lights, intercoms - bullhorn instructions - seeing eyes - black mounds on beach - rockets released - foam pouring down cliff, past mounds into waves - crowd passing through - interviews

---

MONDAY, AUGUST 8 - AM

junked autos - kids' clubhouses dolled up for picnic - goodie car serving - flying machine buzzing hulks - big ballon oozing out of car body - seeing eyes - playtime

SUNDAY, AUGUST 7 - AM

"fire" written inside truck, cops spray with snow bombs - ferry trip, white sheets hung out, loud rock on car radios - seeing eyes - nurses onshore yahooing welcomes - black plastic moving across exit - nurses running off - passed by on highway, nurses stacked five-deep on hospital beds, waving, laughing

In Cooperation With The Dwan Gallery And WCBS-TV

MONDAY, AUGUST 8 - PM

burial pit - black mounds moving slowly down, sea of foam rolling down - cars blaring horns every thirty seconds - blast on whistles, towers of barrels toppled into pit - pushed up incline against flow - seeing eyes still, all over bottom - regular garbage deliveries

Those interested in participating should attend a preliminary meeting at either the VFW Hall, 4 Main Street, Easthampton on Sunday, July 31 - 11 AM; or the CBS Broadcasting Center, 524 West 57 Street, New York City on Tuesday, August 2 - 8 PM (ask at desk in lobby).

General Note

If my work is theatre, it is distinct. It uses neither stages nor arenas. There is no plot. Nor are there rehearsals, actors, audiences, or repeated performances.

Instead, there are planned activities, ritual-like events, adventures, tasks, sudden, hard intrusions into everyday cares; normal undertakings, too, that emerge sharply, italicized by an unusual focus and context. These are enacted by unskilled participants in times and places that are often widely separated, a work extending over days or months, mixing in and out of daily life.

The theatre of Happenings is close in spirit not to Racine or even Beckett, but to the theatre of military war games, archaeological digs, big hunts, drag races, one-day supersales, march-ins, rocket launchings, Pentagon meetings, brain operations, and the subway rush-hour.

Allan Kaprow

Collaborative Note on "Gas"

Our *Gas* started very clearly, in the individual interests and concerns of each of us in the spring of 1966.

Allan Kaprow had been thinking particularly of the Happening idea as bound up with the ritualized needs that all of us, whether we are aware of it or not, are apt to have. From a certain point of view most of the institutions that we call "modern" have already stimulated whole systems of unconscious rituals. The supermarket, for example, overshoots the earlier idea of intimate exchange suggested by the small-town store, and involves us in unconscious daily rituals regarding planning things to buy, exchanges between ourselves and store personnel, traveling down aisles, hearing Muzak, storing away large quantities of foodstuffs upon arriving home. Kaprow had increasingly been concerned with departing from the many quasi, unconscious rituals of our society and focusing on the possibility of conscious rituals. The notion of tribal ritual is of course very old. One of the most essential ideas relating to the creation of *Gas* is that the concept of the tribe and constantly changing rituals may be necessary for us. The peculiar irony of the time artistically may be that the more advanced the civilization becomes, the more archaic the aesthetic needs become.

In elaborating his rituals, Kaprow had been spreading out his events in space and time: a recent occurrence had taken place in three different U.S. cities; he was planning others to take place simultaneously on both sides of the Atlantic. It had therefore become necessary or expedient for him to have others arrange for the practicalities of enactment and, in fact, to have others assume certain managerial responsibilities. This system of subcontracting, which had always been implicit in the structure of the Happening, allowed a great deal of room for shared personal involvements: or collaborative authorship.

Charles Frazier, around the time that *Gas* was initiated, was engaged in implementing a sculptural idea which his many exhibitions, in well-known galleries in both Los Angeles and New York, had led him to: namely, the idea of making sculpture that is free of gallery requirements. It had long seemed to him beside the point to make sculpture according to previous concepts of gallery space when you could make sculpture live in the same space that we live in—or, indeed, make sculpture fly. After a casual meeting early in 1965, Allan Kaprow and Frazier began to work toward a project which would involve both their major current concerns. Frazier had spoken with Virgina Dwan, of the Dwan Gallery, about the possibility of showing flying sculpture at Kitty Hawk—on the old Wright Brothers' field. Envisioning a more public locale, Frazier's dealer suggested that he fly his pieces in the Hamptons, in Long Island, during the forthcoming summer. Frazier and Kaprow began to think about the various possibilities of arranging for a large-scale event in which the role of aerial sculpture would be major, if not primary. The first idea that they agreed upon was that it would be a good idea to have combined aerial and projection events. They then spoke with Mordi Gerstein, who had worked professionally in the area of both sculpture and film, about projection possibilities. A whole series of possibilities was mutually involved: the projection of various film materials on such objects as flying screens, blimps, speeding vehicles, down streets, and against the sides of buildings. The ideas that Frazier and Kaprow had been exploring were not only crystallized, but enlarged by Gerstein, who also suggested that what they were doing would have the character of a news event, and might well be of interest for the medium of TV.

Gordon Hyatt, a CBS producer with a special interest in the arts was contacted; he suggested that the event might well make an appropriate program for his "Eye on New York" series. Gerstein had already given impetus to the creation of situations which were expressly photogenic; now, Gordon Hyatt's involvement intensified this aspect. Ironically enough, Hyatt's film-TV coverage tended to have the effect of shifting the emphasis away from projection events, which would be hard to photograph for television purposes. With Gerstein acting as adviser regarding photographability, Kaprow and Frazier devised a series of twenty-odd events which might easily be subject to treatment by television. Judging the amount of material which "Eye on New York" could handle, Hyatt then selected six basic events: these became, finally, the essence of the Happening.

The title *Gas* was decided upon around this time. At every point events conspired to prove the aptness of this word. The "gas" of almost endless speculation and exchange of ideas might be referred to; or the fact that the event was conceived as "fun": as "a gas." Most significantly, the aerial character of many of the component events was clear. And, too, what delighted us about the piece was the way its elements tended to disperse. Authorship, for example, seemed to be becoming multiple. From the beginning we had considered the possibility of realistically varying the character of the piece according to the demands of particular participants—each of whom, by now, had become a kind of author on his own. Even the authorities in the Hamptons were most helpful—not to mention full of ideas for interesting little variations and changes: we soon enlisted such parties as the Police Department, the Fire Department, the Commissioner of Roads, the Commissioner of Public Works. The expansion of *Gas* now also included a multiplicity of media, locales (we had, of course, thoroughly scouted places around the Hamptons). In the end there had begun to be created an actual concentration on the means of dispersal, with the incorporation of parachuting skydivers, weather balloons, rockets, hovercraft, Kidde-foam, bubbles, an inflatable skyscraper. Allan Kaprow composed a brief working script for the event which we used as an outline for the details of finalization—and the project *Gas* was then in every sense, officially off the ground.

Allan Kaprow, Charles Frazier, Mordi Gerstein

"Happening in the Hamptons"

(The following is a series of notes by *Time* magazine reporter Anne Hollister. They served as the basis for the article on *Gas* which appeared in *Time,* August 19, 1966.)

THE PARADE AT SOUTHAMPTON: Saturday morning, August 6

The CBS team, the inventors of the happening, and volunteer participants assembled at Southampton behind the Polish Hall. While Charles Frazier, the sculptor, dressed as "an American boy mechanic" (Kaprow said) in white coveralls and a white hat tinkered with two hovercrafts which he had built himself, weather balloons were blown up with a vacuum cleaner, children were issued white gloves and told how to handle the perishable balloons with care, and volunteers over fifteen were instructed how to use highway flares—the torches for the planned parade. It was planned as a kind of greeting for the 11:01 train from New York.

Frazier had built a wood and white canvas structure about two feet high over one hovercraft, allowing space for the engine and rider, and he covered the second hovercraft with roughly gathered black plastic.

The CBS producer, Gordon Hyatt, rushed about instructing his crew through a walkie-talkie, or the participants through a bull horn, while his assistant, Carole F. Schwartz helped out, ready to ride the hovercraft dressed in a spangled bathing suit—like the costume which Sonja Henie used to wear, a white plastic space helmet with a gun on top and white boots. Her code name for the event (used by all the happening participants) was "Liquid Hips." Kaprow himself was to represent a second and contrasting hovercraft-mounted figure, dark to Carole Schwartz' white: "The Neutron Kid" was swathed in black plastic, wearing dark glasses and a World War I aviator's helmet.

The train was due to arrive soon, so, even though the hovercrafts were not quite working properly—the parade began. Men and women joined in turning kerosene barrels over and over, rolling them down the main Southampton street and making a terrific, irregular booming sound. They were followed by children bouncing weather balloons over their heads and holding them up there, and by a few people bearing highway flares, and doing little dances as the hot wax from the flares burned their toes. In and around the plaza they marched until finally the train began to arrive. At about this time the hovercraft began operating and the parade began circling around the plaza. "Liquid Hips" waved like a water-skier from her hovercraft, and Allan Kaprow glowered darkly from his. He said later that it had felt like he was crossing the river Styx on the smoking vehicle.

By this time the train had entered the Southampton station. Some of the passengers looked a little dazed at the whole thing, a couple of others walked straight into waiting taxis or chauffeured cars as if this happened every Saturday. "It's certainly not typical Southampton!" remarked one bystander, however.

One of the parade participants described the experience of being in the event as "relaxing—it feels good because there's no distinction between audience and participants." (He had been to other happenings where he had just been an onlooker.)

The train pulled away, the parade broke up, and everything was packed into trunks and despatched for the next location.

EVENTS AT THE BEACH AT AMAGANSETT: Saturday afternoon, August 6

There was a bigger crowd at the beach than usual this Saturday. Most of the people were lying around sunbathing, or jumping the waves, or riding the surf on rubber mats. A few were playing volleyball, and the game continued straight through the happening. Some imperturbable sportsmen said later that they hadn't even noticed what was going on.

As members of the two rock-and-roll bands—"The Neons" and "The Last Words"—combed their long hair, rolled down the sleeves of their polka dot shirts, or struggled out onto the sand with their instruments ("Look, they've even got an organ for classical tastes"), children were pushing and stretching out their arms for giant colored balloons which the happeners were inflating with helium. Messages were inserted in the balloons with the idea that after the balloons were released, aloft, and burst, the messages would be scattered "like dandelion seeds." (Kaprow).[1]

Finally, everything began to happen at once. The band began, a horn was blown, and all the balloons were released; a red smoke bomb went off, and at this signal, four men parachuted out of a plane. They free-fell from 7200 feet to 5000 feet and then opened their chutes. Although they were experienced jumpers, two of the men landed in the water, instead of on the beach. Nobody paid much attention, thinking this was planned, but one of the happeners—a plump lady sculptress who had once been a sky diver in Poland—knew they would be in trouble and watched anxiously as little boys in rubber mattresses paddled out and actually saved the lives of at least one of the two parachutists. Burdened with heavy jump boots, and tangled in their equipment, they had just about given up the struggle.

While a crowd rushed down the beach to greet the parachutists, Charles Frazier, the sculptor, began to inflate his fifty-foot-high, pointed, black plastic "soft skyscraper" (as Frazier called it). It had white windows painted on the sides and a little American flag near the top. A side of the "building" gave away and had to be patched with Scotch tape. "It's a United States sex symbol!" somebody cried gleefully. It was easy enough to pump air into the skyscraper with a vacuum cleaner, but getting it to stand up was another matter. Looking like Lilliputians

[1] The messages ranged in tone from serious to silly: You'd better go home. Your mom is calling you. Quick!/Give me your gum. I need it to hold up my underpants./Chills, thrills and daffodils./Excuse me, but would you know if Afro-Asian albino turtles have warts on their hind legs?/Red bananas on a pickle tree./This is part of an Allan Kaprow Happening entitled "Gas" being performed August, 6, 7, and 8 throughout the Hamptons./Meet me at Times Square. Noon sharp. Wear a silver rose./Bob Dylan is great./Hugh Hefner is a virgin./What gas will come to bear me back to from whence I came?/The delicacy of a thistle belies its toughness, or, the toughness of a thistle belies its delicacy./Many a good man has passed this way./It was an accident.

trying to tie down Gulliver or to get a floppy black rocket to stand up, the children scrambled around, positioning themselves to give the building a push back up whenever it lurched dangerously. It stood upright for about ten feet, and then the rest of it kept weaving and bending.

"This whole afternoon is a great baby-sitting thing," remarked one mother watching her kids scrambling around.

"Got a skyhook?" asked art critic (and coiner of the term "Action Painting") Harold Rosenberg, observing the effort. "The fun is in the struggle," Rosenberg commented to a friend.

Finally the skyscraper was aloft—and someone blew up a huge weather balloon to stand next to it, which made a sort of trylon and perisphere image. The second weather balloon broke, so the intended sexual symbol was never completed.

As a final treat—the skyscraper was allowed to topple and the kids were let loose to pull it apart, which they did with great savagery, reminiscent of a scene from *Lord of the Flies*. There were even some reported cries of "kill it." Into the midst of the kiddie-rippers other children tumbled huge plastic oil drums which had been stacked on the beach. Toward the end of this activity, the rock-and-roll band got into full swing at last. People began frugging on the beach, but the CBS men began asking for repeat takes, and the event developed into a filming.

ON AND AROUND THE SHELTER ISLAND FERRY: Sunday morning, August 7

It was 7 A.M. The mist had risen about thirty feet above the streets of Sag Harbor, and the fake whale, gliding across the harbor (Sag Harbor was once a prominent whaling town) looked a little more real than usual. At the place where the ferry from Sag Harbor docked, a bevy of fifteen especially attractive nurses in pink and white uniforms with white caps and aprons giggled and combed their hair. Their supervisor, who had agreed that they might take part in the happening, didn't fully understand what it was all about, was the lone spectator. The girls, who were being paid five dollars each for their participation (but who probably would have been willing to pay to be in the show) were told about the part they were to play: "Be gay and wave as the ferry pulls in, and then turn poker-faced."

CBS crewmen and happeners piled in their cars and took a ferry over to Shelter Island, and then switched to a larger boat which was to make the return voyage to Sag Harbor. Before boarding, Carole F. Schwartz climbed into a truck labeled "Home Sweet Home Moving and Storage" and sprayed the word FIRE inside the window. Two policemen, who had arrived late, leaped from their squad car and sprayed the entire truck.

The cars drove on board the ferry, and as the ferry churned off and then made lazy, breezy circles around the harbor, the happeners strung up three clotheslines and hung out a lot of sheets with clothespins. All the car radios were turned up and the sheets flapped wildly in the breeze, like luffing sails.

The nurses could be seen waving and laughing as the ferry pulled into the dock, and then someone drew a black curtain in front of them—a sort of black-out. Suddenly the ferry reversed its engines and backed up (one felt like one was in a Keystone comedy, and the reel was being turned backwards). The ferry made another landing, and the cars left the ferry—pushing through and under the black sheet on their way out. The nurses could be seen running away up the hill.

While the nurses gunned their cars to the next location, the happeners and the CBS crew (which had asked for the second ferry landing in order to effect a retake) waited in their own cars.

The crowd looked and responded like one gathered to watch fireworks, or some other festive outdoor event. More surfers left their boards on the beach (Montauk, one assured me, is the best place on the east coast for surfing) and climbed the bluffs to join the crowd. Finally, everybody piled back into their cars and drove off down the highway. About half a mile from the dock, the nurses turned up—piled five in a cot in the middle of the highway, kicking their legs, waving their arms—all very Siren-like. "Maybe we'll be discovered," one said as we pulled by—and at that point they *were* being discovered, by staring people who were going the other way in cars and had no idea what was going on.

The participants pulled over to the beach, and that was the end of the event.

PILGRIMAGE THROUGH THE FIRE-FIGHTING FOAM AT MONTAUK: Sunday afternoon, August 7

The proud, gray-weathered homes of Easthampton do not give way, as one might imagine, to fishermen's shacks as one drives east to the tip of Long Island. The whole nature of the architecture changes to a New Jersey housing development pastel jumble. But behind, there are the brownish bluffs, eroded like the moon. There is a vast expanse of green moor behind the bluffs, and the houses on this moor are ruins, or cover observation bunkers built during the Second World War. The happeners and CBS crewmen gathered on top of the bluffs, shivering a bit in the cold of a misty, windy, overcast afternoon. Two fire-fighting-foam producing machines were adjusted by Walter Kidde Company engineers, dressed in scientistlike white jackets and wearing what looked like white air-raid helmets. Below, on the beach, other participants stretched the ever-appearing black plastic over several wooden frames. These pyramids were designed to echo the crevices and peaks of the dunes, while standing out starkly against the foam.

While the firetruck crawled up the slope, and the firemen began to ready their hoses, the surfers, gawking kids, and the happeners were gathered together and issued walking staffs. They were told that if they wanted to participate, they had to descend the bluffs by an easier side route, and then at a signal walk across the beach, and through the foam which would be released from the fire-fighting-foam machines on top of the bluffs.

When everyone was in place a distress horn sounded, the foam machines began to churn out sudsy stuff which first blew into the air like tiny clouds, and then began to backfire—onto the camera placed on top of the bluffs, onto the firemen who staunchly stayed at their post near the machine and began to look like men getting ready for their morning shaves. The horn on top of the chief's car whoop-whoop-whooped like an emergency horn one often hears in the streets of Paris.

Slowly, like a Pied Piper, or like Moses, Kaprow led his group across the beach and through the foam. "There was a kind of dignity and a kind of apprehension in their approach," someone noted later. The fire department squirted water out overhead which drenched the happeners. The foam poured down the bluffs —a sudsy waterfall which mounted to the knees, thighs, necks of those crossing the beach at the base of the bluffs. A cameraman was in foam up to his armpits, but kept filming (this same intrepid cameraman had filmed the Saturday morning parade from a bicycle).

At the top of the bluffs, while the crowd watched what looked like a pilgrimage ("It looks biblical!"), Charles Frazier ignited one of his two-foot-long rockets—gaily painted blue, red, yellow, and green. The first flew up in the air and then landed behind him, instead of on the beach. The second went into a tailspin and dug back into the bluffs—so Frazier decided to save the rest for another day.

Meanwhile, the fire-fighting foam had spread out to the foam of the waves, which began rolling it back on itself.

"I wanted to stay under longer, but people were falling on me," someone commented. In the midst of the foam people had crouched down, splashed foam at each other, jumped up and down. The plump sculptress sat down calmly and looked like she was sitting in her bubble bath at home.

"A completely irrational environment," someone noted.

Allan Kaprow described it as "tons and tons of danger kissing you like a powder puff."

PICNIC IN THE AUTO GRAVEYARD: Monday morning, August 8

This event was rained out and took place on Tuesday morning. Report on it (paraphrased from Kaprow) follows:

The children arrived in a bus at the auto junkyard. There was a marvelous foggy light. They were divided into four groups of about 4–5 in a group and given instructions. When they had been given paints and brushes and streamers, they went over to some old wrecks of cars which had been cleared of broken glass for the purpose. Sheets covered the dirty old seats.

For about three quarters of an hour the children painted the cars—stripes, flowers—and decorated them with streamers, rubbish—whatever they wanted to. Kaprow noted that the first thing most of them did was to paint the windows of the cars, which created an intimate environment within. The children began to imagine they were in real cars, "Hey, send some heat up here," or missiles, "Countdown: one, two, three . . . blast off!"

At a horn signal they left their "clubhouses" and went over to a stand Kaprow had built of old tires and ate "what kids like to eat"—peanut butter and jelly sandwiches on white bread, ice cream, Cheezits. They took the food back to the cars to eat.

Meanwhile, Kaprow and Frazier spread sheets over some of their junked convertibles and blew up weather balloons, "which emerged through the sheets like the heads of babies being born." The kids played with the balloons, squealing with joy.

Forming up, the kids walked through the woods to the next location, rolling barrels or tires, banging on things from the junkyard, ending up at a clearing. Here Frazier launched another hovercraft—this one three or four feet in diameter, shaped like a funnel and made of light metal. The kids helped to guide it, hanging onto long colored tassels which hung down from the craft.

Taking another walk through the woods, the kids made side excursions to hunt out large (two or three feet in diameter) inflatable colored letters. Returning to the clearing the kids had their letters inflated, and then the group had a countdown, after which Frazier set off the colored rockets he had not used at the bluffs on Sunday.

Covered with paint, the kids were driven back to their rather apprehensive mothers waiting for them in the center of town. (Kaprow particularly liked the fact that in this part of the happening, everyone was a participant—there weren't any inert masses of mere spectators.)

A WALK IN A FOAMING DUMP: Monday afternoon, August 8

The Springs, Long Island, dump looks more like a quarry for brown earth—with one deep and one shallow end. A bulldozer continually plows under the garbage, so there is not much of a mess around.

As the foam machines were adjusted again, and the firemen readied their hoses, Hyatt gave instructions to a mixed group of pre-teens, kiddies, and surfers, who had come all the way over from the Montauk Bluffs, because they'd had such a good time the day before. One teenager had made his walking stick from Montauk into a banner saying "The Rubber Band" (the name of his gang) and the surfers had brought along their walking sticks too as well as a long tube through which one of them was planning to breathe when he sunk under the foam. The surfer with the pierced ear had added two more dangling earrings, and donned a T-shirt which read "Cobra, Cobra, Cobra, Cobra-powered by Ford." "Wish I had my motorcycle, man, to drive up that slope," one said.

Bright-colored barrels were piled three high on a ridge overlooking the deep part of the dump, and the fire-fighting-foam machines were mounted on the slope which led down to the deep portion of the dump. At a signal, the machines began to generate foam. The happeners, who had been instructed to spread over the slope, began to descend, blowing police whistles. The sound of so many whistles blended together in a wild scream. A number of the happeners had been told to drape themselves with some available black plastic sheets, and they walked in front of the group to the edge of the foam which had spread out like a quickly strewn buoyant snowfall over the slope. The bubbles felt light and not even damp to walk through. Allan Kaprow, in the midst of the bubbles walked down the slope with a gentle smile looking like he was daydreaming in the midst of his daydream come true.

When the group reached the edge of the foam the barrels were toppled into the deep end, and then those who had worn black plastic rolled the barrels back up the hill. Their successful ascent signaled the end of the happening.

Afterword

Since most of the more experimental events represented here are the most recent, the reader might be tempted to regard this volume as predicting a trend. Except in the most general sense, this would be incorrect. One of the great pleasures of experimental theatre in the twentieth century, especially when viewed against the background of the commercial theatre, is the range of styles that can exist within it. There is doubtless as much future in the theatre for such a dramatic style as that of Thornton Wilder as there is for the Happening. Indeed, it may be the final fate of the Happening to exert its greatest, most lasting influence on the theatre through its general influence on more traditional twentieth-century dramatic techniques. In any case, it is less interesting at this point to predict or approve of one approach over another in the "Other Theatre," than it is to observe with surprise and enthusiasm its fresh and splendid variety.

M.B.